The Cutting Edge of International Management Education

A volume in
Research in Management Education and Development
Charles Wankel and Robert DeFillippi, *Series Editors*

Research in Management Education and Development

Charles Wankel and Robert DeFillippi, Series Editors

The Cutting Edge of International Management Education

Edited by

Charles Wankel
St. John's University

and

Robert DeFillippi
Suffolk University

INFORMATION AGE
PUBLISHING

80 Mason Street • Greenwich, Connecticut 06830 • www.infoagepub.com

Library of Congress Cataloging-in-Publication Data

The cutting edge of international management education / edited by
Charles Wankel and Robert DeFillippi.
    p. cm. – (Research in management education and development)
Includes bibliographical references.
ISBN 1-59311-204-1 (pbk.) – ISBN 1-59311-205-X (hardcover)
1. International business enterprises–Management–Study and teaching.
I. Wankel, Charles. II. DeFillippi, Bob. III. Series.
 HD62.4.C88 2004
 658'.049'0711–dc22

                                                           2004016003

Printed in the United States of America

LIST OF CONTRIBUTORS

Kirk St. Amant	Texas Tech University, Lubbock, TX
Laura Ancilli	Swinburne University of Technology, Melbourne, Australia
Peter van Baalen	Erasmus University, Rotterdam, The Netherlands
Michela Betta	Swinburne University of Technology, Melbourne, Australia
Allan Bird	University of Missouri at St. Louis
Marta Calas	University of Massachusetts at Amherst
Jean-Luc Cerdin	ESSEC School of Business, Paris, France
Gary Coombs	Ohio University, Athens, OH
Teresa Torres-Coronas	Universitat Rovira i Virgili, Tarragona, Spain
Robert DeFillippi	Suffolk University, Boston, MA
Raffaela Dinelli	Swinburne University of Technology Melbourne, Australia
Paul F. Donnelly	University of Massachusetts at Amherst
Mila Gascó-Hernández	Open University of Catalonia, Barcelona, Spain
Laura Hougaz	Swinburne University of Technology Melbourne, Australia
Bruno Mascitelli	Swinburne University of Technology Melbourne, Australia
Martha Maznevski	International Institute of Management Development (IMD) Lausanne, Switzerland
Jeanne McNett	Assumption College, Worcester, MA
Mark Mendenhall	University of Tennessee, Chattanooga, TN
Lars Moratis	Erasmus University, Rotterdam, The Netherlands

Christine Nielsen	University of Baltimore, Baltimore, MD
Joyce Osland	San José State University, San José, CA
Thomas M. Porcano	Miami University, Oxford, OH
Bruce Rollier	University of Baltimore, Baltimore, MD
Christian Scholz	University of Saarland, Saarbrücken, Germany
David M. Shull	Miami University, Oxford, OH
William B. Snavely	Miami University, Oxford, OH
Mikael Søndergaard	University of Aarhus, Denmark
Wayne Staton	Miami University, Oxford, OH
Volker Stein	University of Saarland, Saarbrücken, Germany
Soifa Su	Shanghai University of Finance and Economics, China
Junko Takagi	ESSEC Business School, Paris, France
Dean Tjosvold	Lingnan University, Hong Kong, China
Charles Wankel	St. John's University, New York, NY
Doris Weyer	University of Vienna, Vienna, Austria
Ed Yost	Ohio University, Athens, OH
Zi-you Yu	Lingnan University, Hong Kong, China

CONTENTS

section II
Cyberspace Perspectives

section III
Teaching Perspectives

NEW VISTAS OF INTERNATIONAL MANAGEMENT EDUCATION

Introduction

Charles Wankel and Robert DeFillippi

INTRODUCTION

The definitive element of business in the 21st century is immense change, such as the creation of global brands, a truly global labor market, and the ability to move money around the world in nanoseconds. How will international management education restructure itself to deal with such issues? (see Bradshaw, 2004). Educating managers to navigate this tumultuous environment successfully is no small undertaking. However, corporations and universities are moving in new and exciting ways to bring international managers up to the level needed to flourish. The multiplicity of directions that business schools around the world are moving in teaching international management is the subject of this volume. While new technologies offer remarkable potential benefits, underlying pedagogical structures must be correspondingly assessed. Evolving new types of learner activity and the

The Cutting Edge of International Management Education, pages xi–xxii

social contexts within which the learning is situated must be addressed (MacLaren, 2004). The excitement of teaching international management in this new epoch translates into excitement by students for learning about it. International management education demands (a) the constant re-evaluation of material relevancy (sidestepping topics and approaches that have become irrelevant); (b) a search for interesting material (curtailing boring course material); (c) an understanding of trends in international management practice; and (d) the development of pedagogies aligned with these practices. These are the values of the distinguished educators whose perspectives we present in *The Cutting Edge of International Management Education*. This chapter will consider current approaches of colleagues around the world to teaching international management and will provide you with an overview of the chapters of this volume.

E-media

In teaching international management, we must provide our students with knowledge of the topics that, through the current business press and other media, engage the leadership of the organizations within which our students will be pursuing their careers. Pollard (2003) observed that, in many business school courses, the globalized business environment is not adequately represented in teaching materials and course textbooks. He recommends moving beyond textbooks. Pollard asks his students to select several well-known, publicly traded companies with international operations. He then asks students to use online resources to analyze the firms, starting with the financial impact of the firms' international operations. Topics new textbooks are struggling to keep pace with include the importance of international e-business, global e-procurement, and international e-commerce (e.g., Stonehouse, Campbell, Hamill, & Purdie, 2004).

Outsourcing and Off-shoring as Current Topics

Labor markets are increasingly global, and the workforces of firms are increasingly internationally distributed (Briscoe & Schuler, 2004). International business instructors should have a focus on "the new rules of the game" (Werwath, 2004). Currently, the foremost international management issue is outsourcing of organizational functions and the off-shoring of business units. This topic is currently of growing interest in the business community with portal sites such http://yourjobisgoingtoindia.com/ providing extensive access to articles that could serve as a basis for student discussion and assignments. Indeed, a first step in educating managers in international management might be a research project on outsourcing opportunities and issues with a focus on such locations as Eastern Europe, China, and India. As educators, we want our students to be knowledgeable about the most important opportunities and threats their organizations will encounter. Moreover, they should understand outsourcing from all sides. That is, they should read the current Indian business press online as well as that of their own region. One free resource for cutting-edge articles from around the world is Google News http://news.google.com/. Students might be asked to sign on to the Google News Alert service http://www.google.com/newsalerts?hl=en to have new articles on this subject funneled to them daily so that they can provide analyses of the trends and strategies they glean from this information. Altavista.com has a free English-to-Chinese translation utility. Students can translate terms such as *outsourcing* into Chinese characters and then search the Web for them. This process enables students to locate Chinese sites to which they otherwise might not have access. These sites can be automatically translated by clicking on the "translate" option in the search results. Other looming topics include global supply chains, global entrepreneurship, and the most effective management of global teams (Werwath, 2004).

Ethics and Social Responsibility

It is clear that international business textbook authors are reacting to calls and requirements for more coverage of ethical issues in international management. Phatak, Bahagat, and Kashlak, in *International Management: Managing in a Diverse and Dynamic Global Environment* (in press), take a "contemporary look at the increasingly important field of ethics and social responsibility that global corporations face today." Griffin and Pustay, in *International Business* (in press), will have a similar new chapter-length treatment of "Ethics and Social Responsibility in International Business." Stonehouse et al. (2004) examine the anti-globalization movement as a context. An examination of recent international management textbooks found a new focus on "appropriate technology transfer." For example, Phatak et al. (in press) introduce the topic of managing technology and knowledge in international business contexts.

What Our Colleagues are Teaching

An inquiry into how our colleagues are teaching international management found the following approaches: (a) a focus on regional issues, (b) a focus on teaching the hazards of ignoring cultural differences, and (c) a focus on how globalization changes the rules of international management. In some European universities, international management courses are framed by the context of the European Union. The expansion of the EU has led some programs to have an important focus on "managing integration across borders" (e.g., Catholic University of Leuven, 2004).

A specialized focus on regional issues was also apparent in "International Management Asia" offered by Li Choy Chong (2004) of the Betriebswissenschaftliches Institut (BWI) in Zurich. His approach included readings that go to the demographic and political core of societies such as Singapore (*South China Morning Post*, 1999, May 6). Chong used a reading on "The People of Asia" from the *Encyclopedia Britannica* to provide very interesting background information. Given the importance of ongoing reform in China, a focused reading such as Ke and Zhang (2004) might provide students with direct insight into the current realities of doing business in China.

Teaching the Hazards of Ignoring Cultural Differences

Dr. Birgitta Wolff at the University of Magdeburg selected a journal article about the Euro Disney case study (Packman & Casmir, 1999) as a vehicle for exploring the hazards of ignoring cultural differences in international business, and more specifically, as a vehicle for showing "that organizations are not distinct, separate entities capable of functioning outside their physical, social and cultural environments." To help her German students understand how cultural approaches to business differ between Americans and Germans, Rachel Lindner (2002) teaches a course at Fachhochschule Düsseldorf on how American culture affects business. Griffin and Pustay (in press) include with their international business textbook a range of country- and region-specific integrated media such as multimedia cases and videos on course topics to help sensitize students to foreign nations. David, Terpstra, and Terpstra (2004) ask how globalization changes the rules of international management. How can management insure ethical behavior throughout the international supply chain? They have created a framework any business can use for monitoring, reporting, and improving performance of suppliers on environmental and social issues, and so forth. This framework ensures that the company's ethical mandate is understood and implemented along the entire length of the international supply chain.

The Elements of International Management

The main international management topics such as international human resource management have their own courses, textbooks, and developments. International human resource management is the focus of Briscoe and Schuler (2004). Contemporary topics include using and managing cross-border teams; creating a global learning organization; training and educating in a transnational organization—including developing managers in the global enterprise, developing a global mindset, developing global competencies, and developing global leadership; global staffing through the global labor market; and cross-national career advancement.

Now that we have provided you with an overview of some cutting-edge topics and trends in the latest textbooks in international management education, we will next briefly summarize the chapters to follow and indicate some of the central themes that recur throughout the chapters, thus suggesting some unifying themes to this rich and diverse set of cutting-edge international management teaching perspectives. Each of the chapters to follow was written by experienced international management educators who summarize their teaching philosophies, review literature related to their particular topics and share with you some of their specific practices, experiences, and reflections. We could not ask more of our contributors, and we invite you to review their work below and in the chapters to follow.

SECTION I: INSTITUTIONAL PERSPECTIVES

Section one of *The Cutting Edge of International Management* features a quartet of articles on the institutional context for university-based international management education. Peter van Baalen and Lars Moratis of Erasmus University's Rotterdam School of Management suggest that pressures for academic accreditation and institutional legitimacy from diverse stakeholders are driving business schools in Europe to evolve into loosely coupled management education partnerships. These management education partnerships are characterized by a number of activities directly relevant to this volume's focus: the sharing of multiple campus locations (e.g., in order to serve different, geographically dispersed markets); ownership of or equity share participation in private business schools (e.g., to exploit foreign markets and to diversify risks); and student and faculty exchanges between management education partners in different countries. In their 2003 survey of more than 40 European business schools, the authors found that about half of the student exchange partnerships were partners located outside their home country. For faculty exchange partnerships, the majority of these agreements included foreign partners. Through their multiple campus locations, especially in regard to foreign campus locations, these business schools engaged in overseas brand-building. The authors' broad findings suggest that both American and European business schools are seeking out partnership relationships to extend their status, their legitimacy, and their reach in a global market for management education.

Junko Takagi and Jean-Luc Cerdin of ESSEC School of Business in Paris next examine how French management education evolved in response to the global institutional forces for change. The authors describe an isomorphic phenomenon whereby North American-based management fields of study and degree programs were incorporated into the French education system. The French business schools themselves were competing for recognition and thereby seeking to diversify their faculty and student populations. In this phase, French business schools perceived international accreditation as recognition that they were "international," and such accreditation-based legitimacy was viewed as vital to accessing transnational markets. In their survey of French business schools, the authors identify globalization and internationalization logics for these French business schools. The globalization logic is characterized by greater emphasis upon the conformity of their programs and practices to international accreditation standards. The internationalization logic is characterized by more nationally oriented programs and practices. This finding is similar to a finding in the van Baalen and Moratis chapter that accreditation forces are playing a significant role in shaping European business school efforts to create truly global international management education offerings.

Bruce Rollier and Christine Nielson of the University of Baltimore detail the principles underlying the international business curriculum designs of leading United States and European business schools. They echo the observations in the preceding chapters on the role of accreditation (among other factors, including the globalization of business practice enabled by information technologies) in driving business schools to design an international management education curriculum. The Association to Advance Collegiate Schools of Business (AACSB) has long emphasized internationalization as a prime accreditation factor, and their current standards explicitly state that an accredited business curriculum must include coverage of global issues. However, AACSB guidelines do not specify what should be included in an international business curriculum. To fill this gap, the chapter authors classify international business (IB) curriculum objectives by the three broad categories of *global awareness, global understanding,* and *global competence.* Then, Rollier and Nielson identify those elements of additional international curriculum development and greater faculty and institutional support required by each of these successively higher levels of international program development. Next, they identify the leading European and United States business schools in international management education and examine their course offerings. Last, the authors identify a number of best practices and offer some practical advice on how other business schools may put these best practices to use in their own institutions.

Laura Ancilli and her colleagues from Swinburne University of Technology in Australia outline the development of an international curriculum integrating foreign language and cultural studies into the business curriculum within the School of Business. They broadly agree with van Baalen and Moratis in their assertion that a transformation process is underway in which business schools are increasingly emphasizing interdisciplinarity of curricula and partnership-based methods of international program implementation. They illustrate these principles in their detailed description of the Italian and European Studies program at Swinburne, which includes a strong Italian language and culture content, as well an international business curriculum supported by a European Study Tour, European Work Experience, and university exchange programs with European universities. In particular, the authors detail the Study Abroad Program in Treviso, Italy, where students from both Swinburne University and the University of Treviso may matriculate in common classes at either campus as part of their programs of study. A further development is a Web site available via the Internet to bring together students of Italian language and culture with the Italian community in Melbourne in order to make their learning more relevant. In conclusion, the Swinburne program represents a highly integrated, international program offering a global competence level of international management education.

SECTION II: CYBERSPACE PERSPECTIVES

Pollard (2003) suggested using the Internet as the bridge between education and the workplace because it provides resources that one can use in getting information on topics such as financial information of international companies that is useful in preparing analyses, both in classrooms and in workplaces. This section features a trio of articles on how information technology is, in some cases, facilitating, and in other cases, constraining virtual learning among geographically dispersed and culturally diverse participants in international management education. The section begins with an international team of United States and European university colleagues (Osland, Bird, Scholz, Maznevski, McNett, Mendenhall, Stein, and Weyer) reporting on a very ambitious program of research and educational pedagogy utilizing Globally Distant Multicultural Teams (GDMT). The four-year GDMT Project experience was a joint effort of United States, Swiss, German, and Austrian universities to provide their students with an innovative, international learning experience modeled on the virtual collaborations found in international organizations. As in multinational corporations, teams composed of members from different cultures and countries completed a task that was primarily conducted and coordinated via the Internet. The GDMT Project was designed to be a vehicle that provides students with an opportunity to practice skills needed to enhance global virtual team productivity. The research team closely monitored the GDMT Project process, performance outcomes, and student and teacher learning experiences. The chapter authors examine these findings in detail and share their insights into why and how team process, culture, and technology are important to both the quality of virtual team project outputs and the quality of team members' learning experiences. The reported findings and lessons learned have valuable implications for educators wishing to incorporate globally distant student teams and virtual team projects into their international management education pedagogy.

Kirk St. Amant of Texas Tech University examines how instructors can use online materials to familiarize students with factors that can affect the management of international virtual teams. The chapter begins with an overview of developments that contribute to the use of such teams. Next, the chapter presents a framework for understanding the management of communication in such teams. This framework is then followed by a series of three Internet-based exercises that management educators can use to familiarize students with how factors of culture and media can affect interactions in international virtual teams. In the first exercise, students experience the limitations of software-based language translation services, such as Babelfish (located online at babel.altavista.com). Through an analysis of the presentation of product information on multinational company Web sites, the second exercise teaches students how cultural expectations can affect online communications between virtual team members. The final exercise examines how different perspectives of *face* (the appearance of dignity and/or prestige) affect the rhetorical styles used by different cultural groups and how face affects the ways in which different cultures convey criticism or bad news between virtual team members. This chapter thus provides both generic pedagogic design principles and specific instructional exercises to help students develop skills for using online media effectively with culturally diverse counterparts at school or in online work situations.

Mikael Søndergaard of the University of Aarhus in Denmark, and Marta B. Calás and Paul F. Donnelly of the University of Massachusetts conclude our section on cyberspace perspectives with a more critical stance toward traditional assumptions of cultural universalism and relativism based on their four years of experience teaching and observing United States and Danish students participating in an international management course using distance learning technologies to foster cross-cultural interactions. The chapter authors describe their experiences in designing and implementing opportunities for their respective United States and Danish classroom-based students to virtually interact on a series of international management cases focused on culture, organizing for transnational management, and ethics in international environments. They report on the subtle and less subtle differences in the "relativistic" arguments made by the Danish students in their virtual casework interactions in comparison to the "universalistic" premises of United States students. Additionally, the authors report that Danish students were more able to detect and report differences in their interactions with the United States students than the other way around, as United States students tended to report more cooperation and agreement than was perhaps the case. The chapter authors conclude that classroom instruction within a specific country with students who belong mostly to that country is not conducive to addressing the problematics of achieving cross-cultural understanding. They suggest that virtual interactions among geographically and culturally distant students and faculty can deepen students' understanding of cultural differences.

SECTION III: TEACHING PERSPECTIVES

Section three concludes our volume with four chapters detailing distinctive approaches to teaching international management. Mila Gascó-Hernández of the Open University of Catalonia (Spain) and Teresa Torres-Coronas of Rovira i Virgili University (Spain) focus their chapter on how stories and storytelling can help business professors worldwide to train students in an innovative and creative way to develop a global mindset while avoiding ethnocentrism. They begin their chapter by carefully reviewing the literature on how management educators have employed storytelling as a pedagogic tool. Next they focus on their own use of storytelling in international management education and development, with specific illustrations from their international management modules on "Building awareness about Japanese culture" and "Building awareness about African culture." They describe their use of stories to help reveal students' hidden assumptions about a country's culture and to provide a means for evaluating and interpreting the differences between their assumptions and the real characteristics of the culture. Finally, the authors' seminars conclude with activities designed to help illustrate how cultural misconceptions influence international management. Ultimately, these storytelling assignments are part of the authors' larger pedagogic goals of assisting students in becoming aware of their own culture and helping them develop a global mindset.

Dean Tjosvold and Zi-you Yu of Lingnan University in Hong Kong and their industry colleague Sofia Su Fang of Shanghai University of Finance and Economics report on their teaching and research experiences with managers in Hong Kong and mainland China on the use of cooperative learning theory and team work in management development. Cooperative learning theory is a research-based approach to developing and utilizing the relationships among students to promote educational objectives. Typically, it involves small groups of students with the goal of helping each student learn and master the course content. The chapter authors offer findings from their own research and teaching practices to refute those who question the effectiveness of Western management ideas and practices in China and who specifically question the cultural appropriateness and utility of high student-involvement approaches like cooperative learning in Chinese classrooms. The authors argue that cooperative learning theory can play a central role in the reform of management education in China to help Chinese managers and management students strengthen their leadership capabilities. The authors provide numerous examples of the successful implementation of cooperative learning theory in their management development work in China, and they conclude their chapter with a useful summary of the basic conditions required for making cooperative learning effective. This chapter provides a positive perspective on utilizing Western-based management education theories with managers in mainland China without contradicting Chinese values and cultural traditions.

Miami University professors Thomas M. Porcano, William B. Snavely, David M. Shull, and Wayne Staton document their experiences in establishing a multi-site Summer Study Abroad program in Europe and compare its benefits relative to the more typical single-site program. They argue that the cultures, lifestyles, and attitudes of British, French, German, Italian, Spanish, and Swiss nationals (and U.S. expatriates domiciled abroad) can be more directly compared and contrasted via a multi-site approach. Differing viewpoints about topics such as the United States, the European Union (EU), other European countries, "foreign" workers, and a plethora of cultural differences become dramatically more apparent in the multi-site approach. The authors' subsequent description of the evolution and implementation of the Miami University Summer Study Abroad program provides a comprehensive look at every procedural detail of their program. Moreover, the authors provide numerous helpful tips for would-be summer study abroad planners to consider. They conclude their detailed review with an enumeration of the benefits of the program for participating students and sponsoring universities and their faculty and administration. This chapter is a must read for anyone seriously considering offering students the opportunity to experience multiple countries and cultural contexts in a single summer study abroad program.

Ohio University professors Gary Coombs and Ed Yost conclude our volume with their examination of the highly successful fifteen-year-old Global Competitiveness Program/Joint Student Consulting Project (GCP/JSCP) that is available to students in both the undergraduate program (GCP) and the MBA program (JSCP). Both the GCP and the JSCP are based on Project Based Learning (PBL), a learner-centered (versus content- or instructor-centered) method that challenges the learners to take progressively increasing responsibility for their own education. Both programs involve their students in international consulting projects with clients in international locales relative to Ohio University. Some of the countries where Ohio University has conducted GCP/JSCP projects include Brazil, China, France, Germany, Greece, Hungary, Italy, Macedonia, Malaysia, South Africa, Spain, Thailand, Denmark and Estonia. In each country, Ohio University professors have developed cooperative relationships with partner universities and institutions that are essential for facilitating site access. They also provide guidance in developing appropriate student projects. The authors share their enormous collective experience with such projects and provide a detailed roadmap for progressing through each phase of consulting project planning and implementation. Thus, this final chapter reinforces powerfully the message in van Baalen and Moratis's opening chapter that business schools must increasingly rely upon networks of partnerships with geographically distant and culturally diverse educational institutions in order to develop and deliver truly global management education.

REFERENCES

Bradshaw, D. (2004, January 26). Decision to go marks a sea change: Interview with Meyer Feldberg of Columbia Business School. *Financial Times*, 9.

Briscoe, D. R. & Schuler, R. S. (2004). *International human resource management: Policies and practices for the global enterprise* (2nd ed). New York: Routledge.

Catholic University of Leuven. (2004). B-KUL-D0138A International Management and Strategy course description. Retrieved March 21, 2004, from http://www.kuleuven.ac.be/onderwijs/aanbod/syllabi/D0138AE.htm .

Chong, L. C. (2004). *International management Asia.* Zurich: Swiss Federal Institute of Technology. Retrieved March 21, 2004, from http://www.lim.ethz.ch/lehre/InternationalMgmtAsia/internatmgmtasia.html

David, K., Terpstra, V., & Terpstra, D. (2004). *Cultural environment of international business, 001* (4th ed). Cincinnati: South-Western.

Griffin, R. W., & Pustay, M. W. (in press). *International business: A managerial perspective* (4th ed). Upper Saddle River, NJ: Prentice-Hall.

Ke, R., & Zhang, W. (2004). Contract disputes and court verdicts involving Chinese private enterprises. In R. Garnaut and L. Song (Eds.), *China's third economic transformation: The rise of the private economy.* New York: RoutledgeCurzon.

Lindner, R. (2002). *Landeskunde United States*. Stuttgart: Klett.

MacLaren, I. (2004). New trends in Web-based learning: Objects, repositories and learner engagement. *European Journal of Engineering Education, 29*(1), 65–72.

Neef, D. (2004). *The supply chain imperative How to ensure ethical behavior in your global suppliers*. New York: AMACOM.

Packman, H. M., & Casmir, F. L. (1999). Learning from the Euro Disney experience. *Gazette, 61*(6), 473–489.

Phatak, A. V., Bhagat, R. S., & Kashlak, R. (in press). *International management: Managing in a diverse and dynamic global environment*. New York: McGraw-Hill.

Pollard, W. B. (2003). Using the Internet to teach international accounting to students of principles of accounting. *Journal of Education for Business, 78*(4), 221–227.

South China Morning Post. (1999, May 6). PM Goh's vision: Nation free of racial tribes. Retrieved March 21, 2004, from http://www.lim.ethz.ch/lehre/International MgmtAsia/PM%20Goh%27s%20vision_Nation%20free%20of%20racial%20tribes .pdf

Stonehouse, G., Campbell, D., Hamill, J., & Purdie, T. (Eds.). (2004). *Global and transnational business: Strategy and management* (2nd ed.). Chichester, England: Wiley.

Werwath, M. (2004). *Globalization and the technical manager: Course outline for IEMS 490-1*. Evanston, IL: Northwestern University, Robert R. McCormick School of Engineering and Applied Science, Department of Industrial Engineering and Management Sciences.

section I

INSTITUTIONAL PERSPECTIVES

CHAPTER 1

FROM GOING ALONE
TO GOING ALONG?

European Business Schools
as Loosely Coupled Networks

Peter van Baalen and Lars Moratis

INTRODUCTION

Amid the turmoil of economic, technological, and social changes in the second half of the 20th century, business schools have become one of the most popular institutions in American and European higher education systems. The MBA program, the most popular program business schools offer, has been widely adopted by these education systems. In the United States, no less than 90,000 students receive MBA degrees from 900 universities each year. One out of every 250 American citizens has an MBA diploma. Although exact figures about the number of graduates who receive MBA degrees annually in Europe are lacking, there is ample evidence of widespread diffusion across the continent (Mazza et al., 1998; the MBA Program Information Site (2004); see Boutaiba & Pedersen, 2003, p. 197).

The Cutting Edge of International Management Education, pages 3–36
Copyright © 2004 by Information Age Publishing
All rights of reproduction in any form reserved.

The route to the success of business schools has not been an easy one. As Macfarlane (1995, p. 8) argues, business and management studies are a classic example of "epistemic drift" whereby knowledge structures have been reorganized into a "dysfunctional" pattern under pressure from external forces. Business schools perform various functions for several constituencies (Trieschmann, Dennis, Northcraft, & Niemi, 2000), particularly for the academic community and for the business community. Each of these constituencies places its own legitimate demands on business schools and holds them accountable to the norms and values of its own culture. Many business schools have not been able to reconcile the often-conflicting legitimacies of academia and business. This inherent "structural ambiguity" (Light, 1983) has caused two severe identity crises in the history of business schools—one in the late 1950s and another in the late 1980s. Business schools managed to survive these crises by choosing new educational strategies and new organizational forms.

Their historical success as tough survivors in higher education systems, however, does not guarantee the future success of business schools. On the contrary, we would argue that, as established institutions in academia, they have to anticipate and to actively accept current and future challenges and to formulate new responses to the highly dynamic, liberalizing, and globalizing market for management education. Business schools see themselves competing with an increasing range of traditional and non-traditional providers of management education. As Crainer and Dearlove put it in their book *Gravy Training: Inside the Real World of Business Schools*, "The education bandwagon is becoming crowded" (1999, p. *xiv*). At the same time, the student population that is enrolling for management education is becoming increasingly diverse.

The question we raise in this chapter is: How are business schools meeting these new challenges now, and how will they meet them in the future? One way is to bring courses online, but this will not be the topic of this chapter. Casual observation suggests that over the past few years, business schools have been actively forming links with other business schools as well as with a myriad of other organizations (Livermore, 2002; "These b-schools make headway," *Business Week*, 2000; "International marriage of b-school giants," *Business Week*, 2001; "New model for global EMBAs, *Business Week*, 2001; "Schools link hands," *Financial Times*, 2003). It appears that several business schools that are engaged in both educational consortia and research collaborations (Baden-Fuller & Ang, 2001) are involved in corporate universities and have linked up with e-learning companies and international publishing houses. Gaddis (2000, pp. 4–5) observes that nearly every top business school in the United States has entered "some sort of strategic alliance with one or more [focused and innovative] greyhound." Other schools have helped set up and have acquired stakes in business schools in developing countries, and some have opened campuses abroad. These observations indicate that business schools are getting organized as networks, or *loosely coupled networks*, as we will call them in this chapter. Data on this particularly promising organizational response is still fragmented and is largely based on business journalism. In this chapter, however, we present the findings of a European survey about this response in order to investigate the extent to which European business schools are "going along" rather than "going alone."

The organization of this chapter is as follows: We first briefly discuss the two main crises for business schools, and the ways business schools in the United States have sought to cope with their structural ambiguities. We then argue that new organizational responses are needed to meet current challenges and to anticipate future challenges. From the perspective of the perceived need for models of management education that balance the two conflicting legitimacies, we propose as an organizational resolution the idea of the business school as a loosely coupled network. Consequently, we will operationalize this idea by using *loosely coupled systems theory* to investigate the ways in which European business schools are responding to the dynamics of the management education market. Finally, we will present and discuss our empirical findings.

IDENTITIES AND CRISES OF BUSINESS SCHOOLS

Over the last two decades, the history of academic business schools in the United States and Europe has been well documented (Amdam, 1996; Daniel, 1998; Engwall, 1992, 1998; Engwall & Zamagni, 1998; Locke, 1984, 1989). A central theme in those histories is the hybrid mission of business schools: On one hand, they have to comply with academic norms and values, while on the other hand, they are expected to serve the needs of the business world. This structural ambiguity has been a persistent burden for business schools, and their hybrid missions have resulted in a balancing act between academic and vocational orientations. The more business schools shifted to academic values, the less they retained the respect of the business world, and vice versa. For business schools, legitimizing themselves and their functions to one constituency meant delegitimizing themselves and their functions to the other constituency. In the United States, this led to two crises for business schools, accompanied with two waves of severe criticism—one in the late 1950s and the second in the late 1980s to mid-1990s (Hugstadt, 1983; Cheit, 1985; Cotton, McKenna, van Auken, & Meuter, 2001). During each crisis, business schools were urged to re-shift their focus to correct an overemphasis on one of these orientations. We will briefly discuss the two business school crises.

The First Business School Crisis

When the first academic business schools were founded during the late 19th and early 20th centuries, they broke with an old tradition of training young high-potential men on the job in an informal way. The rise of modern (functionally organized) industrial enterprise generated a demand for a professionally-trained managerial class ("the visible hand") which could coordinate diverse business functions (Chandler, 1977). The academic business schools took over the responsibility of training and educating these young people to prepare them for managerial jobs. An important issue was how the business schools, as newcomers in the higher education system, could meet academic standards without disregarding the needs of the business world. Until World War II, most business schools in the United States were not able to balance adequately between those divergent educational objectives. The curricula of the schools reflected a vocational orientation: Courses were very descriptive, first-job oriented, fragmented, and hardly scientific. Bossard and Dewhurst seriously criticized business schools for their vocational outlook in their empirical study *University for Business* (1931). The criticism grew massive after World War II when many business firms transformed into multi-divisional enterprises that were trying to integrate functional specialisms while trying to apply abstract and scientific knowledge to industrial technology (Locke, 1989). A new breed of managers was required to supervise the multi-divisional enterprise. Business schools, with their vocational and skill-based training programs, could hardly meet these new demands for scientific and integrated knowledge. The landmark reports of the Ford Foundation and the Carnegie Foundation, both published in 1959, not only criticized business schools vehemently but also suggested a "New (scientific) Look" for business schools (Schlossman, Sedlak, & Wechsler, 1987). These reports recommended that business schools (a) upgrade their teaching to true university education, (b) halt fragmentation and overspecialization of curricula, (c) reallocate resources in favor of graduate programs (MBAs), (d) extend PhD programs, and (e) establish a true science of management. The reason why these reports became so influential is that the Association to Advance Collegiate Schools of Business (AACSB) adopted the New Look ideas into its accreditation standards (Cotton et al., 2001, p. 228). Moreover, business school reforms were financially supported by a large amount of money ($30 million) from the Ford Foundation (van Baalen, 1995).

The Second Business School Crisis

Many business schools in the United States reformed their educational identity and organization according to the recommendations of the two Foundation reports. The MBA became the flagship of the business school. The introduction of basic disciplines, statistics, scientific methods, and rigor into business courses caused the pendulum to swing to a scientific orientation. Until the mid-1980s, only a few critics commented on the New Look of the business schools (e.g., Livingstone, 1971). While business schools were transforming themselves into "normal" scientific institutions, they gradually became disconnected from the world of business. For this reason Schlossman et al. (1987, p. 26) have typified this era (1959–1985) as the "age of autonomy" in which "these schools were free to set their own agendas and to make academic legitimacy the essence of their professional identities."

A new wave of criticism was voiced against the academic drift of the business schools. Criticism came from the business world as well as from prominent management scientists and the AACSB, the accrediting organization of American business schools. In their study *Management Education and Development: Drift or Thrust into the 21st Century?* (1988), which was commissioned by the AACSB, Porter and McKibbin documented and evaluated the development of United States business schools during the New Look era. One important conclusion was that the rapid growth and market success of many business schools had nurtured overall complacency and self-satisfaction, and that, as a consequence, there was little perceived need for major changes. "Failure to make significant changes," the authors argued, "while the environment is currently benign but demonstrably and continually changing could lead to unpleasant consequences—such as perceived irrelevance—later on" (Porter & McKibbin, 1988, p. 298). To equip the business schools adequately for this changing environment, the authors recommended a series of reforms:

- Less standardization and more diversity in missions and pedagogies
- More attention to broad, general education
- Less emphasis on internal firm activities in favor of more attention to the political, legal, economic, and social contexts in which business firms operate
- More attention to international affairs and developments
- More attention to the role of information and communication technology
- More emphasis on cross-functional and interdisciplinary research and education
- More attention to social skills

- More emphasis on closer cooperation with the business world in research and teaching
- More emphasis on framing the portfolio of courses into the concept of lifelong learning

The Porter and McKibbin report initiated a move away from standardization as the norm of accreditation (Cotton et al., p. 229) because the AACSB accepted these recommendations as the foundation for the development of a new set of accreditation criteria. The new criteria should not be perceived as just an attempt to swing the pendulum back to a vocational orientation, nor should the Porter and McKibbin report be perceived as an attempt to promote a universal future direction for business schools. Since the business environment was not changing in a uniform way, Porter and McKibbin favored diversity of missions, goals, and pedagogies. Business schools were allowed to capitalize upon their strengths, to take risks, and to innovate in response to their own environments. The strength of the Porter and McKibbin report is that it broke with the classic "either/or" thinking (academic *or* vocational) about the orientation of business schools. In other words, the idea of a business school could be characterized by multiple legitimate models of management education—at the same time.

A New Business School Crisis?

Porter and McKibbin took a prudent look at a vast number of future studies in order to assess the possible impact on management education. The cumulative and interdependent changes the authors foresaw in 1988 gave only a scant picture of the revolutionary changes that were beginning to take place as symptoms of the rising networked society (Castells, 1996).

A recent report from the AACSB, *Management Education at Risk* (2002), alarms business schools because of the relentless changes that are occurring in the marketplace. Increasing competition from non-accredited schools and the globalization of the business education market are considered to be the roots of the current instability (AACSB, 2002, p. 5). The report points at three critical issues for business schools that are emerging from this changing context: (a) the future shortage of doctoral faculty, (b) the need to ensure the relevance of current curricula to the global business world, and (c) a convergence of degree and non-degree education. In addition, the report draws attention to the fragmentation of the demand side of management education, both in terms of changing student characteristics and of the various kinds of management programs they seek. Like the two Foundation reports of 1959 and the Porter and McKibbin report of 1988, the 2002 AACSB report attempts to lay the foundation for long-term initiatives and calls for business schools to take action to face the challenges of the changing context.

There is much similarity in the ways these different reports call for business school reform and action. The important, and probably disquieting, differences are that the reports of 1959 and 1988 were accompanied by waves of criticism. These waves of criticism expressed the serious involvement of the different stakeholders of the business schools, who worried about the direction (academic or vocational) in which the business schools were developing. Presently, there appears to be a lack of urgency for reform. It is too early to label the current situation a crisis, but it is clear that business schools see themselves confronted with a challenging environment, to say the least. During the former two crises, educational identity was at stake. The main question then was whether or not business schools could legitimize themselves to either the academic or the business community. An outcome of the current situation could be a crisis of a more existential nature. It may not be about the question of the value system (academia or business) under which a school chooses to survive, but whether there still will be a more or less homogeneous value system to which it can legitimize itself in the future. Nowotny (2003) argues that in our modern society, expertise is inherently transgressive and democratized. Knowledge domains are pluralistic, deriving their legitimacy from a variety of sources—practices, institutions, and actors. Moving from "reliable knowledge towards socially robust knowledge" requires interaction between these sources rather than reliance on fellow experts (Nowotny, 2003). From the perspective of management knowledge and management education, this means that the legitimacy of knowledge created and transferred by business schools is co-dependent on the legitimacy of knowledge that is applied by their audiences, and vice versa. We assume that the emerging networked society requires business schools to deal with multiple legitimacies, to ally themselves with divergent academic and business partners, to operate across disciplines and across cultures, and to develop blended learning environments to cater to the learning needs of future managers.

It is not our intention to discuss the characteristics of the networked society and its impact on management education here. (For a detailed discussion, see van Baalen & Moratis, 2001). The main challenge that confronts business schools is how they can respond to their dynamic environments and how they can be responsive to their constituents (Trieschmann et al., 2000). The question we therefore want to raise is: How will business schools respond? How will they cope with the new demands placed upon them in this challenging environment? In this respect, Byrkjeflot (2001), van Baalen and Moratis (2001), and the 2002 AACSB report point to the rise of networks of education providers and opportunities for developing partnerships. Some of those partnerships focus on delivering courses partly through the Internet (see Gaddis, 2000, for examples). An example of this type of partnership is Cardean University, an e-learning consortium that includes an Internet education company and a number of leading international business schools. Other cooperative models of management education include the Community of European Management Schools (CEMS), a network of 17 European business schools that also includes approximately 50 corporate partners, and Universitas 21, an international network of 17 research-intensive universities in ten countries. In 2001, Universitas 21 Global was created as a joint venture between Universitas 21 and Thomson Learning, one of the world's major providers of tailored learning solutions. In May 2003, Universitas 21 Global launched an online MBA program (Universitas 21, 2004). Examples of collaborations between smaller numbers of business schools are myriad and include the AEA Alliance, OneMBA, Trium EMBA, the INSEAD–Wharton Alliance, Columbia Business School–London Business School, and MIT Sloan–IMD. Leading Concepts, a company providing executive education and e-learning solutions in the Middle East, has joined forces with the Stanford Graduate School of Business, the University of Michigan Business School, and the Columbia Business School.

While most of these partnerships focus on developing or delivering management education, several partnerships also focus on research collaboration and faculty and student exchange.[1] As for the former type of partnership, Miguel Villas-Boas, professor of business administration at the University of California's Haas School of Business, and SysIQ, a provider of managed e-business services for retailers and mail order catalogers, recently launched the Internet Consumer Purchase Behavior Study (ICPBS). The goal of ICPBS is to gain insight into how various features of Internet stores impact purchasing behavior, while SysIQ delivers the technical infrastructure and supports the store's front design, order and transaction processing, site usage, and multiple site versioning. Several of Villas-Boas's PhD and MBA students will investigate the effects of site design, product presentation, and price promotion on online purchasing behavior (see "Haas School of Business Faculty Member and SysIQ Launch Study to Understand Online Purchasing Behavior," Market Wire, 2003). An example of the latter type of partnership is the academic exchange partnership between Haute Études Commerciales (HEC) School of Management, known as HEC Paris, and Japan's Nihon University. The corporate university is a specific form of cooperation in the area of management education that has quickly gained popularity over the last years as a strategic vehicle for management, employee, customer, and supplier education and development (Meister, 1998, p. 29). While schools like Henley Management College and Ashridge Business School are active in assisting companies to develop their own corporate universities, other schools have helped set up and have acquired stakes in business schools located in developing countries. For instance, HEC Paris, Copenhagen Business School (CBS), Louvain School of Management (IAG), and the Norwegian School of Economics and Business Administration (NHH) are involved as partners in the Baltic Management Institute (BMI), located in Lithuania. The Norwegian School of Management (BI), is a founding partner of the International School of Management (ISM), also located in Lithuania. A small number of business schools, such as INSEAD and Duke University's Fuqua School of Business, have opened campuses abroad.

These responses represent the different functions and activities of business schools, and, although supportive research is currently lacking, it seems that business schools are exploring ways to "go along" rather than to "go alone" to counter the challenges in their environments. This is a very interesting point since previous discussions and debates about the future of management education have mainly focused on the identity and educational objectives of business schools. Less attention has been paid to the organizational forms that are needed to accomplish these objectives. We have formulated two simple research questions:

1. Are European business schools organizing themselves into networks?
2. If so, what do those business school networks look like?

In order to answer these two questions, we have developed the idea of business schools as loosely coupled networks. We will, however, first discuss different balanced organizational models of business schools. We will then conceptualize and operationalize loosely coupled systems theory for our empirical research, and finally, we will present some preliminary findings.

ORGANIZATIONAL RESPONSES: BALANCED MODELS OF MANAGEMENT EDUCATION

The structural ambiguity of business schools has always been a source of discomfort for both the business schools and their constituents. The conflicting value systems and resulting claims of the academy, in which many business schools reside, and the profession, which values business schools for their relevancy and the employability of graduates, have caused some especially troublesome reforms. Earlier attempts to reform business schools focused attention on a single model that would lead management education into the future—either the professional model or the academic model. The structural ambiguity of business schools was seen as a necessary evil that had to be dealt with. Our brief history shows that business schools dealt with this structural ambiguity by ignoring it and by forcing the management education model in the direction of one specific constituent—to circumvent the inherent structural ambiguity of the business school rather than to acknowledge it.

Null Set Management Education Models

Since the mid-1980s, there has been growing awareness of a need for balanced models of management education that could cope with the conflicting legitimacies of the academic and vocational or business value systems. Balanced models of management education are expected to build on the structural ambiguity of business schools as a source of constructive tension and as a strength rather than as a flaw.

Cheit (1985) explicitly proposed striking a balance between the professional and the academic model because, in his view, the work of business schools and all professional schools in the university is shaped by the schools' dual role as academic and professional institutions (p. 51). The fact that the business school had or should have a place in the academy implied that balanced models of management education could only be built on a certain academic level. The reverse, however, would not be possible: "A school cannot follow the professional model at a high level with a low level of academic demands" (p. 55). This was what Cheit called the *null set.* Interestingly, accepting this notion means that business schools could again become dominated by academic demands, putting them at risk of professional irrelevancy once again, leading to a déjà vu of the second business school crisis.

As a response to the 1991 revision of the AACSB accreditation standards, Cotton et al. have recently supplemented Cheit's conception of feasible management education models by contending that there is a second null set which consists of all the combinations between the two models that include low levels of professional demands. In this view, business schools should show a commitment to both the professional and the academic community. While the pre-1991 AACSB accreditation standards emphasized academic legitimacy and scholarship, the standards that were in force during the period 1991–2003 permitted most schools "a de-emphasis on academic scholarship and allow[ed] applied research and instructional development to substitute in accreditation for the basic research which was once required of all accredited programs" (Cotton et al., p. 229).[2] However, here we should point again to the fact that Porter and McKibbin did not propose a uniform model for management education but allowed for a larger diversity of models. The null set models of Cheit and Cotton et al. are depicted in Figure 1.1.

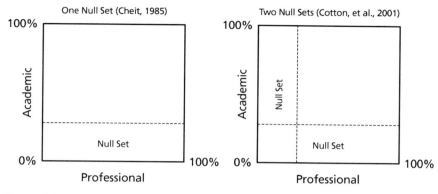

Figure 1.1.   Null sets of management education models.

The new AACSB accreditation standards that came into force in the first half of 2003 seem to pave the way for reforms by endorsing and supporting diversity in business school missions. According to the AACSB, there are various legitimate ways into the future. The new standards contend that "one of the accreditation's guiding principles is the tolerance, and even encouragement, of diverse paths to achieving high quality in management education" (AACSB, 2003, p. 4).

Balanced models of management education not only recognize the simultaneous existence of the academic and the professional model and the demands of the various constituencies of the business school, but also foster constructive tension between these models. Such models are mutually fertile, perhaps complementary, rather than being inherently conflicting or contradictory. This means that management education can be built on the interplay between the business world and the academic world. Balanced models of management education are able to deal with the divergent objectives of these models and the frequently conflicting claims of constituents of the business schools. These balanced models can only emerge when the professional model and the academic model are seen as complementary and accountable to each other.

This issue touches upon on a simple but very fundamental notion that has been gaining increasing support over the last decade—that there are multiple legitimate models of management education that derive their legitimacy from their objectives and their constituents. The AACSB recognized this in the 1994 "mission-linked" revision of its accreditation standards and has emphasized this in the latest revision. Allowing for idiosyncratic approaches to management education means promoting varying legitimate models of management education.

Integrative Models of Management Education

The above contemplative account on the inherent structural ambiguity of business schools and the existence of multiple models of management education is reflected in the works of Miles (1985) and van Baalen and Leijnse (1995). The authors have explored integrative approaches to management education from the perspective of the academic business school. Miles (1985) offered a "six-tiered system of management education" ranging from a broad, non-specialized undergraduate general business major/minor to a wide range of creatively structured executive education programs (pp. 68–72). Although the complementary nature of these programs could be a great impetus for business schools to reorganize themselves along the lines of this comprehensive system, Miles notes that it is unlikely that business schools would attempt a complete, one-time restructuring toward such a system. It is more plausible that business schools would adopt elements from this system independently and develop their own variants. In his idea of a comprehensive business school, Miles seems to recognize structural ambiguity only to a limited extent. Moreover, the current objectives and the current approach to management education ("path dependency") in use at business schools will likely induce idiosyncratic adoptions which would take place at the expense of the potential structural ambiguity of a comprehensive system of management education.

Van Baalen and Leijnse (1995) have proposed the idea of the *synolic business school*. The synolic business school is characterized by interdisciplinary action-oriented pedagogical approaches and new methodologies which force a rethinking of the institutional structures of business schools. The traditional institutional structures of the school are superseded by structures that can accommodate the particular learning needs of managers and future managers in various phases of their careers, in terms of different business programs at different levels. Such structures include learning alliances (Ghoshal, 1992), corporate universities (Meister, 1998), and network learning arrangements (van Baalen & Moratis, 2001). Since lifelong learning is an integral part of the synolic business school, it is the synolic school's goal to provide students with a sound educational basis for a lifelong learning process in business.

The integrative models of management education attempted to deal with multiple missions and tasks within the boundaries of one organization. To investigate the rise and profile of partnerships between networks of business schools, we need an alternative organizational concept. In our opinion, loosely coupled systems theory provides insight into the complexities of those networks. This theory and its relevance for studying business schools as networks will be discussed in the next section.

CONCEPTUALIZING BUSINESS SCHOOLS AS LOOSELY COUPLED NETWORKS

Loosely coupled systems theory presents an approach to studying organizations that incorporates contradictory elements, such as those captured in the idea of structural ambiguity, into one organizational system (Glassman, 1973; Weick, 1976; Orton & Weick, 1990). A very attractive manifestation of this approach is that loosely coupled systems theory recognizes the interdependence between system elements as well as the autonomy (independence) of system elements. Independence of some parts of the system is a necessary precondition for achieving stability over time. It allows a system to absorb distortions, notably those engendered by outside stimuli, without degenerating as a whole. Loosely coupled systems are able to protect themselves from external distortions as well as from disturbances within the system itself. Glassman (1973, pp. 84, 86) has argued that

> a perturbation in any one variable would require readjustment of all of the other variables in the system. In any complex system, there are so many variables that readaptation would then be astronomically improbable. A system whose parts are less richly interconnected, one with interdependence or temporary independence between parts, forms local stabilities which ignore limited perturbations elsewhere in the system.... By virtue of temporary or partial interdependence, new adaptations do not involve complete reorganization of the entire system.

Elements of an organization can be grafted onto or severed from the system with relatively little disturbance to either the elements or the organization (Weick, 1976, p. 3). Through its subsystems or elements, the organization possesses effective local sensing mechanisms that provide the whole system with feedback on the environment. A loosely coupled organization, then, would be more responsive, more flexible, better able to adapt to a dynamic environment, and better able to cope with challenges more rapidly and effectively.

With these properties, loosely coupled systems theory offers very useful starting points for developing an organizational solution for multiple legitimate models of management education.[3] Before elaborating on this, it is important to understand that the term *system* can relate to various levels of analysis. Loosely coupled systems theory has been mainly used to describe intraorganizational phenomena. We argue here that the theory can serve particularly well for analyzing phenomena beyond the traditional boundary of organizations as systems (Orton & Weick, 1990; Brusoni & Prencipe, 2001; Brown, Durchslag, & Hagel, 2002; Schilling & Steensma, 2001).

The key to understanding business schools from a loosely coupled systems perspective is to replace an *intra*organizational level of analysis with an *inter*organizational level of analysis. We approach this interorganizational level from the perspective of partnerships and networks that focus on developing and providing management education. To emphasize our focus on partnerships and networks from intraorganizational phenomena, we will use the term *loosely coupled network* to describe the constellation of relationships entered into by business schools. Figure 1.2 illustrates our conception of the business school as a loosely coupled network and sets it conceptually apart from two other organizational arrangements, namely the business school and the business school network.

Two remarks on this conceptualization should be made. First of all, it should be clear that this approach focuses on the perspective of the individual business school in order to understand the behavior of business schools. Of the limited available studies in this field, some have focused on business school networks and network dynamics (e.g., Spoun, 1998). While this approach has been widely adopted in the study of organizations, particularly business firms, one cannot get a full grasp of the behavior of the individual network members with this approach. When one claims that net-

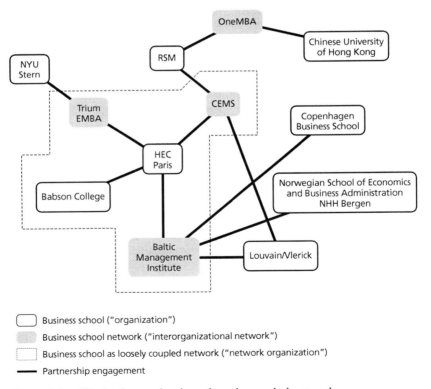

Figure 1.2.   The business school as a loosely coupled network.

works, for various reasons, are viable organizational arrangements for coping with new competitive realities, it would be very relevant to know what motivates individual network members to join the network and what the position and role of the network is in all the activities of the individual organization. It should be clear that the idea of a business school as a loosely coupled network transcends the traditional idea of a business school as a single, uniform entity. Its boundaries also span its outside relationships. The business school as a loosely coupled network, then, is a compound entity that comes in many different compositions. These compositions are the corollaries of the strategic choices made by business schools. We consequently argue here that one can only understand the behavior of business schools when one takes into account their relationships (i.e., partnership engagements).[4] The organizational micro-perspective has become a meso-perspective. The idea of a business school as a loosely coupled network relates to a spherical expansion of business schools, not a morphological expansion per se.

The concept of perceiving a business school as a loosely coupled network possesses great descriptive and explanatory power: It allows for simultaneously analyzing opposing forces or phenomena in organizations, such as objectives and functions of business schools vis-à-vis their various constituents.[5] Seeing the business school as a loosely coupled network allows reconciliation of academic and professional models without sacrificing structural ambiguity.

Within a business school, consequently, different models of management education exist at the same time, and structural ambiguity is seen as a source of constructive tension between the different models. This enables the business school to simultaneously meet the various demands of its constituents, notably the academic and the professional community. In accordance with Miles's idea of a comprehensive system of management education (Miles, 1985), the business school as a loosely coupled network can provide a range of programs varying from undergraduate programs in general management to skill-oriented executive education, thereby enabling business schools to accommodate the learning needs of managers throughout their careers.

The local sensing mechanisms that feed information back into the network enable the business school to respond to the fragmented supply-side and demand-side of the business education market. Based on this information, the business school can adjust its constellation of offerings, if necessary. Another beneficial aspect of the business school as a loosely coupled network is that its elements or subsystems are able to distinguish themselves from each other on several dimensions. For example, a subsystem can (a) focus on offering a particular type of program (e.g., an MBA program) or on serving a particular clientele (e.g., executives); (b) focus on a specific geographic area (e.g., another continent); or (c) focus on a specific learning approach or modality (e.g., online education, workplace learning, corporate universities).[6] Within such a loosely coupled network, it is likely that various microstrategies are pursued. Each subunit of the system has a certain degree of independence or autonomy that allows it to follow its own mission or strategy (Dhillon & Orton, 2001). The business school as a loosely coupled network can balance various models at the same time in this way and can capitalize on the different models within the whole system (e.g., to feed the results of fundamental academic research conducted by one subunit back to other subunits which may put it to their own use). The business school as a loosely coupled network is an organizational arrangement that follows multiple strategies at the same time. For instance, one subunit may follow a high end positioning strategy on the executive education market. The subunit's identity and offerings are academically underpinned but have a strong emphasis on a professional model of management education. Other subunits may have quite different approaches which may be at the other end of the academic and professional spectrum, such as a unit that focuses on offering online pre-experience programs that are continuously fed by a scientific research program. Different elements may operate under different names or labels, while leveraging the reputations of the business schools involved.

OPERATIONALIZING BUSINESS SCHOOLS AS LOOSELY COUPLED NETWORKS

In order to investigate empirically how and to what extent business schools are becoming loosely coupled networks, we developed a multidimensional profile model. This profile model represents a multidimensional construct in that it consists of several interrelated attributes or dimensions. These dimensions can be conceptualized under an overall abstraction (Law, Wong, & Mobley, 1998, p. 747). In our case, the business school as a loosely coupled network represents this abstraction. Within this particular multidimensional construct, combining characteristics of the different dimensions can identify profiles. A multidimensional profile construct should be interpreted as a set of profiled characteristics of the dimensions rather than a single theoretical overall construct that summarizes and represents all dimensions. Hence, it provides an excellent methodological handle for achieving the objectives of exploratory research.

Since we have been particularly concerned with models of management education in this chapter, our operationalization of the loose coupling of European business schools relies primarily on the existence of management education partnerships (the primary dimension) in which European business schools are engaged. When we say *partnerships*, we refer to any formalized, enduring, collaborative endeavors between a business school and another business school or schools, whether public or private institutions, as well as between business schools and other educational institutions. The term *partnership* includes collaborative endeavors like alliances, networks, and joint ventures. Though we are aware of differing interpretations of these terms, we label these endeavors as partnerships for the purposes of this research. The term *management education partnership* in this research does not refer to *ad hoc* partnerships, as opposed to longer-term partnerships, but to partnerships which are meant to be enduring endeavors. The partnerships that are of particular interest to us have the joint design and delivery/offering of management education as their primary focus.[7]

Although management education is one of the most important activities of business schools, it obviously isn't the only one, nor is it the only function of business schools. Therefore, in addition to management education partnerships, we have also taken other dimensions of loose coupling of European business schools into account in our research. It should be noted that, since the focus of our operationalization pertains to management education, these operationalizations of loose coupling are less important here. To obtain a more comprehensive idea of the loose coupling of European business schools, however, we have operationalized loose coupling in management education partnerships by the following dimensions:

- Management research partnerships
- Partnerships with companies
- Involvement in corporate universities
- Multiple campus locations (e.g., in order to serve different, geographically dispersed markets)
- Ownership of, or equity share participation in, private business schools (e.g., to exploit foreign markets and to diversify risks)
- Student exchange partnerships
- Faculty exchange partnerships

Together with management education partnerships, these dimensions comprise an operationalization that provides a comprehensive view of business schools as loosely coupled networks. The full profile model of a business school as a loosely coupled network is depicted in Figure 1.3.

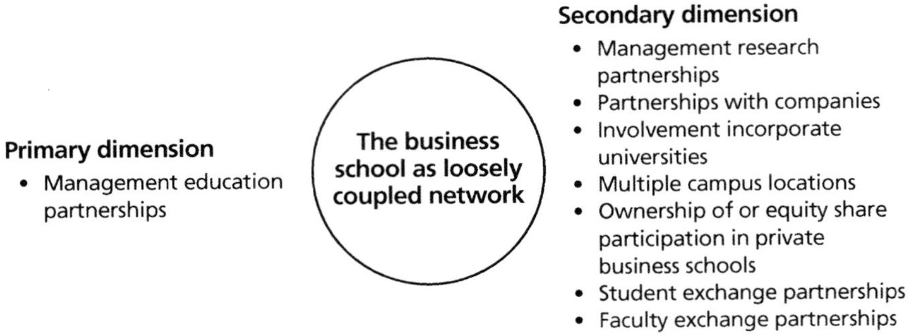

Primary dimension
- Management education partnerships

The business school as loosely coupled network

Secondary dimension
- Management research partnerships
- Partnerships with companies
- Involvement incorporate universities
- Multiple campus locations
- Ownership of or equity share participation in private business schools
- Student exchange partnerships
- Faculty exchange partnerships

Figure 1.3.   Profile model of a business school as loosely coupled network.

EMPIRICAL FINDINGS OF A EUROPEAN SURVEY

In 2003, we conducted a survey among European business schools in order to empirically map them as loosely coupled networks. An extensive survey was developed according to the above mentioned profile model of loosely coupled networks. All European business schools that were invited to join the research project were selected from the membership list of the European Foundation for Management Development (EFMD). This list from several European countries included a variety of schools: public and/or private schools, highly-ranked and/or unranked schools, schools with high and/or low enrollment figures, schools with comprehensive and/or limited program portfolios, and schools which operate locally and/or globally.

In sum, 223 surveys were sent out, and 48 surveys were returned by August 2003, yielding a response rate of 21.5 percent. Some of the results of the survey, based on the data from these 48 surveys, are discussed below. First, the survey results are depicted graphically, and we briefly comment on them. After the results on the primary and secondary dimensions have been shown, we will discuss them and their implications in more detail and draw some tentative conclusions based on these results.

Results on the Primary Dimension

With regard to the primary dimension in our profile model, our survey shows that three out of four schools engage in management education partnerships. Most schools have the intention to engage in more partnerships in the future. While the average number of partners in these partnerships is 3.89, most partnerships involve only two partners in bilateral agreements. This average number includes partnerships such as the Community of

European Management Schools (CEMS) with 17 partners, the European Doctoral Programmes Association in Management and Business Administration (EDAMBA) with 50 partners, and Partnership in International Management (PIM) with 52 partners. At the time of our survey, approximately 25 percent of these schools were planning to engage in more management education partnerships in the short term (within one year). Most of these schools (approximately 87 percent) were planning to engage in more management education partnerships in the medium-term, between one and three years. These results are depicted in Figures 1.4–1.10.

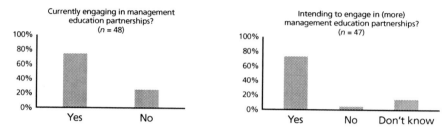

Figure 1.4. Empirical results on the primary dimension: Management education partnerships.

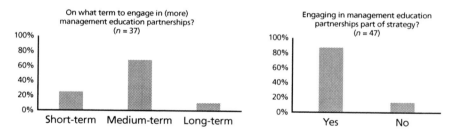

Figure 1.5. Empirical results on the primary dimension: Management education partnerships.

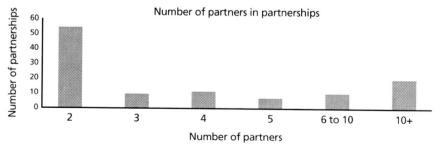

Figure 1.6. Empirical results on the primary dimension: Management education partnerships.

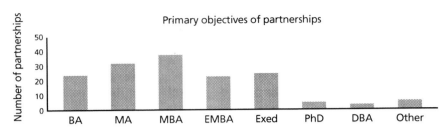

Figure 1.7.

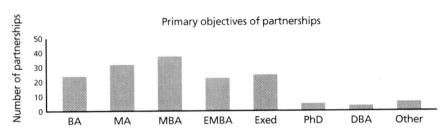

Figure 1.8.

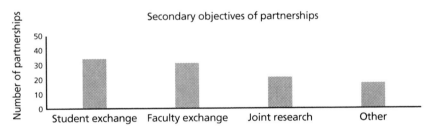

Figure 1.9.

The graphs in Figures 1.4–1.10 also show that most of the management education partnerships of those business schools that were included in our research survey were only recently established. Almost 50 percent of all management education partnerships on which this survey reports were begun during the past three years. When seen in conjunction with the intentions of business schools, there is an apparent tendency towards partnering by European business schools.

As for the objectives of the partnerships, Figures 1.7 and 1.8 show a varied pattern. Most management education partnerships focus on offering MBA programs—either regular MBA programs or Executive MBA (EMBA) programs. Only a few of these partnerships pertain to doctoral education. Of course, this is not surprising since most doctoral work relates to research activities. Secondary objectives of these management education

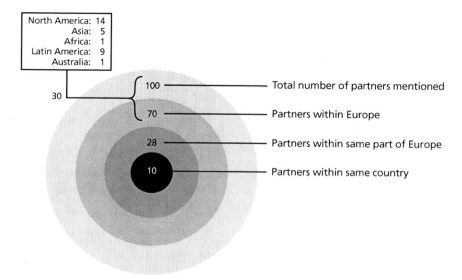

North America: 14
Asia: 5
Africa: 1
Latin America: 9
Australia: 1

30

100 ———————— Total number of partners mentioned

70 ———————— Partners within Europe

28 ———————— Partners within same part of Europe

10 ———————— Partners within same country

Figure 1.10.   Location of most important partners in management education partnerships.

partnerships, represented by the category "Other," include student exchange, faculty exchange, and joint research. Fostering faculty relationships, benchmarking, and recruiting graduates are also secondary objectives that are included in the category "Other."

When we look at the geographical locations of the most important partners of the European business schools in our survey, it appears that 70 percent come from within Europe, while 30 percent are located outside Europe. Of the European business schools with partners outside Europe, most include North American and Latin American partners. This information is represented in Figure 1.10, which shows cumulative numbers.

Results on the Secondary Dimensions

Nearly 60 percent of the business schools in our survey are engaging in management education partnerships with companies. The objective is to offer commercial management education programs to the market. More than half of the responding schools indicated that they intend to engage in more of these partnerships (see Figure 1.11).

24 P. van BAALEN and L. MORATIS

Figure 1.11. Partnerships with companies.

Similar observations were made for management research: A majority of the schools are engaging in management research partnerships and intend to do so in the future (Figure 1.12).

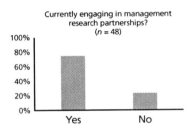
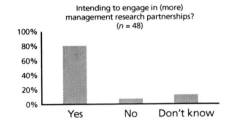

Figure 1.12. Management research partnerships.

With regard to corporate universities, the results (Figure 1.13) show that a little more than 40 percent of the business schools are involved in one or more corporate universities. This involvement particularly relates to providing faculty for teaching, developing course content, and developing program structures.

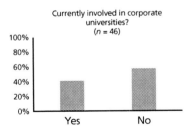

Figure 1.13. Involvement in corporate universities.

More than 70 percent of the European business schools in our survey reported that they engage in partnerships having the exchange of students as the primary focus. A comparable percentage engages in faculty exchange partnerships. The average number of these partnerships differs considerably. While the total average number of student exchange partnerships per business school exceeds 40, the total average number of faculty exchange partnerships is a little above 14. About half of the student exchange partnerships relate to agreements with partners located abroad. For faculty exchange partnerships, the majority of these agreements include foreign partners (Figure 1.14).

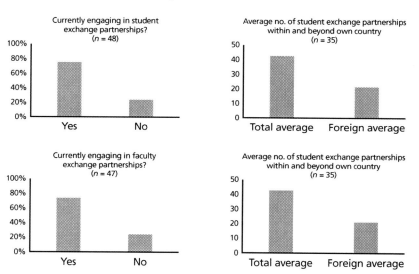

Figure 1.14.   Student and faculty exchange partnerships.

Most schools in our survey don't have campuses at multiple locations. Still, 30 percent do. For the schools which have multiple campuses, the average number of campuses exceeds four, of which one is located abroad. Figure 1.15 shows, with dark gray-shaded bars, the average numbers for the total set of business schools that responded to our survey. It also shows, with light gray-shaded bars, revised average numbers for the total, minus

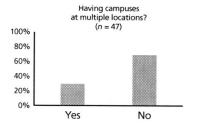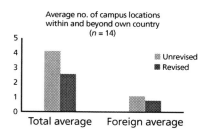

Figure 1.15.   Multiple campus locations.

one school which had a very large number of campuses. Most of these campuses were in the school's country of origin. This school was labeled a *maverick observation*.

A pattern similar to the presence of multiple campuses, only to a much smaller degree, pertains to ownership of or equity share participation in private business schools (Figure 1.16). Three schools in our survey said that they had such equity share participation or ownership, but only one case concerned ownership of, or participation in, a school that was located abroad.

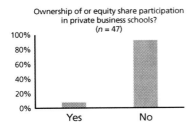

Figure 1.16.   Ownership of or equity share participation in private business schools.

DISCUSSION

The overall picture that emerges from our data about European business schools in relation to our profile model indicates that many schools are in one or more ways loosely coupled. Our data also indicate that there is a tendency towards further loose coupling, judging on the intentions that the business schools in our survey had to engage in more partnerships in the future. Specifically concerning the partnerships focusing on management education, it appears that most of the schools that have these intentions said that they were planning to realize this intention within three years. The large number of business schools that indicated that engaging in management education partnerships is part of their strategies is a strong indication that this tendency will continue in the future. Our empirical findings also suggest that the tendency towards increased management education partnerships is a rather recent phenomenon. The rapid growth of business school partnerships really took off after the year 2000. Our results therefore support suggestions made earlier by casual observations (see Livermore, 2002; "These b-schools make headway," *Business Week*, 2000; "International marriage of b-school giants," *Business Week*, 2001; "New model for global EMBAs, *Business Week*, 2001; "Schools link hands," *Financial Times*, 2003). With respect to the primary dimension, it seems legitimate to say that a rather revolutionary change is taking place on the supply side of the management education market. In the not-too-distant future, competition may emerge between management education partnerships or networks, rather than individual schools. This statement, however, remains speculative for now, and we should be careful about not overstepping our data. The number of entities in partnerships appears to be relatively small. Moreover, only one school appeared to be loosely coupled on both the primary dimension and all secondary dimensions; hence, it is an example of a full-fledged loosely coupled network in our operationalization.

Figure 1.17 shows our aggregate findings on all our dimensions of the business school as a loosely coupled network that were included in our profile model. It provides some insights into the phenomenon of business schools as loosely coupled networks. However, in order to sustain our idea of business schools as loosely coupled networks, a closer examination of our data is necessary. When we search for schools with multiple loose couplings in our data, it appears that out of the total number of 44 schools[8] for which we had all data, 29 were loosely coupled on 4 or more dimensions, 15 schools were loosely coupled on 5 or more dimensions, and 5 schools were loosely coupled on 6 or more dimensions (of which one was loosely coupled on all dimensions).

Of the 10 schools that were not engaged in management education partnerships (our primary dimension), 6 were loosely coupled on 3 or more dimensions. In contrast, 31 out of the 34 schools that did engage in management education partnerships were loosely coupled on 3 or more dimensions. When we adjust this number by excluding the management education partnerships as one dimension (after all, the management education partner-

	Business schools responded:		
	n	YES	NO
Primary dimension			
• Management education partnerships	48	37	11
Secondary dimension			
• Management research partnerships	47	28	19
• Partnerships with companies	48	37	11
• Involvement in corporate universities	46	19	27
• Multiple campus locations	47	14	33
• Ownership of or equity share participation in private business schools	47	3	44
• Student exchange partnerships	48	36	12
• Faculty exchange partnerships	47	13	44

Figure 1.17.   Aggregate findings on business schools as loosely coupled networks.

ships schools engage in already count as one dimension on which they are loosely coupled), 27 out of 34 schools are still loosely coupled on 3 or more dimensions. These data seem to indicate that European business schools are indeed organizing themselves as loosely coupled networks.

When we again distinguish between schools that are and are not engaging in management education partnerships, it appears that those that are engaging in management education partnerships were considerably more likely to engage in research partnerships, too. Another difference relates to faculty exchange partnerships. Of the 10 business schools in our survey not engaged in management education partnerships, five had faculty exchange partnerships. Of the 37 schools engaged in management education partnerships, eight had faculty exchange partnerships. This might imply that management education partnerships should also include a faculty development component in them (e.g., in the form of joint teaching).

European business schools appear to frequently engage in partnerships with companies. While the AACSB report (2002) expressed the fear that in the near future, business schools might lose relevance to the business world, our results may give rise to a less pessimistic outlook. Based on these results, we cannot claim that there is no reason to worry at all, but we may assume that partnering with companies at least helps in improving the relevance of European business schools. Not long after the AACSB report, Pfeffer and Fong (2002) argued that many contemporary MBA programs provide little use for corporate practice and that they are especially falling short of delivering on-the-job training and experience. Doria, Rozanski, & Cohen (2003, p. 8) comment about the Johns Hopkins University–Booz Allen partnership that offers an MBA and a Master of Science in Information and Telecommunications Systems:

> Both programs are conducted at Booz Allen offices and stress shared leadership and teamwork, and the MBA program requires a course in organizational development. Throughout these programs, students learn through team assignments, which try to promote collegiality over competitiveness. With Johns Hopkins getting to know Booz Allen better, the curriculum has evolved to more reliably provide the skills we need. This is an excellent example of a university that recognizes that corporations are also its customers.

Partnerships with companies may indeed serve as a mechanism for gaining and retaining relevance.

A distinction can be made between *traditional* types of business school outreach strategies (research, student exchange, and faculty exchange) and *new* types of business school outreach strategies (management education, companies, corporate universities, multi-campus, equity share). In our opinion, the latter ones are most indicative of the changing nature of the supply side of the management education market and represent some viable strategic options to enable business schools to compete in this market. It should be noted that only a few schools have ownership or hold an equity share in other private business schools. This option may provide business schools a way to expand their geographical reach and explore or develop overseas markets. Such a strategy may be suitable for small, focused niche players that offer one or a few specialized or unique management programs. By acquiring a sufficiently large share in a private business school, they will be able to influence that school's program portfolio in terms of integrating their unique features into the school's offerings. More renowned schools that want to capitalize on their reputations could also consider this as a viable option. Their potential partners may be attracted by the idea of "reputation by association" (Baden-Fuller & Ang, 2001, p. 743). With a multiple-campus location strategy, especially with regards to foreign campus locations, a renowned school may be capable of overseas brand-building. An analysis of the 14 schools ($n = 47$) that had multiple campus locations shows that five of them have campus locations outside their home country. In sum, these 14 schools have 58 campus locations, of which 15 were located abroad. When we adjust this number by including one school that had many domestic campus locations, the numbers are 34 and 11 respectively.

The fact that a relatively high number of schools are engaged in corporate universities could suggest that regular universities and corporate universities are beginning to see each other less as competitors in the same marketplace. Both types of supply structures operate complementarily, emphasizing their own specific functions and roles in the supply side of management education. As with partnerships with companies, corporate universities can also be seen as relevance-enhancing mechanisms.

The emerging loosely coupled networks have a primarily European character, not a global character. Only 30 percent of the partnerships that business schools indicated were most important for them covered partnerships with non-European business schools. Only 14 percent involved United States business schools. It would be interesting to investigate whether this percentage will increase or decrease in the future and to discover whether European business schools will engage in different types of partnerships in the coming years. Several business schools, both European and North American, have started to establish alliances with universities in the Far East, especially in China. The revolutionary growth of China as a leading economic and political world power will, in our opinion, cause a reallocation of resources so that many business schools will establish links with Chinese partners.

LIMITATIONS OF THE RESEARCH

In this chapter we presented the first results of our research on the emergence of business schools as loosely coupled networks. At this stage, we should still be cautious in drawing firm conclusions from the outcomes. Although our research provides several insights, the numbers remain small, and the observations therefore deserve further investigation. We cannot claim that the data about the European business schools that are included in our research represent the entire story of European business schools. The overall picture of this (Western) European story has been dominated by the presence of a few renowned business schools. Not all of those schools have responded to the invitation to complete our survey. Also, the rapid growth of management education programs in Eastern Europe might change the general picture that has been prevalent until now. However, our research does provide some new insights into how European business schools are responding to the challenges they see themselves confronted with in their environments.

Another limitation of the findings is that our survey data only give insight into the complex and dynamic arrangements between business schools and their partners that together make up the loosely coupled network. From a research point of view, there are several other intriguing questions that need to be addressed in further research, such as:

- What are the reasons for business schools to engage in partnerships and develop themselves as loosely coupled networks?
- How and on the basis of which criteria do business schools select their partners? Who will be partnering with whom?
- What are the differences between European, North American, and Asian business schools in terms of their composition as loosely coupled networks? Will they connect to each other?
- How do schools secure their identity and autonomy as a loosely coupled network?
- What kinds of governance structures are used in these loosely coupled networks?
- How will the competition look like when the rise of loosely coupled networks is changing the supply side of the market?

Also, the survey will be followed up by conducting a number case studies on business schools as loosely coupled networks in later stages of our research.

Finally, the market for management education is in a process of continuing transformation, in both the demand side and the supply side. Although our research does address future intentions of European business schools, and therefore casts a prospective view on the development of business schools as loosely coupled networks, it primarily provides a more static view—a map—of the supply side of this market. In order to gain solid evolutionary insight into this transformation process, it will be necessary to monitor qualitative and quantitative changes over a long-term period.

CONCLUSIONS

The fact that business schools have not been able to cope with their inherent structural ambiguity effectively has caused two business school crises. As we have discussed in the beginning of this chapter, the changes that are taking place in the market for management education may evolve into a new crisis. On both the demand side and the supply side, changes are placing new demands on business schools, causing them to rethink their positions and their roles as providers of management education. New competitors, including overseas business schools as well as non-business school providers of management education, are entering the market. Several types of management education providers, such as traditional business schools, new media companies, and consultancy firms, are forming alliances and are becoming strong competitors in the market. Their focused offerings, customer-oriented services, private base, organizational flexibility, and independent position with respect to the academic value system are their competitive strengths in the market. As Gaddis (2000, p. 8) says: "With the e-education market spawning more and more competitors offering specialized and customized products and programs, established business schools will have to respond in kind."

Also, the demand for management education is becoming increasingly fragmented as traditional student bodies are complemented by new types of students that are asking for novel educational solutions. In order not to become victims of their structural ambiguity again, business schools need to develop balanced models of management education that enable them to exploit this structural ambiguity as a strength rather than a liability. In our opinion, if business schools are unable to develop these models, they may lose their once uncompromised position as leaders in management thinking and as primary providers of management education.

The idea of business schools as loosely coupled networks presents an organizational response to changes within this dynamic market for management education and provides an organizational framework to develop balanced models of management education. Gaining empirical insights into the responses of business schools as one of the most popular divisions of the higher education system is important to counterbalance the all-too-wild speculations on the future of business schools and the educational strategies to which they will adhere. For this reason, we started our research on the rise and profiles of business schools as loosely coupled networks in Europe.

The findings of our research as presented in this chapter clearly indicate the emergence of business schools as loosely coupled networks. Since 2000, European business schools have been especially active in establishing partnerships with other business schools and companies. Moreover, many business schools intend to engage in new partnerships or additional partnerships in the near future. The number of partnerships in which schools are engaged and the variation in types of partnerships are still limited, however, as is the average number of schools involved in these relationships. The geographical scope of these business schools as loosely coupled networks is mainly confined to Europe. Our research indicates that the supply side of the management education market is changing and that European business schools are pursuing strategies of "going along" rather than "going alone" to meet the demands their environments are placing on them.

The networks in which university-based business schools participate should profile on high-quality research, reputation, and university status of the schools (AACSB, 2002). The evolving market for management education schools may bring about a new sort of business school and a new type of competition in which different types of supply structures of management education engage. The concept of the business school, as it has reigned for over a century, is changing.

NOTES

1.   A partnership or network may of course focus on all of these activities.

2.   In a way, however, we also see this reflected in Cheit's approach. While both these notions accept the inherent structural ambiguity of business schools, the approach of Cotton et al. seems to recognize this structural ambiguity more than Cheit's, since the latter allows for models characterized by high academic levels and relatively low professional levels.

3.   It should be noted that this solution is a *re*solution rather than a *dis*solution for these conflicts and tensions. In the former case, structural ambiguity is recognized and capitalized upon, while in the latter case, structural ambiguity is eliminated.

4.   This corresponds with Benson's principle of totality in dialectical analysis (Benson, 1977).

5.   Thompson (1967) called this "the duality of organizations." As a corollary of the duality of organizations, the duality of business schools can thus be seen as residing in the structural ambiguity that arises from tensions between academic and professional models of management education.

6. As a loosely coupled network as a whole, the business school may also distinguish itself through its particular set of subsystems which sets it apart from other loosely coupled networks.

7. The term *partnership* was chosen because of its neutral nature. In a recent article named "A Lexicon of Inter-Institutional Co-Operation" by Daniel W. Lang (2002), the following forms of "co-operation" between educational institutions are distinguished: program closure; responsibility center budgeting (RCB); management by contract, consortia, federation, affiliation, merger; and merger with RCB. Lang does not distinguish networks at all, though some will argue that networks are synonymous with federations (while others, in turn, will contradict such a view). Duysters, de Man, and Wildeman (1999) have elaborated on a network approach to forming and managing alliances, opposing dyadic alliances to network alliances. With so much opportunity for nuance and distorted interpretations, researchers find themselves walking a thin line using a differentiated terminology. One only has to glance at a small selection of articles from literature on strategic management or organization studies in order to become aware of the wide range of conceptions and interpretations of coordinating mechanisms that are regularly distinguished. Using a differentiated terminology may well result in distortions in questionnaire completion and consequently may compromise the validity of the data gathered. What one respondent may identify or interpret as one form of coordination mechanism may not be considered to be as such by another respondent. The only thing a partnership implies, in our view, is multiple parties coordinating certain activities for certain reasons in certain ways. Such a perspective is therefore beneficial to the purposes of this research project. By implication, this means that a range of coordination mechanisms can be mapped by using the term *partnership* as an umbrella term; it does not exclude any coordination mechanism the research aims to identify in advance.

8. Out of the 48 responses, only 44 responses were complete. On three occasions, data were missing for one dimension. On one occasion, data were incomplete for two dimensions.

REFERENCES

Amdam, R. P. (Ed.). (1996). *Management education and competitiveness: Europe, Japan and the United States.* London: Routledge.

Association to Advance Collegiate Schools of Business International (AACSB International). (2002). *Management education at risk* (Report of the Management Education Task Force to the AACSB International Board of Directors). St. Louis, MO: Author.

Association to Advance Collegiate Schools of Business International (AACSB International). (2003). *Eligibility procedures and standards for business accreditation.* St. Louis, MO: Author.

Baden-Fuller, C., & Ang, S. W. (2001). Building reputations: The role of alliances in the European business school scene. *Long Range Planning, 34*(6), 741–755.

Benson, K. J. (1977). Organizations: A dialectical view. *Administrative Science Quarterly, 22*(1), 1–21.

Bossard, J. H. S., & Dewhurst, J. F. (1931). *University education for business: A study of existing needs and practices.* Philadelphia: University of Pennsylvania Press.

Boutaiba, S., & Pedersen, J. S. (2003). Creating an MBA identity: Between field and organization. In R. P. Amdam, R. Kvåshaugen, & E. Larssen (Eds.), *Inside the business school. The content of European business education* (pp. 197–218). Copenhagen: Copenhagen Business School Press.

Brown, J. S., Durchslag, S., & Hagel, J., III. (2002). Loosening up: How process networks unlock the power of specialization. *McKinsey Quarterly, 2,* 23–33.

Brusoni, S., & Prencipe, A. (2001). Managing knowledge in loosely coupled networks: Exploring the links between product and knowledge dynamics. *Journal of Management Studies, 38*(7), 1019–1035.

Byrkjeflot, H. (2001). *E-learning alliances. The new partnerships in business education.* Bergen, Norway: Stein Rokkan Centre for Social Studies. Retrieved March 23, 2004, from http://los.rokkan.uib.no/losforsk/PDF/2001/Notat/N0102.pdf

Castells, M. (1996). *The rise of the network society.* Cambridge, MA: Blackwell.

Chandler, A. D. (1977). *The visible hand: The managerial revolution in American business.* Cambridge, MA: Harvard University Press.

Cheit, E. F. (1985). Business schools and their critics. *California Management Review, 27*(3), 43–62.

Cotton, C. C., McKenna, J. F., van Auken, S., & Meuter, M. L. (2001). Action and reaction in the evolution of business school missions. *Management Decision, 39*(3), 227–232.

Crainer, S., & Dearlove, D. (1999). *Gravy training: Inside the real world of business schools.* Oxford: Capstone.

Daniel, C. A. (1998). *MBA: The first century.* London: Associated University Presses.

Dhillon, G., & Orton, J. D. (2001). Schizoid incoherence, microstrategic options, and the strategic management of new organizational forms. *M@n@gement, 4*(4), 229–240.

Doria, J., Rozanski, H., & Cohen, E. (2003, Fall). What business needs from business schools? *Strategy+Business,* 2–8.

Duysters, G., de Man, A. P., & Wildeman, L. (1999). A network approach to alliance management. *European Management Journal, 17*(2), 182–187.

Engwall, L. (1992). *Mercury meets Minerva.* Oxford: Pergamon Press.

Engwall, L. (1998). Mercury and Minerva: Modern multinational academic business studies on a global scale. In J. L. Alvarez (Ed.), *The diffusion and consumption of business knowledge.* London: Macmillan.

Engwall, L., & Zamagni, V. (1998). *Management education in historical perspective.* Manchester, England: Manchester University Press.

Gaddis, P. O. (2000, 4th qtr). Business schools: Fighting the enemy within. *Strategy+Business,* 1–8.

Ghoshal, S., Arnzen, B., & Brownfield, S. (1992). A learning alliance between business and business schools. *California Management Review, 35*(1), 50–67.

Glassman, R. B. (1973). Persistence and loose coupling in living systems. *Behavioral Science, 18*(2), 83–98.

Haas school of business faculty member & SysIQ launch study to understand online purchasing behavior. Market Wire. (2003, December 17). Retrieved from http://www.marketwire.com/mw/home

Hugstad, P. S. (1983). *The business school in the 1980s: Liberalism versus vocationalism.* New York: Praeger.

International marriage of b-school giants. (2001, March 29). *Business Week.*

Lang, D. W. (2002). A lexicon of inter-institutional cooperation. *Higher Education, 44*(1), 153–183.

Law, K. S., Wong, C., & Mobley, W. H. (1998). Toward a taxonomy of multidimensional constructs. *Academy of Management Review, 23*(4), 741–755.

Light, D. W. (1983). The development of professional schools in America. In K. Jarausch (Ed.), *The transformation of higher learning, 1860–1930* (pp. 345–367). University of Chicago Press: Chicago.

Livermore, C. (2002). *Getting down to business (schools).* Retrieved March 23, 2004, from http://www.pathfinder-one.com/Pages/articles/mar02bus.htm

Livingstone, J. S. (1971, January–February). Myth of the well-educated manager. *Harvard Business Review,* 79–89.

Locke, R. R. (1984). *The end of practical man: Entrepreneurship and higher education in Germany, France and Great Britain, 1880–1940.* Greenwich, CT: JAI Press.

Locke, R. R. (1989). *Management and higher education since 1940: The influence of America and Japan on West Germany, Great Britain, and France.* Cambridge: Cambridge University Press.

Macfarlane, B. (1995). Business and management studies in higher education. *International Journal of Educational Management, 9*(5), 4–9.

MBA Program Information Site. (2004). Retrieved March 23, 2004, from http://www.MBAinfo.com

Meister, J. (1998). *Corporate universities: Lessons in building a world-class work force.* New York: McGraw-Hill.

Miles, R. E. (1985). The future of business education. *California Management Review, 27*(3), 63–73.

New model for global EMBAs. (2001, October 26). *Business Week.*

Nowotny, H. (2003). Democratising expertise and socially robust knowledge. *Science and Public Policy, 30*(3), 151–156.

Orton, J. D., & Weick, K. E. (1990). Loosely coupled systems: A reconceptualization. *Academy of Management Review, 15*(2), 203–223.

Pfeffer, J., & Fong, C. T. (2002). The end of business schools? Less success than meets the eye. *Academy of Management Learning and Education, 1*(1), 78–96.

Porter, L. W., & McKibbin, L. E. (1988). *Management education and development: Drift or thrust into the 21st century?* New York: McGraw-Hill.

Robins, K., & Webster, F. (Eds.). (2002). *The virtual university? Knowledge, markets, and management.* Oxford: Oxford University Press.

Rowan, B. (2002). Rationality and reality in organizational management: Using the coupling metaphor to understand educational and other organizations: A concluding comment. *Journal of Educational Administration, 40*(6), 604–611.

Schilling, M. A., & Steensma, H. K. (2001). The use of modular organizational forms: An industry-level analysis. *Academy of Management Journal, 44*(6), 1149–1168.

Schlossman, S., Sedlak, M., & Wechsler, H. (1987, Winter). The "New Look," the Ford Foundation, and the revolution in business education. *Selections,* 11–31.

Schools link hands across the globe. (2003, October 20). *Financial Times.*

Spoun, S. (1998). *Internationalisierung von Universitäten. Eine Studie am Beispiel der Community of European Management Schools.* Doctoral Dissertation. Bamberg, Germany: Difo-Druck.
These b-schools make headway by consorting with the competition. (2000, October 6). *Business Week.*
Thompson, J. D. (1967). *Organizations in action: Social science bases of administrative theory.* New York: McGraw-Hill.
Trieschmann, J. S., Dennis, A. R., Northcraft, G. B., & Niemi, A. W., Jr. (2000). Serving multiple constituencies in business schools. *Academy of Management Journal, 43*(6), 1130–1141.
Trow, M. (2002). Some consequences of the new information and communication technologies for higher education. In K. Robins and F. Webster (Eds.), *The virtual university? Knowledge, markets, and management* (pp. 301–317). Oxford: Oxford University Press.
Universitas 21 (2004). *Universitas 21: A network for higher education.* Retrieved March 23, 2004, from http://www.Universitas21.com
van Baalen, P. J. (1995). *Management en hoger onderwijs. De geschiedenis van het academisch management-onderwijs in Nederland.* Doctoral dissertation. Delft, the Netherlands: Eburon.
van Baalen, P. J., & Leijnse, F. (1995). Beyond the discipline: Inserting interdisciplinarity in business and management education. In P. J. van Baalen (Ed.), *New challenges for the business schools.* Delft, the Netherlands: Eburon.
van Baalen, P. J., & Moratis, L. T. (2001). *Management education in the network economy: Its context, content, and organization.* Dordrecht, the Netherlands: Kluwer Academic Publishers.
Weick, K. E. (1976). Educational organizations as loosely coupled systems. *Administrative Science Quarterly, 21*(1), 1–19.
Weick, K. E. (1982). Management of organizational change among loosely coupled elements. In P. S. Goodman and Associates (Eds.), *Change in Organizations* (pp. 375–408). San Francisco: Jossey-Bass.

CHAPTER 2

INTERNATIONALIZING FRENCH MANAGEMENT EDUCATION

A Contextual Analysis of Strategies in French Business Schools

Junko Takagi and Jean-Luc Cerdin

INTRODUCTION

Although most international business education literature takes a linear, non-contextual view of the internationalizing process by assuming that it is a universal phenomenon, the French context seems to contradict these assumptions. In this chapter, we identify differentiated internationalizing logics coexisting in the French business school population which explain variance in strategies found among these schools. We argue that internationalization can take different meanings, implying the necessity to take into consideration contextual factors in analyzing internationalizing strategies.

In the academic literature on the internationalization of management education, there is general agreement that the globalization of economies

The Cutting Edge of International Management Education, pages 37–61

37

has strongly influenced the internationalization process (e.g., Aggarwal, 1989; Gniewosz, 1996, 2000; Goldberg, 1992–1993; Kwok, Arpan, & Folks, 1994; Kyj, Kyj, & Marshall, 1995; Luuostarinen & Pulkinnen, 1991; Nehrt, 1987; Pitt, Berthon, & Robson, 1997; Schoell, 1991). There is an implicit assumption that a direct relationship exists between economic pressures in the business environment and the content of management education. It is also assumed that the internationalization of management education is a universal phenomenon with common meanings and objectives. Attention is thus restricted to the organizational level of analysis, and studies focus on the extent to which schools and programs are "internationalized." While some studies emphasize the national specificities of management education and its impact on internationalization (see Gnieswosz, 1996; 2000), none investigate the role and meaning of internationalization within different contexts to discover whether the assumptions in the literature are correct.

For example, the French management education field seems to contradict these assumptions. A study of this field indicates an evolution towards an Anglo-Saxon model over the past thirty years (Takagi & de Carlo, 2003). During that period, it is possible to identify three phases and two different logics of internationalization. We see changes not only at the organizational level but also at the institutional level, and the meaning of *internationalization* has evolved along with the institutional framework. The means of internationalization have also evolved from imitation to legitimation, while the institutional focus has shifted from the national to the transnational, a distinction elaborated on by Djelic and Quack (2003). Even though internationalizing practices in French business schools strongly resemble strategies generally found in the literature, a contextual approach underscores variance in objectives, target markets, and the importance placed on each strategy.

In this chapter, we present the internationalizing of French management education through a contextual analysis of the evolution of the field in general, and of the strategies of a selection of business schools in particular. We show how the field has evolved and what this entails for the definition of the term *international.* We investigate how different strategies fit the meanings that are available, and we also analyze market expectations regarding internationalization through a survey of French business school students. Finally, based on our analysis, we discuss potential consequences for the future.

THE FRENCH CONTEXT

In France, due to an active effort on the part of French public administration to encourage the proliferation of management education since the

1960s (Takagi & de Carlo, 2003) which was motivated in large part by the observation that the French economy was lagging behind that of the United States (Servan-Schreiber, 1967), French management education as an organizational field has in fact been internationalizing for several decades. We argue that while the concept of internationalization has become more strategic at the organizational level (i.e., individual business schools) over the past decade, it has been a recurrent theme in the development of these schools since the 1960s. During that period, the locus of action or the level at which internationalization has taken place has shifted from the organizational level to the field level, and from that, to the level of the institutional environment. These shifts reflect the nature of institutional change as elaborated by Tolbert and Zucker (1996) where new logics are first incorporated into action patterns at the micro-level and over time attain "habituation" status. These logics are gradually incorporated into governance structures, a stage identified as "objectification," and are eventually institutionalized as a regulatory and normative system.

Periods of Internationalization

We can clearly identify periods and levels of internationalization of French management education beginning in the latter half of the 1960s. First, there was imitation of certain aspects of the North American model, particularly related to content. This phase occurred in conjunction with a period of accommodation in which there was an active incorporation of this model into the national institutional framework resulting in local legitimation of the model. More recently, we observe the expansion of the institutional field from the national to the transnational.

The Ministry of Education and the Fondation Nationale pour l'Enseignement de la Gestion (FNEGE) propagated the first period simultaneously. The FNEGE was initiated in part by the Ministry of Industry in 1968 with the goal of encouraging global competitiveness of the French economy and identifying management education as a key component. The FNEGE helped to develop a certain level of internationalization in management education in France by implementing a program to send French academics to North American and European universities to acquire academic training in management fields (Chessel & Pavis, 2001). Before this period, instruction in business schools was based around economics and law. More business-oriented subjects such as marketing and accounting were incorporated into the curriculum at this time. Also, a permanent faculty body began to be established in business schools around this period, and full-time faculty with degrees in management science started to appear. The first French doctoral program in management was established in the university system, although graduates with doctoral degrees in management did not appear until the mid-1970s.

The first university completely dedicated to management issues was founded in 1968–1969, and management fields (in both teaching and research) were introduced into the French university system at the same time. The establishment of doctoral programs in management in French universities has helped increase the number of faculty members with doctoral degrees in management as well as the more traditional disciplines of economics and law. Since the university system has almost a complete monopoly of doctoral degrees,[1] the introduction of management as an academic field within this system has accorded an important place for universities in French management education despite their late entry into the field.

In considering internationalization, it is also important to take into account the role of competitors and potential role models, and in particular the placement of INSEAD in France in 1958–1959. As Bjorkjeflot (2003) indicates, INSEAD is still one of the few fully international management programs in Europe.[2] The benchmark role that INSEAD played in the process of internationalization at this stage is undeniable.

In this first phase of internationalization, imitation occurred in two different organizational populations. Changes occurred in the teaching and research fields in the already existing business schools. A system of permanent faculty was inaugurated, and academic departments were formalized, incorporating both North American and French academic traditions in management. The university system, which until this time had not accommodated management education, became a new entry into this field, also structuring programs around the North American model.

The second period may be defined as the objectification and institutionalization stage (Tolbert & Zucker, 1996). For example, the role of the Ministry of Education has been mostly as a local accrediting agent, but since the late 1960s, it has played an active role in legitimating management as an academic field in France by incorporating it into the university system and creating doctoral programs and degrees in management.

Also, in the face of increasing internal competition from universities created by the active participation of the state to bring French management education up to international standards, there was an endeavor to strengthen credibility and legitimacy of the traditional *grandes écoles* by bringing together interests of the business and engineering schools. The Conférence des Grandes Écoles, created in 1973, groups both engineering and business schools, providing a source of peer legitimacy for member schools. Membership serves an accreditation function and permits the prestigious label of *grande école* to member schools.[3] One requisite of a grande école is the international dimension comprising compulsory foreign language requirements, the possibility of internships abroad, and the acquisition of double diplomas with foreign management institutions. More recently, the business school chapter has actively participated in EQUAL (European Quality Link), which brings together national-level accrediting bodies from European countries to assess accreditation systems in Europe and to develop European quality assurance for management education (Hedmo, 2003).

In the third and most recent phase of internationalization, there is a search by individual business schools for international recognition through accreditation at either the school or program level. Whereas local institutions have encouraged French management education to develop the international dimension in the first two periods, the past decade has witnessed an increasing interest on the part of some French business schools to seek accreditation from non-French institutions such as the American AACSB, the Brussels-based EFMD (EQUIS), and the AMBA for specific MBA programs. To date, ten French business schools have been accredited by EQUIS. Three schools have also been accredited by the AACSB. While EQUIS is a joint European conception forged by its member schools, the AACSB can be considered an external legitimating body. There is also more attention in French higher education to the labeling of degree programs, resulting in an increase in programs with the MBA label. Thus, a recent trend has been to expand the institutional field of management education and of business schools in particular, from the national to the transnational arena.

The initial phase of internationalization concerned the development of the organization (establishment of management fields such as marketing and finance) and content to accommodate North American management perspectives through a preoccupation on the part of French institutions to increase the level of national economic competitiveness. We observe an isomorphic phenomenon whereby North American management fields and degree programs were incorporated into the French education system. This is followed by assimilation and legitimation of these practices as witnessed by the development of rules and local institutions. These two phases see developments at both the local institutional and the organizational field levels. The third phase of internationalization is centered around the schools themselves with a goal to compete in the global management education market for recognition and to diversify faculty and student populations. In this phase, schools perceive international accreditation as recognition that they are international and as a key to accessing transnational markets.

The first two phases are an elaboration of the same institutional logic, the goal being to operate within the national institutional framework to incorporate perspectives on management that were considered to be the most competitive and to add more international dimensions (internationalization). We argue that the most recent phase embodies a paradigm shift (Djelic & Quack, 2003) in which the meaning of *international* is no longer solely embedded within a national institutional framework. Schools seek to align themselves to global definitions and participate in the creation of a new transnational institutional framework (globalization).

Table 2.1 summarizes and contrasts the three stages of evolution of the international dimension in French management education. The study of the French system allows us to identify distinct motivations for internationalization in the French context and underscores the importance of investigating the institutional environment of management education in order to understand the process of internationalization.

Table 2.1.   Periods of Internationalization in French Management Education

Period	1960s–1970s	1970s to now	mid-1990s to now
Institutional Field	National	National	Transnational
Logic	Americanization	Internationalization	Globalization
Means of internationalization	Imitation (disciplines/ structure)	Institutionalization National accreditation	Globalization Transnational accreditation
Key institutional actors	1. FNEGE 2. Role models (e.g. INSEAD) 3. Ministry of Education	1. Ministry of Education; Creation of management programs in the local university system; Creation of doctoral programs 2. Conférence des Grandes Ecoles	1. International accrediting agents (AACSB, EQUIS, AMBA, etc.)
Organizational Strategies	• introduction of management disciplines • development of permanent business faculty • faculty with North American and European management degrees • internationalization of local market	• membership in Conférence des Grandes Ecoles • recognition of programs and degrees by the Ministry of Education • local legitimation of international dimensions	• membership in EQUAL, AACSB, etc. • international accreditation of programs • international legitimation of programs

Evaluation of Internationalizing Strategies in French Business Schools

Having described the context of internationalization of French management education, we look at the current status of internationalization through an evaluation of strategies found in a sample of business schools. First, we list dimensions used in the literature to ascertain the degree of internationalization, and we compare this to dimensions used by French business schools to describe their programs. The business school data is based on information obtained through official websites of business schools recognized by the Conférence des Grandes Écoles, Chapitre des Écoles de Commerce. The business school chapter of the Conférence des Grandes Écoles lists twenty-seven business schools. Ten of these schools are currently accredited by EQUIS, and three are also accredited by the AACSB. Following our analysis of the evolution of internationalization in the French management education context, we distinguish between schools that are aligned to the internationalization logic and those that adhere to the globalization logic. In the following analysis, we operationalize this variable by international accreditation such that schools with accreditation follow a globalization logic while those that are not accredited follow an internationalization logic.

Table 2.2 presents dimensions for the internationalization of management education that are discussed in the academic literature. Most studies investigate a range of dimensions, but there are variations in the combination of dimensions used. We use these dimensions to evaluate internationalizing strategies of our sample of French business schools.

Table 2.2.   Dimensions Used in the Academic Literature to Assess Internationalization of Management Education

Dimensions	Strategies	Studies
Internationalization objectives	School or departmental mission	Arpan and Kwok (2000), Kwok et. al. (1994), Kwok and Arpan (1994), Tyagi (2001)
Internationalization of curriculum	Curriculum	Arpan and Kwok (2000), Ahwireng-Obeng (1999), Gniewosz (1996, 2000), Kwok and Arpan (1994), Kwok et. al. (1994), Nehrt (1987), Luuostarinen and Pulkinnen (1991), Tyagi (2001)
	Languages	Gniewosz (1996, 2000), Luuostarinen and Pulkinnen (1991)
	Teaching style and methodology	Ahwiren-Obeng (1999), Salehi-Sangari and Foster (1999)

Table 2.2.   Dimensions Used in the Academic Literature to Assess Internationalization of Management Education (Cont.)

Dimensions	Strategies	Studies
	Textbooks/ Information sources	Francis and Globerman (1992/3), Salehi-Sangari and Foster (1999)
	Student evaluation	Salehi-Sangari and Foster (1999)
Organization	Organizational issues	Arpan and Kwok (2000), Gniewosz (1996, 2000), Luuostarinen and Pulkinnen (1991), Kwok and Arpan (1994), Kwok et al. (1994)
Faculty	Faculty	Arpan and Kwok (2000), Kwok and Arpan (1994), Kwok et al. (1994), Tyagi (2001)
	Research	Luuostarinen and Pulkinnen (1991)
International experience	Exchange programs and alliances	Arpan and Kwok (2000), Ahwireng-Obeng (1999), Gniewosz (1996, 2000), Luuostarinen and Pulkinnen (1991), Nehrt (1987), Kwok and Arpan (1994), Kwok et al. (1994), Tyagi (2001)
	Student internship	Arpan and Kwok (2000)
	Overseas campus	Nehrt (1987)

Dimension 1. Internationalization Objectives

Some studies focus on the content of the school mission statement and whether or not internationalization objectives are stated. This is assumed to indicate the perceived strategic importance of the international dimension for the image of the school and how serious the school is regarding internationalization.

Figure 2.1 shows the percentage of French business schools in our sample with mission statements and objectives that include the international dimension in some form. Schools corresponding to the globalization logic are more likely to have mission statements, and to also include the international dimension in them. In the three schools with both AACSB and EQUIS accreditation, the international dimension is an integral element in the identity of the school as stated in their missions and objectives. This is much less so for schools under the internationalization logic, with less than 50% including the international dimension in their objectives.

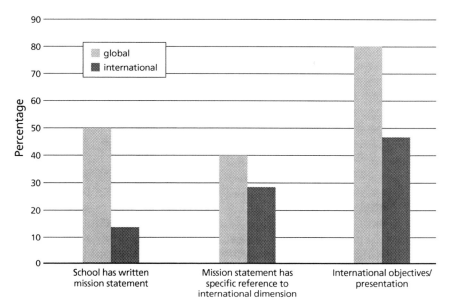

Figure 2.1.   International objectives of French business schools.

Dimension 2. Internationalization of Curriculum

Kwok et al. (1994) identify three objectives for international management education—awareness, understanding, and expertise. This taxonomy corresponds to methods for incorporating international content into educational programs. International topics may be introduced into already existing courses through infusion. If the objective is to generate deeper understanding of cross-national differences in management fields, then courses may be created either at a general level or with specificity. Where expertise is required, whole programs may be created. Some studies have found that objectives for international management education differ across academic levels. Awareness was more important at the bachelor level as compared to master's and doctoral levels, whereas understanding and expertise were more important for the master's level (Arpan & Kwok, 2000; Beamish & Calof, 1989; Herremans & Wright, 1992). Studies focusing on the internationalization of management education in non-North American settings also focus on language acquisition in programs as an indication of the level of internationalization of a program (Gniewosz, 1996; 2000; Luuostarinen & Pulkinnen, 1991).

Dimension 3. Organization

The concept of substance (content) versus structure (organization) is frequently found in the literature. It is presented as a linear continuum along which internationalization progresses. In contrast, Amdam, Kvålshaugen and Larsen (2003) present the juxtaposition of the two concepts according to neo-institutional theory. Various studies look at the structure or organization of international content within schools. For example, Kwok et al. (1994) and Kwok and Arpan (1994) investigate the presence of international business (IB) programs and departments. Programs reflect recognition of IB as a functional field while IB departments reflect a perception of IB as an academic field. Similar studies also look at who organizes IB programs (Arpan & Kwok, 2000), and program requirements (Andrus, Laughlin, & Norvell, 1995).

Our analysis combines the curriculum and organization dimensions. Figure 2.2 shows that the percentage of schools in our sample with IB departments (e.g., "international affairs and management" and "business and international environment") that correspond to the globalization logic is greater than for other schools. A similar relationship holds for accreditation and IB-related research centers and institutes. In fact, accredited schools are more likely to emphasize the importance of research and to provide detailed information on faculty and research activities. Since foreign language training is an integral part of French management educa-

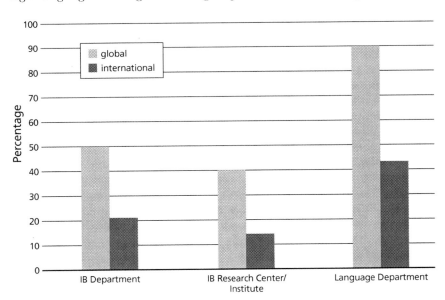

Figure 2.2.   Percentage of IB departments, language departments and IB research centers.

tion, most of the schools have a department combining language and culture. From the information available, international accreditation is positively correlated with the presence of a language department with full-time faculty. Some of the courses offered in intercultural management are given by these language departments (See the chapter by Ancilli, Betta, Dinelli, Hougaz, & Mascitelli in this volume).

Figure 2.3 depicts the percentage of schools in each category with IB programs or majors. We have separated the main grande école program in all of the schools[4] in our sample from other master's level programs, and we look at IB specialization in this program. A majority of schools claim to have both compulsory and elective IB courses, some of which are given in English. As the figure indicates, a slightly higher percentage of schools with a global focus have IB majors in their main program. Three accredited schools mention infusion of international business issues in all their courses. Language requirements for these programs vary from two to three foreign languages. Usually, two are compulsory, and the third is either an elective or based on the student's ability in the first two languages. Accreditation correlates inversely with the mention of either the TOEFL or TOEIC as a graduation requirement.

We also distinguish between MBAs and other types of master's level programs since the MBA is often presented as an indication of internationalization in which the language of instruction is predominantly English. Again, we find the greatest differences between accredited and non-accredited

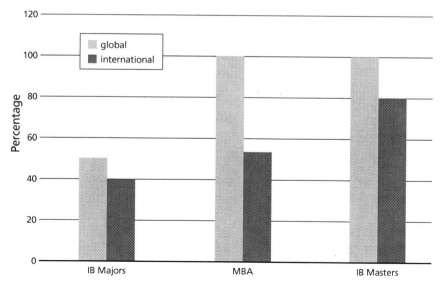

Figure 2.3.   Percentage of schools with international programs.

schools. Accreditation ensures the presence of MBA programs, with an average of four MBA programs in the schools with double accreditation and 1.5 programs for schools with single accreditation. Although all schools have non-MBA master's level programs, the globalization logic is also positively correlated with the presence of IB-related programs. In addition, it increases the likelihood that international business programs are taught in English than in French.

Dimension 4. Faculty

A number of studies discuss issues related to faculty. According to Arpan and Kwok (2000), European business schools are much more likely than United States schools to appoint a non-national as dean, indicating a higher level of internationalization for schools with non-national deans. There is also discussion on different methods employed by schools to encourage faculty acquisition of international expertise. Schools that are more developed along the international dimension encourage and reward participation in international conferences, teaching in other countries through exchange programs, and research in international business (Kwok & Arpan, 1994; Andrus et al., 1995).

Information on faculty is not systematic, and it is difficult to verify in our data source. If we look at what is presented in the official website of each school, some give a percentage of non-French full-time faculty members. The percentage of foreign faculty is presented as an indication of the level of internationalization of a school. The average percentage of foreign faculty for each category increases from just over 20% in schools corresponding to the global logic to 50.7% in the other schools. Part of the inflation of this figure for the latter schools is probably a reflection of the comparatively small number of permanent faculty. Also, in cases where there is no detailed faculty information, it is difficult to determine whether or not this figure also includes visiting professors. (The figure does include language professors.) Due to the inconsistent nature of information available for this dimension, it is difficult to draw any conclusions.

Dimension 5. Internationalization of Students

Most of the studies reviewed look at the opportunities provided by schools for students to gain international experience through exchange programs with other schools, alliances, overseas internships, the presence of an overseas campus, and the number of foreign students and their countries of origin (e.g., Schoell, 1991). Often, these studies report the types of exchanges/alliances and the number of schools with which the target school is linked (e.g., Luuostarinen & Pulkinnen, 1991; Nehrt, 1987; Kwok et al., 1994).

All schools in our sample communicate the number of alliances and exchange opportunities they have. They range from 52 to 96 in accredited schools and 40 to 120 in other schools. While accredited schools systematically mention their double diploma programs (range: 3 to 13), this information is not systematic for non-accredited schools (range: 6 to 43). Most schools provide information of the foreign student population either in raw numbers (range: 160 to 400) or as a percentage of the student population (16% to 42%). Overseas experience is compulsory for all accredited schools, though there is some variation in the minimum length of stay (three months to six months) and in the destination (one school has specifically designated the United States). Only two accredited schools have overseas campuses in our sample.

DISCUSSION

The above analysis of internationalizing strategies in French business schools indicates that practices differ according to the institutional framework in which the school is embedded. We therefore observe significant differences between accredited and non-accredited schools. Schools often emphasize accreditation by the AACSB and EQUIS as the recognition of the internationalization of the school and its programs. We find statements such as "[EQUIS accreditation] is the recognition that the school meets international standards," and "[recognition of] efforts made by the school to become more international." As compared to the North American schools for whom the AACSB serves as a guideline for internationalization, French schools perceive accreditation to be a goal in itself, equating accreditation with "being international."

Many French schools have also changed their names to include English terms such as *school of business and management, graduate school of management, European school of management,* and *management/business school.* Figure 2.4 shows the differences between schools corresponding to the two logics; we observe that greater differences exist for schools with English names. Both categories of schools are less likely to have English logos. Here, there is a tendency to consider using English as being synonymous with becoming international. This phenomenon is also visible in the language of instruction of international business programs, particularly in MBA programs. Increasing numbers of programs are either bi-lingual (French and English) or completely in English.

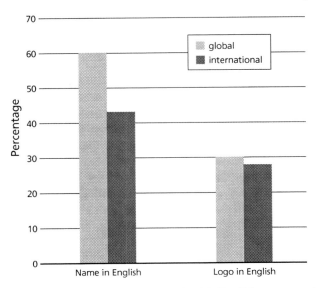

Figure 2.4.   Percentage of schools with English names and logos.

Another parallel phenomenon is the number of MBA programs in the French business schools. In France, EQUIS- and AACSB-accredited schools tend to have more MBA programs, which are in turn more likely to be accredited by the AMBA. Many schools have a general full-time MBA and an executive MBA program. Some schools have up to six different MBA programs, which are either industry specific (e.g., luxury-brand, wine, aerospace) or based in different regions. Meyer (2002) perceives the global diffusion of MBAs as a potential cause for the diffusion of American-style corporate governance and management practices. Byrkjeflot (2003) discusses two possibilities for interpretation—either as convergence to global systems (Crainer & Dearlove, 1999) or differentiation based on a "translation of ideas and concepts that take a very different shape in different contexts" (Byrkjeflot, 2003, p. 226). Our analysis leads us to support the more contextual perspective since, although the MBA is generally perceived by French business schools as an internationally recognized degree and consequently a label that adds international credibility to the school, we expect to find content differentiation across programs (Amdam et al., 2003; Takagi & de Carlo, 2003).

We found that it was important for most schools in our sample to give the impression of diversity in their faculty and student populations. It was, however, often difficult to objectively confirm these impressions through the data source used. Only a handful of schools, mostly those with double accreditation, provide extensive information on the nationality and background of their permanent faculty. We observe that where this information is systematic, programs to diversify the student population, such as exchanges, double diplomas, and in some cases, overseas campuses also exist. We predict that there are differences in the level of diversity achieved between these and the other schools.

In general, we find increasing diversity along with more English labels and English as the language of instruction in the sample corresponding to the globalization logic. It may be the case that the use of English is a prerequisite for the internationalization of French schools and more generally of non-Anglophone schools. To a certain extent, this follows the Americanization of management education proposed by Amdam (1996). We argue, however, that French business schools continue to have strong ties to the French institutional framework. The use of English in itself is not going to profoundly change their national identity, although English does permit more possibilities for international experience and interaction. We propose that an emerging characteristic of a more global logic is the emphasis placed on international exchange and interaction opportunities as opposed to international content.

The analysis does not allow us to determine whether schools corresponding to the internationalization logic have chosen to stay at that stage, or whether these schools are looking for resources to move into a more global framework. It is therefore difficult to refine the finding that differences exist between accredited and non-accredited schools. The results nonetheless clearly show these differences and support the notion that two logics of internationalization currently exist in this field.

MARKET EXPECTATIONS

In this section, we discuss and evaluate internationalizing dimensions in regards to their utility and impact for clients of management education (i.e., students and businesses). Although Reynolds and Rice (1988) found that managers valued international experience over management education for international expertise in their workforce, most other studies of management interests show that managers appreciate the importance of education in international training (Ball & McCulloch, 1993; Kohers, 1985). There is little in the literature concerning student interests (see Albers-Miller, Prenshaw, & Straughan, 1999). We provide data from responses to a survey of the perceptions of a sample of 120 first-year French business school students from one business school in France concerning the internationalizing strategies of French business schools. Our main objective in this section is to identity what factors are perceived by this population as adding value for working in an international context. In the discussion, we compare our findings from the student survey with the existing literature on business interests.

Figure 2.5 shows the results of a factor analysis of sixteen international elements that were identified by students in our sample as more or less important. Four components were identified by the analysis as significant: International recognition, intercultural exchange opportunities, language of instruction of management courses, and research-related faculty activities. The figure presents the response means for each component from "not at all important" (1) to "extremely important" (5). The international recognition cluster includes accreditation by an international body, the international renown of the school, and a degree that is recognized abroad. This dimension was perceived by students in our sample as most important for a school to be considered international. In a survey of 300 recruitment managers from firms in the French top 3000, managers rank ordered graduates of business schools along the international dimension. According to Ipsos, a survey-based multinational market research group with its head office in Paris, the top three positions were occupied by schools with double accreditation, and all ten internationally accredited schools were ranked in the top thirteen (Ipsos, 2000). Thus, recognition of a school or degree through international accreditation corresponds with both business and student expectations.

Intercultural exchange opportunities are also perceived by students to be important for a school to be considered international. This dimension groups physical exchange opportunities such as exchange programs, double diplomas, and overseas campuses with more socially interactive opportunities such as diversity of student and faculty populations. Students are far less concerned with the relevance of English as the language of instruction, and show little interest in faculty research activities.

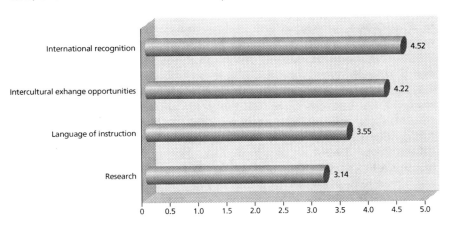

Figure 2.5.   Student perceptions of the importance of elements for a French Business School to be labeled as International.

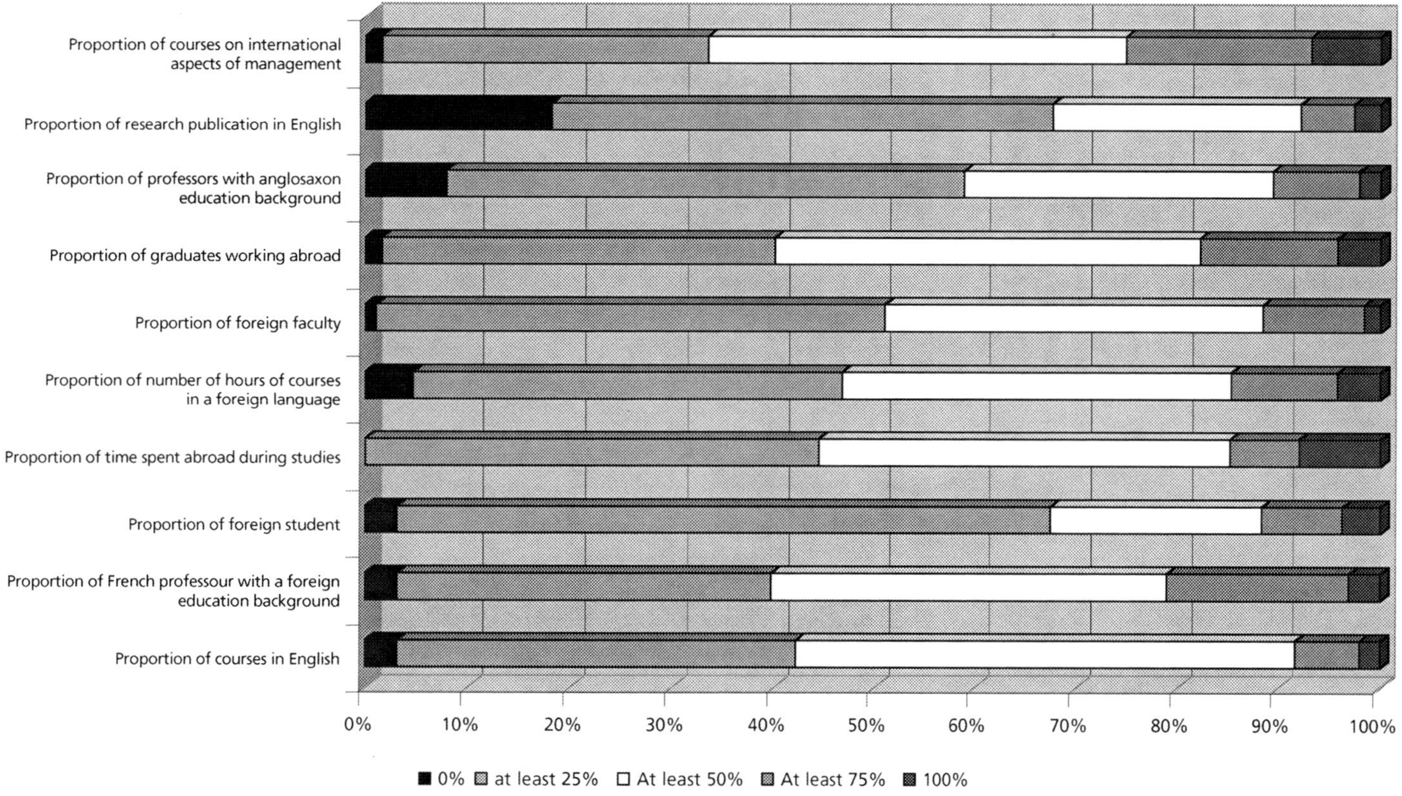
Proportion of courses on international aspects of management
Proportion of research publication in English
Proportion of professors with anglosaxon education background
Proportion of graduates working abroad
Proportion of foreign faculty
Proportion of number of hours of courses in a foreign language
Proportion of time spent abroad during studies
Proportion of foreign student
Proportion of French professour with a foreign education background
Proportion of courses in English
0%
10%
20%
30%
40%
50%
60%
70%
80%
90%
100%
0%
at least 25%
At least 50%
At least 75%
100%

Figure 2.6. Minimum percentage of dimensions to consider a French Business School as international.

Figure 2.6 shows the proportion of each internationalizing dimension that is perceived by students to be necessary in a program for it to be considered international. All students in our sample perceived time spent abroad during studies to be compulsory in an international program. The highest percentage of students also replied that 100% of studies should be spent abroad in order to consider a program as international. In terms of courses, students again seem less concerned with language issues and place more importance on the international content. As in the previous analysis, research-related dimensions are perceived to be least relevant to internationalization.

Figure 2.7 reports student perceptions of the most important criteria used by firms to assess international capabilities of potential new hires. By far, the most important items relate to foreign language proficiency, with more students perceiving multiple language skills to be more important than simply English proficiency. This is followed by items concerning international experience. Students perceive firms to be more interested in candidates with multiple international experiences, with emphasis on the length of those experiences.

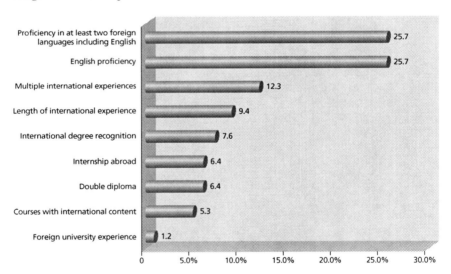

Figure 2.7.   Student perceptions of the importance of international criteria for firms.

DISCUSSION

In articles that investigate managerial perceptions of existing practice and corporate needs (Beamish & Calof, 1989; Herremans & Wright, 1992; Ball & McCulloch, 1993; Lundstrom, White, & Schuster, 1996), researchers often arrive at the conclusion that, while managers perceive a need for international management knowledge in their recruits, they do not see a direct connection between program content and expertise, attaching more value to actual international experience of individuals. Both Kobrin (1984) and Ball and McCulloch (1993) report that over 70% of their executive respondents perceive that employees will learn international business skills on the job. In a study of professional members of the American Marketing Association interested in international marketing, Lundstrom et al. (1996) also found that respondents considered general business/marketing skills as more important for job candidates than international skills and knowledge. These results correspond to Beamish and Calof's (1989) findings that Canadian senior managers distinguished different international skills and knowledge needs for different hierarchical positions within a firm. Senior managers expected new hires to show cultural awareness and language skills. International positions were more likely to be filled by post-experience candidates than new graduates, and international experience and functional skills were desired for post-experience hires. The students in our French sample support these findings in the literature by placing importance on international experience and language skills. They are also aware that firms may place little value on the international course content but nonetheless appreciate this type of knowledge acquisition in an international management program.

For students, faculty research ranks lowest in terms of importance for the internationalization of a school. It is interesting to note that Beamish and Calof (1989) in their study of business perceptions of international management education report that executives do not find academic research useful for business interests. Research continues to be perceived as academic and removed from business practice by both managers and students.

The emphasis on international experience and language skills leads us to conclude that French students perceive international interaction opportunities to be important in international management education. The interaction may be in an academic context as in courses with a diverse student and/or faculty composition, and/or through exchange programs and double diplomas; but it can also include work experience abroad, and also simply time spent abroad. For students, the international dimension is mostly experiential in nature in contrast with more content-based perspectives. This experiential approach is easily incorporated into the transnational institutional framework discussed in the previous section. French business schools corresponding to the globalization logic also emphasize interaction opportunities through a combination of strategies such as diversification of faculty and students, exchange programs, and overseas campuses.

The current study was confined to first-year French students with limited work experience. This is a fairly homogenous population across the business schools in our sample. It is also the most significant population in the schools in our study, and thus we may argue that they represent a majority opinion. However, in a field that is seeking to diversify, it is also important in future studies to take into account expectations of students with other backgrounds in order to claim a representative sample.

CONCLUSIONS

In this chapter, we distinguish between two coexisting institutional arenas for French business schools and identify corresponding logics of internationalization. The internationalization logic provides a somewhat static vision that emphasizes content and structure. It is tied to national institutions and caters mostly to the local market. The globalization logic focuses more on action and accentuates interaction and exchange in the management education system. In this framework, the locus of legitimation expands to include transnational institutions. The literature on internationalizing management education applies to the former logic and cannot address how a school may vacillate from one logic to the other. Institutional arguments consider conditions for institutional persistence and change (Djelic & Quack, 2003) and may also be applied to understand organizational change processes. This perspective allows us to take into account the complexities of the local environment as well as the potentially unifying globalization forces and to present some possible future scenarios for the internationalizing process in French business schools.

In Figure 2.8, we present evolutionary paths of internationalization. Paths 1 and 2 apply to schools that are currently operating within what we have termed the internationalization logic. These schools may remain within their present framework or may transfer to the global framework in the future. The deciding element may be related to structural features of a school. For example, Shetty and Rudell (2002) discuss the effects of size and resources on internationalizing strategies. It may also depend on the target market of the school. There is obviously no need for all business schools to compete on the global market for faculty, students, and firms. As some schools move into this new environment, they will leave more local opportunities for those who remain. At the same time, there is also an imitation effect, which is affected by issues of status and prestige. To the extent to which the initiating schools are perceived to have high status and pres-

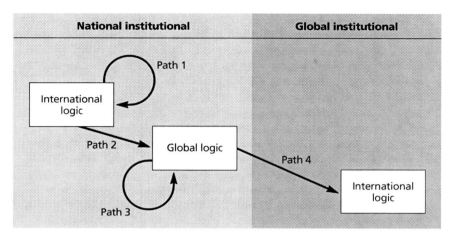

Figure 2.8.   An evolutionary path model of internationalization of French business schools.

tige, there will be more imitation on the part of other schools to shift to the transnational framework.

Currently, all schools operating in the globalization logic are also firmly attached to the local institutional environment. Although they are seeking to extend their frame of reference by seeking connections with transnational institutions in the form of accrediting agents, they are nonetheless dependent upon local institutions such as the Ministry of Education for their legitimation and survival. These schools may remain in this operating mode as indicated by path 3 straddling the two institutional environments, or they may terminate ties with the local environment and move to a transnational existence (path 4). Both these paths are in fact problematic.

First, there are potential inconsistencies between the national and transnational institutional frameworks. When this is the case, the organizational field becomes unstable, and the legitimacy of organizational actors may be jeopardized according to institutional theory (Scott & Meyer, 1991). Scott (1993) notes that in order for new institutional frameworks to be legitimated, old ones need to be delegitimated. Thus, we can hypothesize that in the presence of inconsistencies, business schools may abandon ties to the local institutional environment and move to the transnational arena. The problem here is that the global institutional environment is only just emerging, and there is need for institutional building in the transnational space to support these schools. We note in the chapter that some schools have already participated in this type of process at the European level through the creation of EQUAL. Djelic and Quack (2003) propose that this type of institution building at the transnational level is "a marker and defining characteristic ... of the recent episode of globalization" (2003, p. 25). The model of student expectations regarding internationalization that emerges from our analysis in this chapter fits the globalization logic quite well. This suggests a potential internal force within business schools to move in the transnational direction.

In this chapter, we have focused on the importance of contextual factors in analyzing and understanding internationalizing strategies in management education. Highlighting international elements of the evolution of the French management education field allows us to observe the evolution of internationalizing logics: Americanization, internationalization, and globalization. It also allows us to expand the level of analysis to include not only organizational perspectives but also field and institutional perspectives on internationalization, which together provide a dynamic approach to understanding strategies. It permits us to observe coexisting logics currently present in the field that impact strategies found in different business schools, leading us to conclude that it is a field in transition.

A contextual approach to the internationalization of management education opens up avenues for future research at different levels of analysis. One challenge is to study institution-building processes in the transnational space of management education and the impact of these processes for individual school strategies. Another challenge is to carry out a longitudinal study of internationalizing processes in schools to refine the discussion in this chapter and to better understand why some schools correspond to a particular logic and others do not. Also, as discussed above, empirical studies on student and business expectations should be carried out to extend arguments made in this chapter.

NOTES

1. The single exception for business schools being HEC (Takagi & de Carlo, 2003).
2. The others being IMD–Lausanne and the London Business School (Byrkjeflot, 2003).
3. In 1996, 78 out of 222 business schools were officially recognized by the Ministry of Education, and 57 of these delivered diplomas with ministry visas (Groupe ESCP 1997 Rapport EQUIS). In 2003, 27 business schools are members of the Conférence des Grandes Écoles.
4. See Takagi and de Carlo (2003) for a detailed description of the French business school system.

REFERENCES

Aggarwal, R. (1989, Fall). Strategies for internationalizing the business school: Educating for the global economy. *Journal of Marketing Education*, 59–64.

Ahwireng-Obeng, F. (1999). Internationalizing economics education in South Africa. *Competitiveness Review*, 9(1), 30–39.

Albers-Miller, N. D., Prenshaw, P. J., & Straughan, R. D. (1999). Student perceptions of study abroad programs: A survey of U.S. colleges and universities. *Marketing Education Review*, 9(1), 29–36.

Amdam, R. P., Kvålshaugen, R., & Larsen, E. (2003). The power of content revisited. In R. P. Amdam, R. Kvålshaugen, & E. Larsen (Eds.), *Inside the business schools: The content of European business education* (pp. 11–26). Oslo: Abstrakt forlag AS.

Andrus, D. M., Laughlin, J., and Norvell, W. (1995). Internationalizing the marketing curriculum: A profile of the international marketing course. *Marketing Education Review*, 5(2), 9–18.

Arpan, J. S., and Kwok, C. C. Y. (2000). *Internationalizing the business school: Global survey of institutions of higher learning in the year 2000*. [Report]. University of South Carolina, The Center for International Business Education and Research, The Darla Moore School of Business.

Ball, D. A., and McCulluch, W. H., Jr. (1993, 2nd quarter). An integrative study of the importance of international business education. *Journal of International Business Studies*, 383–391.

Beamish, P., and Calof, J. (1989, Fall). International business education: A corporate view. *Journal of International Business Studies*, 553–564.

Byrkjeflot, H. (2003). To MBA or not to MBA? A dilemma accentuated by the recent boom in business education. In R. P. Amdam, R. Kvålshaugen, & E. Larsen (Eds.), *Inside the business schools: The content of European business education* (pp. 219–246). Oslo: Abstrakt forlag AS.

Chessel, M.-E., and Pavis, F. (2001). *Le technocrate, le patron et le professeur: Une histoire de l'enseignement supérieur de gestion*. Paris: Belin.

Crainer, S., and Dearlove, D. (1999). *Gravy training: Inside the business of business schools*. San Francisco: Jossey-Bass.

Djelic, M.-L., and Quack, S. (2003). Theoretical building blocks for a research agenda linking globalization and institutions. In M.-L. Djelic and S. Quack (Eds.), *Globalization and institutions: Redefining the rules of the economic game*. Cheltenham, UK: Edward Elgar.

Gniewosz, G. (1996). International business education at Australian universities in 1993. *Journal of Teaching in International Business*, 7(3), 1–16.

Gniewosz, G. (2000). Australian management education for international business activity. *Journal of Management Development*, 19(3/4), 318–332.

Goldberg, M. A. (1992–1993). Managing the internationalization of management education: Moving on diverse mutually reinforcing fronts simultaneously. *Journal of Business Administration*, 21(1 & 2), 317–325.

Hedmo, T. (2003). The Europeanization of business education. In R. P. Amdam, R. Kvålshaugen, & E. Larsen (Eds.), *Inside the business schools: The content of European business education* (pp. 247–266). Oslo: Abstrakt forlag AS.

Herremans, I. M., and Wright, M. E. (1992). The international accounting education needs of employees in international firms. *Journal of Teaching in International Business*, *3*(4), 1–22.

Ipsos (2000). [Report] See www.ipsos.com

Kobrin, S. (1984). *International expertise in American business*. New York: Institute of International Education.

Kohers, T. (1985, Summer–Fall). Corporate employment needs and their implications for an international business curriculum. *Issues in International Business*, 33–37.

Kwok, C. C. Y., and Arpan, J. S. (1994). A comparison of international business education at U.S. and European business schools in the 1990s. *Management International Review*, *34*(4), 357–379.

Kwok, C. C. Y., Arpan, J. S., and Folks, W. R. (1994, 3rd quarter). A global survey of international business education in the 1990s. *Journal of International Business Studies*, 605–623.

Kyj, L. S., Kyj, M. J., and Marshall, P. S. (1995, November–December). Internationalization of American business programs: Case study Ukraine. *Business Horizons*, 55–63.

Lundstrom, W. J., White, D. S., and Schuster, C. P. (1996). Internationalizing the marketing curriculum: The professional marketer's perspective. *Journal of Marketing Education*, *18*(2), 5–16.

Luuostarinen, R. and Pulkinnen, T. (1991). *International business education in European universities in 1990* [FIBO project]. Helsinki: Helsinki School of Economics and Business Administration.

Meyer, J. W. (2002). Globalization and the expansion and standardization of management. In K. Sahlin-Andersson and L. Engwall (Eds.), *The expansion of management knowledge*. Stanford: Stanford University Press.

Nehrt, L. C. (1987). The internationalization of the curriculum. *Journal of International Business Studies*, *18*(1), 83–90.

Pitt, L., Berthon, P., and Robson, M. (1997). The internationalization of management knowledge dissemination: A dialectic. *Journal of World Business*, *32*(4), 369–385.

Reynolds, J., and Rice, G., Jr. (1988). American education for international business. *Management International Review*, 3, 48–57.

Salehi-Sangari, E., and Foster, T. (1999). Curriculum internationalisation: A comparative study in Iran and Sweden. *European Journal of Marketing*, *33*(7/8), 760–771.

Schoell, W. F. (1991). International students: An underutilized resource in internationalizing marketing education. *Journal of Marketing Education*, *13*(2), 31–35.

Scott, W. R. (1995). *Institutions and Organizations*. Thousand Oaks, CA: Sage.

Scott, W. R., and Meyer, J. W. (1991). The organization of societal sectors: Propositions and early evidence. In W. W. Powell and P. J. DiMaggio (Eds.), *The New Institutionalism in Organizational Analysis*. Chicago: University of Chicago Press.

Servan-Schreiber, J.-J. (1967). *Le défi américain*. Paris: Denoel.

Shetty, A., and Rudell, F. (2002). Internationalizing the business program—a perspective of a small school. *Journal of Education for Business*, *78*(2), 103–110.

Takagi, J., and de Carlo, L. (2003). The ephemeral national model of management education: A comparative study of five management programs in France. In R. P. Amdam, R. Kvålshaugen, & E. Larsen (Eds.), *Inside the business schools: The content of European business education* (pp. 29–57). Oslo: Abstrakt forlag AS.

Tolbert, P., and Zucker, L. (1996). The institutionalization of institutional theory. In S. Clegg, C. Hardy, and W. Nord (Eds.), *Handbook of Organization Studies* (pp. 175–190). London: Sage.

Tyagi, P. K. (2001). Internationalization of marketing education: Current status and future challenges. *Marketing Education Review, 11*(1), 75–84.

CHAPTER 3

APPROACHES FOR INTERNATIONALIZING THE BUSINESS SCHOOL CURRICULUM

International Business Curriculum Approaches

Bruce Rollier and Christine Nielsen

INTRODUCTION

While the importance of international education for students has been widely recognized for decades, the momentous events of recent years have made the need much more critically apparent. The World Trade Center and Pentagon disasters in 2001 made it obvious that a better understanding of other cultures and religions is vital to our security and to the Earth's future. Turmoil and conflict in Iraq, Israel, Kosovo, Afghanistan, Liberia, Indonesia, and many other countries have been featured in television news and on the front pages of newspapers and magazines. International issues

The Cutting Edge of International Management Education, pages 63–87
Copyright © 2004 by Information Age Publishing
All rights of reproduction in any form reserved.

have been given greater coverage than in any period since the Vietnam War. Potential nuclear threats from North Korea and from the India/Pakistan standoff in Kashmir require careful monitoring. The AIDS devastation in Africa and Asia and the SARS epidemic of 2003 demonstrate that a deadly virus can spread from country to country with lightning speed.

The reasons for the swift spread of internationalization are many, including the break-up of the Soviet Union, the unification of Europe, and the invasion of national markets by foreign companies that required retaliation by the home countries. The major enabling factor, however, has been information technology (IT), particularly computerized telecommunications, which has made it possible for firms to control operations at widely dispersed sites and to respond rapidly to threats and opportunities. IT breaks down the barriers of time and location and makes applications equally accessible to everyone (Conger, 1993).

Another major factor is the rapid diffusion and standardization of technology. Such developments as computer-aided design, electronic data interchange, object-oriented technologies, and relational database systems have been adopted around the world much faster than earlier technologies (Mann, 2000). Fiber optics, satellites, wireless, and other communications technologies have enabled developing countries to build effective networks (Gilder, 2000). The long-term increases in computer power and software sophistication make it possible for firms to greatly reduce their product life cycles and customer order cycles, to reduce inventory costs, and to build more reliable systems. Dramatic reductions in the costs of transmission and of computing power make these developments economically feasible for even the smallest of firms, and for nearly every country.

Commerce and industry are also increasingly global (Germain, 2000; Lechner & Boli, 2000). The advent of the Euro and the standardization among member countries promoted by the European Union facilitates international trade. Communist China is rapidly becoming a behemoth of capitalism and is gradually more becoming more democratic. Electronic commerce can potentially make the products of every country available to the residents of every other country. Ebay operates in 22 countries, and many major corporations maintain Web sites in several languages. Wireless technologies and the "mobile Internet" (PriceWaterhouse Coopers, 2001) are vastly expanding the number of people using the Internet—including those in developing countries—and are providing important new applications for current users. Enterprise Resource Management (ERM) systems integrating worldwide operations are spreading rapidly.

Most business careers in the future are likely to involve systems that operate internationally, at least to some extent. Many students will be employed by foreign firms, or will work on projects in foreign countries as expatriates. A native United States student may work in Turkey or France or China; a Thai citizen may be employed in Russia or Argentina. Outsourcing of programming, data entry, and telemarketing jobs to countries such as India and Ireland has been common for years, and recently this practice has spread to high-skilled white-collar positions (Madigan, 2003). Systems will increasingly be globally integrated, and many of today's students will have opportunities to participate in projects in other countries. Even those who remain in one country throughout their careers will need to be aware of the differences in language and culture among areas of the world as more and more products are sold in multiple countries and as Web sites operate in many languages. An international perspective is also critically important for those who will work with or manage someone with different values or a different cultural background.

International training is increasingly popular with business employers. Many business schools are trying to adapt to this demand in various ways, including establishing foreign campuses and research centers, forming alliances with foreign business schools, initiating exchange programs, and setting up overseas internships (Celestino, 1999). Some of the alliances include offering credit for the other school's courses and even joint degrees.

In 1988, the United States Congress amended the Higher Education Act of 1965 "to include the Centers for International Business Education and Research (CIBER) Program" (Kedia and Cornwell, 1994, p. 13). These centers are located at various universities and are to provide resources and research for the teaching of critical foreign languages and international business topics.

AACSB International has long emphasized internationalization as a prime accreditation factor (Nehrt, 1987), and the need has become much more apparent in recent years. Current standards explicitly state that the curriculum should include coverage of global issues (AACSB, 2004). However, the guidelines do not specify what should be included, although AACSB publications and studies frequently address the need for international programs and provide guidance for curriculum planners and faculty (AACSB, 2002; Bisoux, 2003; Corlett, 2004).

WHAT DO STUDENTS NEED TO KNOW?

There seems to be widespread agreement among academics who have published their opinions that international education is important for business students. However, that does not mean that there is concurrence on the specifics of international programs. Thinking about that question is somewhat overwhelming: There are so many different countries, languages, cultures, economic systems, and political systems. How can any curriculum do justice to such a vast field of knowledge? In considering such questions, it quickly becomes obvious that international programs must be designed to meet the needs of the students the school wishes to attract and to provide them with knowledge and skills required by potential employers. To an increasing degree, business employers value an international orientation, but often functional competency is even more important. Ideally, one should not be sacrificed for the other. In this chapter we will explore approaches for adding an international perspective without omitting vital functional material. The skills of the faculty and their willingness to teach the international courses and to maintain their competence with international research must also be considered in designing the curriculum.

Another critical question that needs to be addressed is: Are the students for which the international curriculum is designed all English speakers born in the United States? An unspoken assumption is often that American students need to learn about other cultures and other economies. But if the commercial world is now globalized, would it not follow that students everywhere need this knowledge? Many global corporations employ multicultural teams (Corlett, 2004), and it is entirely possible that a student from China or Pakistan might work for an American firm in Argentina or Belgium. Another assumption is that students from other countries are international experts, whereas in reality, they are usually from a single-country background and as much in need of international and intercultural knowledge as American students.

Students from other countries are attending universities in the United States in unprecedented numbers, especially students from Asia. In the 2000/2001 school year, there were 548,000 foreign scholars studying in the United States, up 6% from the previous year (McMurtrie, 2001). The top four countries were China, Japan, South Korea, and India, in that order. However, the United States is losing market share. Foreign students in the United States as a percentage of the total of students enrolled outside their native country declined from 39% to 30% between 1982 and 1995 (McMurtrie, 2001). Several countries have been competing aggressively for these students, especially Britain, Australia, Germany, and Japan. Australia has established a nonprofit organization to coordinate international enrollments among its 39 public universities. This has brought Australia a 73% increase in international students since 1994, while the increase for the United States was only 21% during the same period (McMurtrie, 2001, A45).

Foreign students can bring big advantages to international education programs. After all, one of the best ways for students to learn about other cultures and global issues is to have a diverse mix of nationalities in the class. At this writing, because of security concerns subsequent to the 9/11/ 2001 attacks, the United States Justice Department is pursuing policies that discourage foreign visitors, including potential scholars. Johnson (2003) argues that such policies are shortsighted and actually an endangerment to national security. The government is not intentionally undermining these international exchanges, but the system of inefficient visa screening, the poor implementation of a foreign-student monitoring system that is a heavy burden for university administrations, and very aggressive enforcement of immigration laws is having that effect. "The most important benefits that the United States has gained from educating successive generations of future leaders are in the realms of foreign policy and national security. Foreign students and scholars, who constitute an exceptional reservoir of good will for our country, are perhaps our most undervalued foreign-policy asset." (Johnson, 2003, p. 1). It is to be hoped that international tensions and fear of terrorism will ease soon so that these onerous policies might be relaxed.

Some foreign students will return to their home countries to work after graduation, and some will remain in the country in which they obtained their education (Hazelhurst, 2001). Those students who do not return to their home country are a particular problem for many African countries, which have a great need for highly-skilled people and a shortage of first-class universities. When the best students cannot obtain the education they need in their native country, they will enroll in European or United States universities and often do not return. The labor market for IT employees has become globalized, with workers relocating to the countries with higher salaries (West & Bogumil, 2001). Many manufacturing plants have been relocated to countries with low wage scales, and in recent years, an increasing number of service jobs, including high tech jobs, are performed by teleworkers in low-wage countries via high-speed networks (Madigan, 2003). One estimate is for nearly 600,000 high-skilled United States jobs in office support, business operations, computer programming, and other occupations to be moved offshore by 2005, with 3.3 million jobs to be moved offshore by 2015.

As older workers retire, the young people coming of age and moving into the work force will be predominantly from minority groups and lower economic classes who have not traditionally attended college (Peterson, 2000). At the same time, the fastest-growing occupations are mostly high tech. Of the ten fastest-growing job categories in the 2000 to 2010 projections made by the Bureau of Labor Statistics, nine of the ten require high skills and advanced education to at least the Bachelors degree level (Bureau of Labor Statistics, 2004).

THE BLEAK OUTLOOK FOR HIGHER EDUCATION

At this time, public universities and colleges in the United States are facing a tuition crisis (Quinn, 2004) which requires them to raise tuitions rapidly and cut down on costs wherever they can. Over the last ten years, average tuitions for four-year institutions have increased by 53%, nearly twice the inflation rate, and in the last year alone (2003) they are up by 14%. Over the long term, conditions are not likely to improve for higher education or for international programs, for the following reasons:

- Annual U.S. deficits are already massive and, as the baby boomers retire, there will be an intense budgetary squeeze as tax revenues decline and health care costs increase.
- Raising taxes could solve the problem, but that may not be feasible politically.
- Affluent taxpayers whose children have finished school may resist having their taxes used for higher education rather than for health care.
- Tuition hikes mainly affect the poor. For affluent families, college costs have increased at about the same rate as their incomes. For middle-income families, the costs are 19% of income, and for low-income families, the costs are 71% of income in the latest year surveyed (Quinn, 2004). As Quinn says, "Higher education is getting less, not more public financial support. That's astonishing, in a country that knows the jobs of the future will require more knowledge and technical talent" (p. 49).
- Unfortunately for the United States economy, after the baby boomer retirements start, the children of low-income families will predominate in the labor force (Peterson, 2000). Birthrates for wealthy families have declined, and the younger population is increasingly African-American or Hispanic; traditionally, a much lower percentage of these groups have attended college. Whereas 51% of children from wealthy families (incomes greater than $90,000) complete their college degree before age 24, only 4.5% of low-income children do. Yet, the fastest growing occupations are high tech, and in the future we will need people who have the skills to take these positions and to perform them with quality. One of the biggest challenges for universities will be to enroll non-traditional students when tuition rates have risen far beyond the students' means.
- Some universities may not survive. Those that are able to continue will need to cut costs to the bone. While international programs are seen as necessary in good economic times, administrators, curriculum designers, and faculty may have less enthusiasm for international programs if they have to choose between functional specialties and the international curriculum.
- Educators who desire international programs will have to make a very strong case for their value, and make sure the programs are of high

quality, meet the needs of a significant number of students, and require minimal resources. If not, international programs may be the first to go if the institution faces financial exigency or even bankruptcy.

THE PROMISE OF THE INTERNET

The World Wide Web may provide at least part of the solution to the looming higher-education crisis. An emerging trend toward strategic partnerships exists among universities and colleges, similar to those partnerships employed by industry for many years. Although the trend is likely to be resisted by many in academia, it may be the only way to survive. Recently, three community colleges in Baltimore County, Maryland, merged into one institution, enabling students to take classes at any of the three locations. This type of merger saves faculty resources and accommodates a broader curriculum. One campus can specialize in international programs rather than all three campuses competing with one another with redundant programs. It seems likely, in our opinion, that there will be a trend toward consolidation in higher education, just as there has been in other industries, and that this will also result in international consolidation.

However, sharing resources does not necessarily require a formal merger. Strategic partnerships may be formed on a temporary and less formal basis. The Web enables cooperative programs between countries far from each other, even across oceans. The number of institutions teaching on the Web is increasing rapidly, and a number of business schools offer a full MBA on the Web. For example, the University of Baltimore has had such a program for several years, and students from a number of different states and several countries have enrolled. One MBA marketing course was successfully taught with the instructor located in Botswana and most of the students located in the United States.

"Virtual universities" are already emerging, with entire programs available for which students do not have to attend physical classes (Niederman & Rollier, 2001). The Internet makes it possible for students to take classes from any location, and it is common in such programs for students to be widely separated and working from various countries. Although increasing fairly rapidly, the number of such institutions offering Web degrees is still comparatively small because the technology is still somewhat primitive. The classes must be almost completely asynchronous. This makes them very convenient for working adults who can perform their course work at unscheduled times, but some educators are skeptical about such things as the difficulty of administering closed-book examinations and the quality of the education for students who may not be highly motivated. From the standpoint of the instructor, the classes are highly labor-intensive because all the communication requires typing, and there are normally many one-on-one communications. However, this is likely to change in the near future.

Software for synchronous operations is already available, but has not been introduced by the major vendors (Blackboard and WebCT) because the programs require broadband access. As soon as a critical mass of potential students have broadband capability (such as cable modems or DSL) courses will likely start to become more interactive. Instructors will be able to see students and vice versa; instructors can demonstrate concepts and conduct lectures on screen rather than trying to explain them through email; closed book quizzes and examinations can be administered with the instructor monitoring; and human voices can be used for communication as an alternative to keyboards. Asynchronous capabilities will still be available, so course designers will have great flexibility in constructing courses that are highly adapted to the needs of the learner. Synchronous features should make it feasible for a single instructor to teach more students in a class, thus bringing down the cost per student. Increasing volumes should rapidly lower the technology costs.

In parallel with the growth of virtual universities, there will be a trend toward "cafeteria-style" programs, with students picking some courses from one university and some from others. This has already happened with some multi-campus universities, community colleges, and virtual consortia such as Western Governors University, which has no teaching faculty and offers no courses itself (Carnevale, 2003). This trend will lower overall costs significantly while offering students much greater choice. It will also require increasing standardization of curricula, and the standardization will be international. Courses should have the same learning objectives no matter where they are taught, although different methods and materials might be used. In a few years, we may start to see MBA requirements increasingly standardized. Courses will need international content in order to be relevant to all the students taking them, and this trend will give many more students an opportunity to take a much greater variety of international courses, whatever their location.

INTERNATIONAL BUSINESS EDUCATION
AS A PUBLIC GOOD

Since September 11, 2001, there has been a paradigm shift in the views of public and private leaders toward international education. The majority view now is that international education is essential to the national interest, both for the United States' continued leadership in the world economy and as a matter of national security. There is increasing recognition that institutions of higher learning share responsibilities for economic development and public welfare, as noted in these remarks from the Chancellor of the University of Maryland System (Kirwan, 2002):

> Higher education must produce a new generation workforce that is worldly wise, culturally aware, and foreign language literate. At the national level, 9/ 11 was a wake-up call to this generation as Sputnik was to mine. We have gotten a wake-up call that we are not creating a generation of internationally educated students.... We must learn about foreign countries' economies, customs and cultures, language and politics, or we will certainly be at a large disadvantage. They certainly know everything about us.... Our national security depends on creating specialists educated about different regions of the world.... There are too few course requirements with an emphasis on international [issues].... International issues are on Maryland university presidents' minds as they never have been before.... As a public good, we need to encourage the investment of funds in international education, and create more public–private partnerships to deal with the challenges we face.

Clearly it is of great importance for students to consider international issues and to be able to analyze problems from a global perspective. Having a global perspective means that they learn to consider the international implications of decisions that are made. This is not as simple as it may seem. One of the authors was previously employed by IBM, and for several years was assigned to World Trade Corporation, an international subsidiary of IBM. Some decisions were made by individuals that seemed incredibly unaware of international implications. For example, the first IBM copier was designed with the assumption that the United States standard for paper size was recognized all over the world. Thus, that copier was unusable in Japan, a huge market for other products. Despite experiences such as this, the author found it very difficult to maintain and foster an international perspective after his reassignment to the United States division of the company.

Students will have to function as citizens, employees, managers, and entrepreneurs in an increasingly international world. The challenge for educators is in determining the specifics of what should be taught, and in determining the best approach for providing an international perspective strong enough that it will be retained after graduation. In the remainder of this chapter, we will discuss the difficulties of developing curricula with adequate international content, and then we will explore various approaches to teaching international material.

THE CHALLENGE OF CURRICULUM BUILDING

Although the importance of internationalizing the curriculum is widely recognized among business school faculty and administrators, there is a major problem for curriculum designers and for professors who wish to include international material in their courses: How do you fit it in? How can it be crammed into a curriculum already bursting at the seams? How do you justify adding this international material rather than other important topics? How do you decide what material to drop to make room for it?

A curriculum is, or should be, analogous to architecture. The outer structure—the four years allotted to an undergraduate degree or the one or two years required for a graduate degree—is quite rigid, as are the internal divisions (semesters and courses). For economic as well as traditional reasons, it is not realistically possible to increase the size of the structure. A university that attempted to require a fifth year for a bachelor's degree would likely lose students.

Once created, this structure is filled with requirements: English composition, science courses, mathematics, the business core, requirements of the major and minor disciplines, and a small list of acceptable electives. It is often necessary, at least in some of the business disciplines, to add new material and sometimes entirely new courses, but additional content requirements are difficult to accommodate without modifying or eliminating existing courses. Like rearranging furniture within a limited space, curriculum changes occur every year as courses are added, dropped, or altered, but the changes at any one point in time are seldom extensive, and they affect a very small proportion of the total curriculum. Yet, this slow rate of evolution does not accurately reflect the rapid and accelerating pace of change in the business world.

The conflict between a rigid curriculum structure and the need for dynamic adaptability and swift implementation of changes is a particularly severe problem for curriculum designers who wish to add international topics, a relatively young discipline in a stage of rapid knowledge acquisition. The great majority of changes are for new content and new skills; rarely do topics become obsolete. Just as it is sometimes easier to knock down a building and erect a new one in its place rather than making extensive modifications to the old one, it may be simpler to completely redesign a course or a curriculum than to make major modifications.

The problem of trying to pack too much into a structure cannot be easily resolved. It will require painful decisions to eliminate seemingly vital material. The long-term solution may involve full faculty acceptance of the concept of lifelong learning, ridding ourselves of the notion that education is a process that ceases upon graduation. Undoubtedly almost all faculty would agree that we cannot possibly cram everything into students' minds that they will need for the rest of their lives; yet, in designing courses and curricula, it often seems that this is what we are trying to do. However, the trend to online education and strategic partnerships may at least change the perception that each institution must provide complete programs independently of other universities.

CURRICULUM INTERNATIONALIZATION APPROACHES

The term *internationalization* needs to be carefully defined for each institution. If the objective is to prepare a self-selected segment of the student body for careers in international management, then a strong major in that field may need to be designed specifically for that segment, perhaps with foreign language competency an additional requirement. If, on the other hand, the objective is for every student to achieve a level of global awareness, then the material must be part of the required curriculum for everyone.

International business (IB) curriculum objectives may be classified broadly by the three broad categories of *global awareness, global understanding,* and *global competence* (Arpan, 1993; Kedia, 1993). Institutions may provide a different level for different academic programs. Kedia & Cornwell (1994, p. 16) provide these definitions of the three levels:

1. *Global awareness* is at the lowest level of the three categories and requires the fewest resources. Rather than employing new faculty specializing in international programs, the institution can satisfy the requirements of this category by "internationalizing" the existing faculty and embedding international material in every course in the curriculum. In solving problems, students should take a world view and be aware of the international implications of their solutions.

2. *Global understanding* is at the middle level of the three categories. The institution can add new International Business faculty; establish awards for international teaching and research; add a general international course to the core, plus individual courses in functional areas; and establish a concentration in IB. This level should provide understanding and knowledge about foreign cultures and global markets.

3. *Global competence* is the highest level of the three categories, and it requires the most resources as well as the sharpest focus on internationalization. Programs may include graduate and/or undergraduate IB degrees, a Master's degree in International Business Studies, and an International MBA. The curriculum may involve overseas internships, extended stay programs, and work abroad programs; it should also provide sophisticated IB training to enable executives to

function in overseas positions. Global competence programs are designed with in-depth courses for students who are planning for international careers. This level may require intensive and highly-authentic language training leading to complete fluency; cultural and political courses for a particular world area; a series of courses in global economics and international finance; and internships in other countries, which are often difficult to set up effectively (Pickert, 1992). There may be a shortage of faculty qualified for international business topics or a shortage of faculty who have sufficient interest in acquiring the requisite knowledge and experience (Conger, 1993). Setting up high-quality training in several world languages can be extremely expensive. Knowledge of disciplines must be broad—encompassing practices of countries around the globe—as well as deep. International programs are often expensive to administer and may require that resources be diverted from other important areas. It must be kept in mind that there are hundreds of countries in the world, and there are very significant differences between them, including such seemingly closely-related countries as Japan, China, and South Korea. The world has great variety, and the areas of concentration must be chosen very carefully.

Arpan (1993) explains these terms as follows: "*Awareness* is where it all begins. If students don't know there's a wider world 'out there,' they can hardly be expected to understand it or learn how to deal with it. From a curriculum standpoint, the 'awareness' goal can be achieved generally and relatively easily by the *infusion* method; that is, placing/infusing some international content in existing courses throughout the curriculum" (p. 16). "*Understanding* begins when awareness is established and represents a significantly higher order of learning for the student and educational commitment and complexity for the institution. It's one thing for the student to understand why a deficit exists or how a trade deficit influences economic conditions, government policies, and so forth. From a curriculum standpoint, achieving the 'understanding' goal requires more than infusion. It requires *specific international courses* and international course *requirements*" (pp. 16-17). "*Competency* provides the necessary skills to operate in a foreign environment. From a curriculum standpoint, true international business competency is facilitated by a *specialized degree* of an international and multidisciplinary nature" (p. 17).

According to the latest rankings in *U.S. News & World Report* (USNews, 2004), the five highest-rated international management programs (for United States universities only) are at Thunderbird Graduate School, the University of South Carolina, Columbia University, the University of Pennsylvania, and New York University. Thunderbird Graduate School, in Glendale,

Arizona, has been exclusively devoted to international management education since its founding in 1945, and its program has consistently rated first for several years. The University of South Carolina's highly rated International MBA (IMBA) has been so successful that its regular MBA has been dropped. All the other schools ranked in the top twenty are wealthy private schools such as Columbia, Wharton, New York University, Harvard, Duke, and Stanford, or large, prestigious state universities such as the University of Michigan and the University of California at Berkeley. Both Thunderbird and South Carolina offer language tracks in Chinese, French, German, Japanese, and Spanish. Thunderbird also offers Russian, and South Carolina includes Italian. Most of the top-ranked schools offer opportunities for overseas internships. There are, of course, many highly regarded schools in other countries, such as the International Institute for Management Development (IMD), London Business School, INSEAD, and the University of Western Ontario that provide excellent preparation for careers in international business.

This is not to imply that public universities and small private institutions cannot excel in the provision of international programs. For example, the Merrick School of Business at the University of Baltimore, despite its small size and limited resources, is recognized as a regional leader in global business education. Specializations in International Business at both the undergraduate and graduate levels are among the five most popular majors at the Merrick School of Business, and demand for international courses is growing. As Hornbacher (2002) points out in the following quotation from the *Baltimore Sun*, public recognition over the past several years underscores the success of this program.

> Give educators in UB's Merrick School of Business high marks for helping shape a now solidly established international business program that has drawn admiring glances from other educational institutions and kudos from students, regional and state international economic development officials, and from the Maryland business community as well.

The success of Merrick School of Business derives from external partnerships with the business community and foreign universities. Language training is available through an agreement with a Mexican university with an international reputation for Spanish language training. The strongest, most active sector of business community support for the Merrick School of Business is from the international business community. The Merrick School's Wright Global Business Scholars Program was made possible by a gift from an executive of a leading financial institution with additional support from several international corporations. However, strong internal support is of equal importance, as international programs cut across traditional functional areas of the business curriculum, a factor which could lead to bureaucratic entanglements without a supportive administration and a dedicated faculty.

TOP-RANKED UNIVERSITIES IN INTERNATIONAL BUSINESS EDUCATION

A recent study of graduate international business curricula at top-ranked universities recognized for their leadership in global business education revealed substantial agreement regarding priority course offerings (Nielsen, 2003). Sixteen leading universities in the United States and abroad were included in this study. The institutions are listed in Table 3.1.

Table 3.1.   Leading Universities in Global Business Education

U.S. Institutions

American School of International Management (Thunderbird)

Columbia University—Columbia School of Business

Harvard University—Harvard Business School

New York University—Leonard Stern School of Business

Stanford University—Stanford Graduate School of Business

University of South Carolina—Darla Moore School of Business

University of Pennsylvania—Wharton School

University of California–Los Angeles—Anderson School of Business

University of Michigan—Michigan School of Business

University of California—Haas School of Business

Foreign Institutions

INSEAD—France

International Institute of Management Development (IMD)—Switzerland

London Business School—United Kingdom

SDA Bocconi—Italy

University of Navarra—Madrid, Spain

University of Western Ontario—Canada

Twenty international business courses are offered at two or more of the top universities. Five of these courses provide broad coverage of general skills required for success in the international arena, including Global Economy and International Economics, International Business Environment, International Management, International Business Negotiations, and

Global Strategic Management. Another five courses are in regional studies (Asia, China, Latin America, Japan, and Emerging Markets). Eight offerings relate to specific business functions, with International Finance and Global Marketing representing the most popular. One course focuses on Ethics in International Business. One offering available at only two of the top schools is the Global Business Practicum, which places teams of MBA students in the field, working on real-world projects for corporate sponsors. The leading institutions and their course offerings are summarized in Table 3.2.

Table 3.2. International Business Courses Offered by Leading Universities in Global Business Education

Courses	Universities Offering Courses	Description of Courses
Doing Business in Asia	New York University, Michigan School of Business, INSEAD, U. of South Carolina	Provides students with an understanding of the region, focusing on geographic, political, social and economic factors.
Doing Business in China	INSEAD, New York University, Michigan School of Business, London Business School	Provides students with an understanding of the region, focusing on geographic, political, social and economic factors.
Doing Business in Latin America	Michigan School of Business, U. of South Carolina	Provides students with an understanding of the region, focusing on geographic, political, social and economic factors.
Doing Business in Japan/The Japanese Economy	Columbia School of Business, New York University, Michigan School of Business	Surveys the post-WWII economy, including the most recent recession of the 1990s. Specific institutional arrangements examined are the large firm, industrial relations, groups of related firms, the financial system and general trading companies. Japan's foreign economic relations are considered.
Emerging Markets	Columbia School of Business, UCLA, New York University, Harvard	Analysis of changing economic, political, demographic, and sociocultural conditions in developing countries as they affect the business environment.
Ethics in International Business/ International Business Law	U. of South Carolina, Stanford Graduate School of Business, UC Berkeley, Michigan School of Business, Thunderbird, UCLA	Considers ethical issues in the context of corporate headquarters' solutions and their appropriateness for the international environment. Legal environments of international business. How multinationals resolve issues in a fashion consistent with the laws and polices of the home and host countries.

Table 3.2.   International Business Courses Offered by Leading Universities in Global Business Education (Cont.)

Courses	Universities Offering Courses	Description of Courses
Global Business Practicum	Michigan School of Business, U. of Pennsylvania	Teams of MBAs apply knowledge to international projects such as market entry, joint ventures, and strategic alliances. Spending time in-country, student teams work to produce valuable results for corporate sponsors.
Global Economy/ International Economics	New York University, UC Berkeley, Michigan School of Business, Columbia School of Business, Stanford Graduate School of Business, UCLA, U. of Navarra, Thunderbird, INSEAD	Provides analytical framework required for understanding how changing macroeconomic conditions in the world economy affect environment faced by modern decision-makers and business leaders.
Global Strategic Management/ International Business Strategy	Stanford Graduate School of Business, U. of Pennsylvania, London Business School, UC Berkeley, U. of South Carolina, Thunderbird, INSEAD, University of Western Ontario	The course examines the sources of international competitive advantage; alternative strategies for entering foreign markets; headquarter-subsidiary relations and other organizational design issues; alliances; strategies for sustaining growth; and the particular challenges of implementation in international and global operations.
Global Technology Management	U. of Pennsylvania, Thunderbird	An introduction to the world of networked information and the role information technology in a global business environment.
International Accounting	IMD, SDA Bocconi, UCLA, U. of Pennsylvania, Michigan School of Business, U. of Western Ontario	Comparative analysis of accounting concepts and practices in other countries. Study of contrasts between various systems. Problems of accounting for international corporations.
International Banking/Global Banking	U. of South Carolina, Columbia School of Business, U. of Pennsylvania, New York University	Examine major aspects of international banking using reading, case studies, and an international bank management simulation. Analysis of the competitive performance and strategic positioning of financial institutions in multinational capital markets. Considers international aspects of raising capital in multinational, multi-regulatory settings.

Table 3.2. International Business Courses Offered by Leading Universities in Global Business Education (Cont.)

Courses	Universities Offering Courses	Description of Courses
International Business Environment	U. of South Carolina, IMD, New York University, Columbia School of Business, UCLA, Stanford Graduate School, U. of Western Ontario	Learn how to analyze political, economic, social and technological factors that impact global business decisions, including market entry strategies.
International Business Negotiations	U. of South Carolina, Harvard, New York University, Thunderbird	Examines how decision-makers in business and government settings manage the process and outcomes of negotiations, cross-cultural negotiations in a global business environment.
International Financial Management/Markets	UC Berkeley, Michigan School of Business, U. of Pennsylvania, London Business School, U. of South Carolina, New York University, U. of Navarra, Columbia School of Business, Stanford Graduate School of Business, UCLA, Thunderbird, INSEAD, IMD, U. of Western Ontario	Introduction to financial institutions and operations of the international macroeconomic environment. Special attention paid to international financial arrangements relevant for mangers of multinational corporations. Provides a framework for making corporate financial decisions in an international context. Conceptual understanding of foreign exchange markets, Euro-currency market, international bond market, and equity markets in various countries.
International Human Resources	INSEAD, IMD	
International Management	U. of South Carolina, U. of Western Ontario, IMD, Michigan School of Business, U. of Navarra, Thunderbird, Harvard, SDA Bocconi, IMD, Stanford Graduate School	Examines key aspects of international management, as applied to both small companies and multinational corporations. Emphasizes human relations skills, including cross-cultural communications and negotiations; and technical skills required for strategic operation of global organizations.
International Marketing/Global Marketing Strategy	Columbia School of Business, Harvard, IMD, Michigan School of Business, New York University, Standford Graduate School of Business, Thunderbird, UC Berkeley, UCLA, U. of Navarra, U. of Pennsylvania, U. of South Carolina	Examination of marketing strategy and management within the context of international markets and increasing globalization. Covers the management of international marketing strategy.

Table 3.2.   International Business Courses Offered by Leading Universities in Global Business Education (Cont.)

Courses	Universities Offering Courses	Description of Courses
International Taxation	SDA Bocconi, New York University, U. of Pennsylvania, Thunderbird	Introduction to comparative tax systems outside the U.S. Reviews the major issues in multinational income taxation.
International Trade and Investment	U. of South Carolina, New York University, UC Berkeley, Michigan School of Business, Harvard	Focus on the determinants of global trade flows, patterns of international competition, and governmental policies affecting international trade.

Source: Nielsen, 2003. "Study of Top-Ranked Universities in Global Business Education." Research assistance provided by Rhoda Lee and Martin Flachsland.

SOME PRACTICAL INTERNATIONAL ISSUES

Some students will question the value of spending time on international topics. They may feel that they will be working in a single country throughout their careers and may have little interest in learning about cultures in other parts of the world. Students tend to focus on getting that first job and may not look far enough ahead to the international opportunities that may become available to them. Students also may not realize how many organizations today operate internationally. Even though their job may always be in the United States, the customers, the workforce, the management, and the organization's owners may represent many different countries. Studying issues (e.g., those discussed in this section) with experiential techniques such as case studies can make the international courses more realistic and relevant.

Many students (and even some professors), especially those who have always lived in the same country, tend to think of the way things are done in their native country as the only right way to do them. The fact that we have much to learn from other countries and other cultures, even from tiny non-European nations such as Singapore or Chile, is not readily recognized There are opportunities for learning all over the globe.

Many of those who pursue business careers, especially the most successful students, will probably be engaged at some point with projects that involve countries other than their own. Perhaps they will live in another country, perhaps not, but in any event they will need to be aware of factors such as the following:

- *Time zone differences.*
- *Language differences.* English may eventually become a universal language, but the great majority of people in the world do not know English (Wallraff, 2000). Even people who can communicate in English may not have a large enough vocabulary to understand technical terms peculiar to the industry. In projects involving multiple languages, not everyone will have the same degree of understanding of the common language (Carney & Franciulli, 1999). Language immersion classes for expatriates and their family members before departure and continued language classes after arrival at the project site can facilitate cultural adjustment and effectiveness (Andreason, 2003).
- *Cultural differences.* A variety of cultural differences may manifest themselves in work practices, education of the work force, and management of projects and business operations. When United States employees are sent to a distant country to implement a project or to occupy an operational or management position, they should be very carefully chosen (Freedman, 2003; Vance, Paderon, & Paderon, 1993). Employees (and their families, if possible) should be given an exploratory trip to the assigned country to make certain that they understand the living conditions there and the cultural differences to which they may need to adapt (Andreason, 2003). Locally hired personnel may be resentful of expatriates, who are often brought in at high positions and with much higher salaries and benefits than those available to the locals. Convincing employees to accept foreign assignments, especially in geographic areas assumed to be dangerous, can be challenging for organizations (Lublin, 2003). In the current world environment, it has become critically important to provide concrete policies for assuring employee safety in the assignment (Belisle & Cuthbertson, 2003).
- *Project management.* If a project is being performed in a particular country with personnel primarily from other countries, the project manager must have excellent human relations skills as well as administrative and technical expertise. Off-site projects can be difficult because normal home office support may not be locally available (Welch, 2003).
- *Locality differences.* Symbols may be different, particularly in Asia. Common standards may be different; for example, most of the world measures quantities and distances with the metric system rather than with pounds, ounces, feet, and inches. Name protocols may cause problems. In China, the last name is usually given first. In Spanish-speaking countries, the mother's last name is traditionally appended after the father's last name. Therefore, it would be offensive to refer

to Pedro Almodovar Garcia as Senor Garcia. Kanji characters are sorted by the number of "strokes" in the character rather than by the alphabet. The telecommunications infrastructure in a country may be inadequate or poorly maintained (Garfield & Watson, 1997). Government regulations may restrict what a company is allowed to do and may also limit the transfer of money and data across national borders. Such factors as European unification and cross-border mergers can create very complex problems.

- *Technology transfer.* Until recently, this was a major problem for Third World countries (Conger, 1993). Because of the phenomenal growth of the World Wide Web, the availability of high bandwidth communications channels (Gilder, 2000), and plummeting hardware costs due to the continuance of Moore's Law (Mann, 2000), this problem is rapidly being alleviated. Students should understand the importance of these factors for global economic health.

TECHNIQUES OF INFUSION

One learning objective, applicable to all three of the internationalization levels, should be to provide awareness, not just a specific body of content knowledge. Infusion (embedding international content into every course) is desirable because it exposes *all* students to international issues and concepts *within the context of other material.* It also requires fewer faculty resources than other methods of internationalization. If carefully and thoughtfully implemented, the integration of international topics into existing courses can encourage students to think of the concepts as relevant to their careers, rather than just isolated topics. It is particularly important to provide some degree of international awareness in a variety of courses as an alternative to displacing other important material.

If infusion is to work correctly, however, it is critical that all faculty members be knowledgeable about relevant international issues and enthusiastic about including them in their courses. Infusion requires creativity and careful planning on the part of the instructor. Students from other countries within the class can often be an excellent resource for providing a distinctive point of view.

Curriculum designers must be extraordinarily creative in internationalizing the curriculum without displacing other necessary material. There are hundreds of countries in the world, and hundreds of different cultures. Each is unique, and it would be impossible to teach about any significant number of them (as well as self-defeating). The idea is to broaden the students' perspective and to encourage openness to differences as well as similarities. The ability to look at issues from someone else's point of view will be an extremely valuable asset throughout the students' lives. The methods have to match the teaching objectives and the type of course, but the most effective courses involve experiential learning rather than lecturing.

For management-oriented courses, cases are ideal. There are many excellent international cases from a variety of sources, including Harvard Publishing, Ivey Publishing, Thunderbird Graduate School, several Web sites, and many textbooks. The best cases are multi-faceted and cover a variety of issues. They are realistic because they represent situations that actually happened and people who actually exist. An important advantage is that cases provide a strong link to the world of practice, which students may not receive from a textbook or from lectures (Armstrong, 1997). The instructor should strongly encourage students to visualize themselves in the situation portrayed in a case, and to analyze the situation from different perspectives as if it were actually happening to them. The closer students can come to that ideal, the more they will benefit from the experience and internalize the lessons of the case for later use.

A simple technique for hands-on term projects is to instruct the teams to imagine that they are carrying out the project in some other part of the world. A short project can be designed which involves a foreign company as a framework for the project, allowing the students to get a realistic idea of the problems of implementing the project in that country. With the availability of the Web, it has become feasible to set up multi-country projects with global teams. In recent years, many such exercises have been conducted on the Web with participation by multiple schools from different countries. Kopczak and Fransoo (2000) have described the Global Project Coordination course in which "three students from each of two universities in different parts of the globe form a joint project team to work on a company-sponsored project that addresses a global business issue" (2000, p. 91). This particular project involved supply chain management, but it should be adaptable for virtually any course that includes a team project. Recently, a Web site was set up by Robert Davison of the City University of Hong Kong to facilitate the forming of virtual teams (Davison, 2002). Some schools have provided a virtual "study tour" of other countries to provide international exposure (Porth, 1997).

CONCLUSIONS

This chapter addresses the problem of providing an appropriate level of international content for business students in an already crowded curriculum. Students planning for international business careers require competency programs in courses providing both a broad understanding of the global business environment and specialized skills in functional areas such as international finance and international marketing. Beyond course work, these programs are enhanced by foreign language training, study trips, and practicums that provide students with practical in-the-field experiences. Such programs are very expensive to provide unless the school (e.g., the University of South Carolina) specializes in international programs with a significant share of its resources devoted to international content. Thunderbird Graduate School is unique in that all its resources are devoted to international content. Students in other majors need to be cognizant of international issues while acquiring other skills. In the business curricula, there is little room for even one required course devoted exclusively to international information systems issues. If such courses are electives, not every student would take them, and every student needs to be aware of these issues and how to deal with them.

Embedding international content (infusion) into the existing required courses is an effective approach that provides every student with a global perspective, at least for that class. By presenting it within the context of the course material rather than as an isolated, separate topic, students can comprehend international content more readily and understand its importance to their careers. Infusion is efficient because the international issues are taught in parallel with the regular content of the course. Students can relate to these issues and understand them because they are seeing actual examples applied to real life situations. When they encounter similar situations later in their careers, this awareness may contribute to better decisions. Most of them will probably never move to another country to perform a project, but surely the great majority will work with companies that have customers or suppliers in more than one country. Many students will eventually participate in multicultural teams or manage a staff of employees from a variety of countries. It is critically important for business faculty to make students aware of the special problems that might be encountered in a global environment.

Are these techniques effective in meeting the learning objective of global awareness? It is difficult to measure their value, and perhaps impossible to measure them with any degree of precision. There is much anecdotal evidence, however, that suggests these techniques can provide a significant level of global awareness. Most students enjoy case studies and other realistic exercises, so they tend to participate actively in class discussions and to demonstrate understanding of the issues. Such exercises generate a high degree of interest and curiosity about the countries and cultures being studied. It is possible even for schools with limited resources to provide high-quality, low-cost international programs with financial support from business institutions who benefit from the programs.

However, international programs and higher education itself are already facing formidable challenges which will likely become much more intense.

The future looks bleak—for both financial and political reasons—with huge budget deficits, anti-tax fervor, baby boomer retirements, competition for funding with major health programs, looming deficits in Social Security, and other factors. As tuitions rise and universities are forced to cut expenses to the bone, advocates of international programs will have to persuade the university administrators, students, politicians, corporate executives, and the general public that the programs are necessary and deserve to be funded. Advocates must also convince these constituencies that the programs are highly beneficial for the economy, that they are designed to be relevant and of high quality, and that they can be administered with maximum efficiency (Gibbs, 1994). It is essential to take a globally integrated approach to curriculum design. For most universities, separation of domestic issues from international issues will no longer be an option.

REFERENCES

Andreason, A. W. (2003). Direct and indirect forms of in-country support for expatriates and their families as a means of reducing premature returns and improving job performance. *International Journal of Management, 20,* 548–554.

Armstrong, E. G. (1997). A hybrid model of problem-based learning. In D. Boud & G. Feletti (Eds.), *The challenge of problem-based learning* (pp. 137–150). (2nd ed.). London: Kogan Page.

Arpan, J. (1993). Curricular and administrative considerations: The Cheshire cat parable. In S. T. Cavusgil (Ed.), *Internationalizing business education: Meeting the challenge* (pp. 15–30). East Lansing: Michigan State University.

Association to Advance Collegiate Schools of Business (AACSB). (2004). *Eligibility procedures and standards for business accreditation.* Retrieved March 24, 2004, from http://www.aacsb.edu/accreditation/business/standards01-01-04.pdf

Association to Advance Collegiate Schools of Business (AACSB). (2002). *Management education at risk* (Report of the Management Education Task Force). St. Louis, MO: Author.

Belisle, B., & Cuthbertson, W. (2003). Anticipate expat crisis instead of responding. *Canadian HR Reporter, 16*(5), 13.

Bisoux, T. (2003, January–February). New directions in global education. *BizEd,* 34–37.

Bureau of Labor Statistics (2004). *Employment projections.* Retrieved March 24, 2004, from http://www.bls.gov/emp/home.htm

Carnevale, D. (2003). Western Governors U. wins key accreditation. *The Chronicle of Higher Education, 49*(27), p. A32.

Carney, C. V., & Franciulli, M. (1999). Stereotypes of Latin Americans among graduate students of international management: Determining cultural needs of the United States-trained business professional. *Journal of Language for International Business, 10*(2), 29–45.

Celestino, M. L. (1999). Graduate education programs with international vision: How graduate business schools are transcending borders. *World Trade, 12*(7), 86–91.

Conger, S. (1993). Issues in teaching globalization in information systems. In M. Khosrowpour & K. D. Loch (Eds.), *Global information technology education: Issues and trends* (pp. 313–353). Harrisburg, PA: Idea Group

Corlett, G. E. (2004). Enhancing international programs. *eNewsline.* The Association to Advance Collegiate Schools of Business. Retrieved March 24, 2004 from http://www.aacsb.edu/publications/enewsline/archive_deans/dc-gcorlett.asp

Davison, R. (2002). Introduction to the virtual teams page. Retrieved March 24, 2004, from http://www.is.cityu.edu.hk/research/resources/isworld/virtualteams/

Freedman, R. (2003, June). Creating global leaders. *Chief Executive,* 20–22.

Garfield, M. J., & Watson, R. T. (1997). Differences in national information infrastructures: The reflection of national cultures. *Journal of Strategic Information Systems,* 313–337.

Germain, R. D. (2000). Globalization in historical perspective. In R. D. Germain (Ed.), *Globalization and its critics* (pp. 67–90). London: Macmillan.

Gibbs, M. C., Jr. (1994). Contemporary strategies for internationalization of the business curriculum. In M. C. Gibbs, Jr. (Ed.), *Internationalization of the business curriculum* (pp. 11–29). New York: International Business Press.

Gilder, G. (2000). The end is drawing nigh. *Forbes, 165*(8), 171–172.

Hazelhurst, S. (2001). Developing IT skills internationally: Who's developing whom? *Communications of the ACM, 44*(7), 27–28.

Hornbacher, G. (2002, September 22). Open for business: The world [Special section on education]. *Baltimore Sun,* pp. 1 & 5.

Johnson, V. (2003). The perils of homeland security: When we hinder foreign students and scholars, we endanger our national security. *The Chronicle of Higher Education, 49*(31), p. B7.

Kedia, B. L. (1993). The CIBER agenda. In S. T. Cavusgil (Ed.), *Internationalizing business education: Meeting the challenge* (pp. 15–30). East Lansing: Michigan State University.

Kedia, B. L., & Cornwell, T. B. (1994). Mission based strategies for internationalizing United States Business schools. In M. C. Gibbs, Jr. (Ed.), *Internationalization of the business curriculum* (pp. 11–29). New York: International Business Press.

Kirwan, B. (2002, November 18). Unpublished remarks to the Maryland International Education Association Annual Meeting.

Kopczak, L. R., & Fransoo, J. C. (2000). Teaching supply chain management through global projects with global project teams. *Production and Operations Management, 9,* 91–104.

Lechner, F. J., & Boli, J. (Eds.). (2000). *The globalization reader.* Malden, MA: Blackwell.

Lublin, J. S. (2003, September 29). Workplace security (A special report); No place like home: Companies face a dual problem with overseas assignments: First, persuading employees to accept them; And second, protecting them if they do. *Wall Street Journal*, pp. R7–R10.

Madigan, K. (2003, August 18–25). Outsourcing jobs: Is it bad? Yes.... *Business Week*, 37–38.

Mann, C. C. (2000). The end of Moore's Law? *Technology Review, 103*(3), 42–48.

McMurtrie, B. (2001, November 16). Foreign enrollments grow in the United States, but so does competition from other nations. *The Chronicle of Higher Education*, p. A45.

Nehrt, L. C. (1987). The internationalization of the curriculum. *Journal of International Business Studies, 18*(3), 83–90.

Niederman, F., & Rollier, B. (2001). How are you going to keep them in the classroom after they've seen MTV? Online education in a virtual world. In L. Chidambaram & I. Zigurs (Eds.), *Our virtual world: The transformation of work, play and life via technology* (pp. 56–73). Hershey, PA: Idea Group.

Nielsen, C. (2003). *Study of top-ranked universities in global business education.* Unpublished internal study at the University of Baltimore.

Peterson, P. G. (2000). Gray dawn: How the coming age wave will transform America—and the world. New York: Three Rivers Press.

Pickert, S. M. (1992). *Preparing for a global community: Achieving an international perspective in higher education.* Washington, DC: George Washington University.

Porth, S. J. (1997). Management education goes international: A model for designing and teaching a study tour course. *Journal of Management Education, 21,* 190–199.

Pricewaterhouse Coopers. (2001). *Technology forecast: 2001–2003: Mobile Internet: Unleashing the power of wireless.* Menlo Park, CA: Author.

Quinn, J. B. (2004, February 2). Colleges' new tuition crisis. *Newsweek*, 49.

USNews. (2004). *America's best graduate schools: 2004 edition.* Washington, DC: Author.

Vance, C. M., Paderon, E., & Paderon, S. (1993). An ethical argument for host country workforce training and development in the expatriate management assignment. *Journal of Business Ethics, 12*(1), 635–641.

Wallraff, B. (2000). What global language? *The Atlantic Monthly, 286*(5), 52–66.

Welch, D. E. (2003). Globalisation of staff movements: Beyond cultural adjustment. *Management International Review, 43,* 149–162.

West, L. A., & Bogumil, W. A. (2001). Immigration and the global IT work force. *Communications of the ACM, 44*(7), 34–38.

CHAPTER 4

THE INTERNATIONALIZATION OF THE BUSINESS CURRICULUM THROUGH LANGUAGE AND CULTURE

A Theoretical and Practical Approach to Interdisciplinary Cooperation

**Laura Ancilli, Michela Betta, Raffaela Dinelli,
Laura Hougaz, and Bruno Mascitelli**

INTRODUCTION

Undoubtedly, business education is gradually becoming more global. As a consequence, educators are regularly addressing and debating prominent issues in internationalizing the business curriculum, such as (a) which subjects should be taught in order to improve the global and international skills of business students and (b) how to determine the methodological steps to follow to best incorporate these subjects into the curriculum. The internationalization of the business curriculum is no simple task, and no definitive

The Cutting Edge of International Management Education, pages 89–112
Copyright © 2004 by Information Age Publishing
All rights of reproduction in any form reserved.

and exclusive strategy has yet been devised. On the one hand, educators will argue endlessly for a long list of competencies that must be included in the program (e.g., Abboushi, Lackman, & Peace, 1999; Arthur & Bennett, 1995) according to the needs of specific faculties, the operational areas, and the educational aims pursued by single educational units. On the other hand, the business community has its own position and requirements, the most urgent of which is that graduates be equipped with an international perspective (Deutschman, 1991; Javalgi, Vogelsang-Coombs, Lawson, & White, 1997; White & Griffith, 1998). Students also have their own attitudes and perceptions (Turley & Shannon, 1999) along with the desire to be exposed to real international challenges and environments.

In the following paragraphs, we will present a compelling case (emerging from the following two aspects) for internationalizing the curriculum of the traditional school of business.

1. The introduction of language study in addition to content which targets global business education as a vehicle for a successful implementation of new business didactics.
2. The emphasis on culture and cross-cultural education as a vehicle for understanding specific countries and economic areas of the world, local markets, and commercial traditions and customs.

These topics are addressed in a sequential format, moving from (a) the theoretical debate on the internationalization of business curricula, to (b) the empirical work and activities performed in our unit concerning the development of a study abroad curriculum, and to (c) the organization of the resources (knowledge, skills, and practice) that will help students to broaden and strengthen their academic and professional profiles. Our academic work is therefore structured according to specific needs, but not in terms of hierarchy. None of the activities that we are presenting is secondary to the others. Students will need the technological resources and the intellectual challenges from academics and external experts in the same way that they will need a strongly articulated language program, a study abroad program, and training.

The material presented in this chapter traces a number of teaching and learning approaches developed for the Italian language and European studies curriculum which were integrated into the business courses at Swinburne University of Technology in Melbourne, Australia.

Purpose

The chapter begins with a theoretical discussion of the literature on the internationalization of business schools in general, and on the curricula of business schools in particular. The argument we present is that proficiency in language and understanding of culture cannot be simply reduced to supplementary tools but must be understood as a crucial feature of any internationalization strategy. In the course of our analysis, and specifically in our case study, we will use the terms *global* and *international* and *globalization* and *internationalization* interchangeably. Figure 4.1 describes the components of the unit, which include (a) face-to-face teaching programs, (b) language training programs, (c) the resource components given by technological support, (d) the expertise provided by external institutions; and

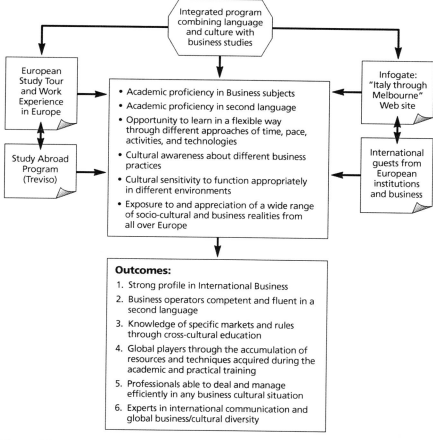

Figure 4.1.

(e), the study abroad and training abroad curriculum. The five crucial sub-units are interrelated in their programmatic work, and the work of the entire unit leads to the outcomes that students can expect at the completion of their studies.

Limitations

Admittedly, the content of this report is subject to several limitations. The report is written from the perspective of active participants closely associated with the project who may be too involved to critically assess all its aspects and dimensions. In addition, this report aims at highlighting possible alternatives for those who may be interested in pursuing similar goals. This is not a fixed framework, but in some contexts, it may not be easily or successfully reproduced. Finally, limits to the length of the report impose upon us the necessity to prioritize some aspects and neglect others. We therefore propose to offer a more complete and detailed description of the programs of study and current program developments in a subsequent publication.

THEORETICAL JUSTIFICATIONS FOR THE INTERNATIONALIZATION OF A BUSINESS CURRICULUM

In some exceptionally interesting case studies dealing with the universities and business schools of the future, some observers and writers have identified global responsibility as the driving moral force that will turn the current university system into a "multiversity" (Moratis & van Baalen, 2002, p. 161) and turn business schools into "global business schools" (Lorange, 2003, p. 127) or "synolic business schools" (Moratis & van Baalen, 2002, p. 161). We will expand briefly on these terms in an attempt to introduce the theoretical background that supports our work and initiatives.

According to Moratis and van Baalen (2002), the term *multiversity* describes a transformation process that has already changed universities into "hybrid organizations" (p. 161). Universities have become many things in a competitive environment that requires new teaching contexts and contents, knowledge transfers and knowledge differentiation, and an understanding of global management. In the internationalization debate, multiversity is understood as a new entity that connects diverse communities and constituencies together. The business school located in such a tertiary entity is understood to be a *synolic business school*.[1] The basic principle of the synolic business school is interdisciplinarity, and its method of implementation is networking. In this new debate, reorganized schools of business are considered the central starting point. Less relevant to these reorganized synolic schools seem the critical voices that condemned the inability of business schools to anticipate trends and to react to the changing needs of managers, or those voices that condemned business schools for not creating links to business and for failing to internationalize their curriculum (Albers-Miller, Sigerstadt, and Straughan, 2000, pp. 57–58). Also less relevant to the synolic business school are criticisms of the passive role of business schools in responding only to developments initiated by others (Albers-Miller, Prenshaw, & Straughan, 1999; Tesar & Moini, 1998). Business schools have indeed turned into key players in the debate on the internationalization of commerce. Despite this, Scherer, Beaten, Fall Ainina, and Meyer (2003, pp. 36–37) still speak of a multifaceted "resistance to internationalization" that they are inclined to classify as "administrative resistance" (e.g., budget, organizational structure, lack of incentives for internationalization efforts of their staff) and as "faculty resistance" (e.g., senior management resistance, questioning of the added educational values of internationalization programs, lack of cognitive shift). However, Scherer et al. suggest the possibility of overcoming such resistance through a series of actions aimed at gaining administrative and faculty support: (a) identifying an International Business (IB) champion as well as a "critical mass," (b) articulating an international vision and objectives, (c) developing the faculty's IB expertise through research and practice, and (d) encouraging travel abroad as well as course modification (pp. 40–44). This strategy is important not only because it encourages the development of a comprehensive IB program, but also because it offers solutions to the practical problems that always accompany the creation and implementation of an international business curriculum.

THE IMPORTANCE OF LANGUAGE AND CULTURE

Theory supports the argument that language, culture, and the business environment are interdependent; this is historically well documented (Hall, 1959, 1976; Hofstede 1980, 1990, 1991; Tropenaars, 1993). The fundamental importance of learning a language other than English in order to understand different (business) cultures has been emphasized in numerous works (e.g., Albers-Miller, Sigerstadt, et al., 2000; Lascu & Kenman, 2000; Albers-Miller, Prenshaw, et al., 1999; Tesar & Moini, 1998; Kahal, 1998; Kaynak & Kucukemiroglu, 1997; Teck-Meng, Aik-Meng, & Liang, 1997; Osman-Gani & Ser Toh, 1997; Mockler, Chao, & Dologite, 1996; Kuhne, 1990). Our contention is that the study of languages and the ability to understand different cultures are the *conditio sine qua non* for the internationalization of the curricula of business schools.

This chapter will supply new arguments and empirical evidence in support of the internationalization of a traditional business curriculum through knowledge of languages and cultures. We will outline a model adopted by Swinburne University of Technology, which integrates languages and business study. The model will describe the very successful interdisciplinary developments that have been devised and implemented across the curricula to give business students unique international opportunities and experiences resulting from the interlinking of business, language, and culture courses. The result is a program that specifically develops students' competence in business practices, improves their awareness of international issues, and increases their knowledge about the impact of the European Union (EU), particularly focusing on Italy as one of the key players in the EU. Other program goals are the improvement of student competence in the Italian language, an appreciation of the significance of cultural diversity, and an understanding of the European and Italian business environments.

The internationalization of business curricula has been a topic of discussion since the early 1960s (e.g., Fugate & Jefferson, 2001). As relevant literature on the topic of international business communication has began to appear, outcomes have been well documented, and discussion is still ongoing (e.g., Beamish & Calof, 1989; Larson, 1991; Beamer, 1992; Victor, 1992, Martin & Chaney, 1992, Kwok, Arpan, & Folks, 1994; Lundstrom, White, & Schuster, 1996; Nash, 1997; Vielba & Edelshain, 1997; Turley & Shannon, 1999; Domke-Damonte, 2001; Siaya, Porcelli, & Green, 2002). The benefits deriving from modernization through a curriculum targeting global and international perspectives have been minutely described by Lundstrom & White (1997). They assert, among other things, that

> by establishing and maintaining an open dialogue with the business community [and students], academicians can benefit in two ways: They can better tailor course offerings to fit the outcomes desired by practitioners, and they can reduce the criticism that they are insular and out of touch with the needs of the business community. (p. 24)

In spite of this intensive and extensive work, White and Griffith (1998) report that the majority of business schools have internationalized their programs "to only a small extent" and that the courses are still not successfully producing the much sought-after "high quality global managers" (p. 111). Turley and Shannon (1999) support this view, reporting that "students do not feel adequately prepared for careers in international marketing." In addition, Kwok, Arpan, and Folks (1994) emphasize that "internationalization efforts continue to fall short of fulfilling the need of businesses for personnel who can think and act in a global context." Kwok et al. describe four different approaches that may be followed to initiate or accelerate the internationalization of a business curriculum: (1) infusing an international dimension into existing business courses; (2) offering a general course in international business to all students; (3) offering specialized international courses in one or more functional fields, and (4) integrating subjects such as world geography, world politics, and comparative economic systems into the business course. In addition, Kwok et al. emphasize the necessity for out-of-country experiences in order to "broaden and deepen students' understanding about the complexities and realities of international business."

Admittedly, in the meantime, much has been written about infusion, inclusion, internship, exchange programs, and educational joint ventures as well as the creation of core programs to achieve a productive internationalization of business faculties and curricula in a global educational market (Albers-Miller, Sigerstadt, et al., 2000, p. 60). Albers-Miller, Prenshaw, et al. (1999, p. 35) speak of the creation of new programs devoted to the internationalization of students and their business faculties, whereas Teck-Meng et al. (1997, pp. 23–24), Osman-Gani and Ser Toh (1997, pp. 2–3), and Kaynuk and Kucukemiroglu (1997, p. 54) speak of an internationalization of all subjects offered in a business school. Kahal (1998, pp. 12–13) expresses the desire to make business education a political task by calling for complete modernization of business schools through government intervention. Tesar and Moini (1998, pp. 87, 94) emphasize the urgency to modernize faculties and their management as a "prerequisite for faculty globalization."

On a more critical level, Mockler, Chao, and Dologite (1996, pp. 34–36) speak of the creation of new private schools and universities in China and Russia to address the internationalization of their schools of economics. However, coming from a practical business perspective, Lundstrum, White, and Schuster (1996) agree that the needs of the business community have not yet been met. They suggest that "an interdisciplinary, andragogical approach" (p.15) combining different areas of studies, such as general business and marketing classes, political science, communication, and language training, would better reflect today's changes in the global educational market. Fortunately, the idea of including language training in the business curriculum is steadily acquiring more credibility. In spite of this development, however, the necessity of introducing the study of a second language within the International Business (IB) curriculum of English-speaking countries has only been recognized in the last few years. In the course of a survey of a group of undergraduate marketing students, Turley and Shannon (1999) ascertained the students' strong wish to learn and speak a second language fluently and to develop an appreciation of cross-cultural issues.

Although the importance of language competence and cultural fluency within the International Business programs has been well documented in the academic literature and has been widely accepted, one unresolved issue is how to integrate these aspects successfully into the curricula so that language courses may become accessible and relevant to the needs and aspirations of business students.

Learning a language is an intensive exercise that requires, among other things, a cumulative acquisition of vocabulary and grammatical understanding over a prolonged period of time. Students undertaking a business undergraduate degree often have difficulty in integrating a language sequence of subjects into their course structure which will enable them to gain a reasonable level of proficiency. Wherever the integration of language subjects into business curricula has been attempted, the approaches adopted have varied greatly. Since academics and the managerial staff of business schools have begun to take an interest in developing courses in the international business area (Green and Scott, 1996), a variety of different approaches are being accepted and implemented. Moreover, there is now general support for the view that in the process of learning a language "one gets culturally sensitive, which is also essential to conducting international business" (Cavusgil, 1994), regardless of the specific approach adopted.

THE INTERNATIONALIZATION OF THE BUSINESS DEGREE

In order to produce a relevant international business program, Swinburne University of Technology has adopted a combination of approaches suggested by Kwok et al. (1994). Recent developments in University policy have given priority, among other things, to internationalization and entrepreneurship. The infusion model has been implemented, which provides all existing business courses with an international dimension. In addition, an international business major with a strong focus on three economic global regions, (Europe, the United States, and Asia), has been developed into a successful Bachelor of International Business degree. This course of study gives students the opportunity to combine business practices and networks with an awareness of international issues, intercultural understanding, and language competence. It must be added, at this stage, that one of the strategic priorities of Swinburne University is to be engaged in the process of internationalization—extending international networks, and in particular, providing its students with a successful internationalized curriculum.

In 1999 language teaching at Swinburne University of Technology, which in Australia is traditionally undertaken within the Faculty of Arts, was integrated into the School of Business in an attempt to enhance the international focus of the Swinburne University business courses and to provide a fresh and unique setting for the teaching of languages. On this occasion, the languages staff acted as the "IB champion" and "critical mass" in the sense proposed by Scherer et al. (2003, p. 42). The languages staff were therefore instrumental in the changes that led from the creation of a double degree in Business and Arts, to the subsequent integration of languages into the School of Business, and the development of the IB program. The languages staff also gained the support of senior management at the university level, which additionally strengthened their position. The languages staff, who were consulted at all times during the process and who were heavily committed to this new approach, were encouraged to develop and extend their own interests beyond their traditional disciplinary and cultural boundaries. They were given an opportunity to broaden their own visions, skills, and interests, the results of which were then absorbed into new courses and programs.

The initial goal was to review, restructure, and reposition the Italian language and culture program in order to make it more relevant to a business environment and to the environment of the European Union. However, in practice, changing the traditional boundaries of a long-standing program, accepting a new context and new parameters, and developing new ways of thinking about it are just some of the initial challenges which staff have had to face. The greatest barriers in the repositioning of languages study within a business framework have been (a) in understanding how the two areas of business and languages could actually interrelate and (b) in identifying new opportunities for interaction. Both areas of study have traditionally been viewed as discrete and have existed as separate programs, usually with totally unrelated curricula. Thus, there was a risk that the language programs would continue to be viewed as marginal within the educational curricula. In order to avoid this, a relevant connection between the Italian and European programs and the Business program at Swinburne University of Technology was created by developing courses that appealed to business students with an interest in Europe through the introduction of the option of studying the Italian language to support the international business focus of the program. The languages staff made a radical and deliberate decision to integrate a business focus into the program while decreasing their emphasis on the more traditional literary component, thus developing a new approach which had greater appeal to business students and in which all aspects of the program were perceived as relevant and related. This process, which was gradually implemented over a number of years, involved

1. Establishing a new European Union program with a business perspective (taught in English)

2. Developing an Italian business environment focus (taught in English), linking it in content to both the European Union program and the language program.

3. Incorporating new components of Italian business language into the Italian Studies major (taught in Italian and English).

A new Bachelor of International Business degree and a new European Business minor have developed from the closer interaction between staff from the language and business disciplines. The Italian language curriculum has been completely redesigned and redeveloped to ensure that it has a clear business perspective that therefore complements the business courses. The European Union program, which is aimed at emphasizing Italy's role in a thriving new Europe, complements and supports the Italian program perfectly. Italy is presented as the *gateway* to Europe, and the staff at Swinburne University of Technology have developed strong contacts with Italian authorities and industry links in both Italy and Australia. In addition to the changes concerned with content of the curriculum, Swinburne University of Technology has made a deliberate attempt to infuse issues of cultural diversity and cross-cultural understanding into the curriculum.

Thus, we can assert that the Italian and European Studies programs at Swinburne University of Technology have developed unique characteristics which have grown over recent years to become important points of reference within the School of Business.

The double degree program in Business and Arts (Italian) offered at Swinburne University of Technology is unique in Australia in that it allows students the opportunity to obtain

- A full specialization in Business (with majors in marketing, international business, human resource management, accounting, finance, and IT)
- Professional accreditation (e.g., in Accounting), and in addition, competence in Italian with a special focus on business language
- An understanding of the political and social environments of Italy and Europe, including competence in the policies and regulations governing the European Union
- An appreciation of the business cultures of Italy and the European Union
- An appreciation of cross-cultural issues
- A range of Asian language and culture studies similar to European Studies

The internationalization of the business curriculum involves a complex and finely balanced interplay between all these components and the traditional business curriculum. The double degree program at Swinburne University of Technology also creates links between the European Union and the Italian business environments as viewed from an Australian perspective. It guarantees a complete integration of three different areas (EU, Italy, and Australia) and their economic and cultural systems into the academic curriculum. It improves students' skills, increases their resources, and facilitates the development of new relationships between Australia and Europe through individuals who have gained a competent knowledge of the European Union and its marketplace.

The restructured European Studies and Italian programs currently offer various options which provide students with the flexibility to select the most appropriate combination of courses to suit their perceived requirements for their future careers. In addition, students are given great opportunities to extend their experiences and their horizons in a variety of stimulating ways. The following sections will outline some of the different strategies adopted by the European Studies and Italian sections, which will provide a more complete picture of the sections' activities and a discussion of some of the results achieved to date.

EUROPEAN STUDY TOUR AND WORK EXPERIENCE IN EUROPE

From the outset, the idea was to develop a European Studies program at Swinburne University of Technology which would complement and support the Italian language and culture program in its new business direction, placing it within a wider learning context. The European Studies program would have a strong curriculum content but would also be supported by extra-curricular programs, including a European Study Tour, European Work Experience, and an exchange program with European universities. The close relationship between the Italian and European Studies programs with their emphasis on business studies, business language, and business practical experiences is at the core of Swinburne University's success, which has been recognized by other universities and by the business and academic community at large.

Methodology

The combination of curriculum, different modes of subject delivery, and extra-curricular experiences offered by the Italian and European programs is constantly revised and updated to create a finely tuned and well-balanced program which is relevant, viable and innovative. As a result, European subjects and programs have been integrated into the Business degree, in particular into the International Business program, allowing students to undertake some specialization in European and Italian business. Following completion of the introductory courses covering the political and business framework of the European Union, students can elect to undertake the European Business Study Tour and European Work Experience.

Aim

The European Business Study Tour complements and enhances the European Studies program. The tour is an annual event whose academic rigor compares favorably with executive-style study tours with high professional standards. The basic aim of this initiative is to provide students with "hands on" meetings with the institutions that operate within the European Union, along with the relevant Australian trade and diplomatic representations in Europe. Students visit key European institutions, including the European Commission, the European Council, the Committee of the Regions, the European Parliament, and the European Central Bank in Frankfurt. In order to gauge Australia's role in Europe, especially from a business perspective, the tour also enlists the expertise of Australian diplomatic and trade representatives, who explain Australia's role in Europe. These officials provide students with interesting reports about the issues that companies in Australia need to consider when doing business in Europe. The visits range from meetings with ambassadors, who offers their appreciation of Australia's bilateral relationship with the host country, to meetings with trade representatives who explain the extent of Australia's competitive advantage in specific markets in Europe. The staff at Swinburne University of Technology has developed these professional links and personal contacts over many years.

Outcomes

The students participating in the European Business Study Tour gain a more operational and practical appreciation of the relationships between Australia and the EU along with an analysis of a particular aspect of that relationship—the Italian perspective.

The European Business Study Tour is offered on an annual basis in November–December. It has a duration of three weeks and is conducted outside the existing semester structure so that it does not interfere with semester course work or exam timetables.

Assessment and Preparation

Students are expected to participate in a series of seminars prior to departure and to research information for the meetings that will take place during the tour. In some circumstances, students are provided with industry briefings on European companies and their involvement in Australian trade. Throughout the European Business Study Tour students are in constant "assessment mode." They are expected to listen, question, discuss, brief, and debate the meetings that they attend. In addition, students are called upon to represent their institution and to be ambassadors for Swinburne University of Technology and Australia. At the completion of the tour, students are expected to submit an extensive report on a specific topic selected prior to their departure.

Another special experience offered by Swinburne University's International European Business program is Work Experience in Europe. Every year a small but select group of students undertake this experience, which involves work placement in an appropriate company in Europe for a minimum of 12 weeks and a maximum of 24 weeks. Competence in a second language may be a requirement, thus rendering the experience even more challenging. Students receive the equivalent of a full semester's academic credit once the academic assessment criteria have been satisfied. Students are required to complete a project based on a comparative study or on a topic related to potential for trade between the European Union and Australia. In addition, students are required to submit a professional diary of their activities during the placement. The Work Experience in Europe program is always quite challenging for students since they are engaged in an experience with minimum support infrastructure, often on their own, with only their limited personal experience and resources on which to rely. The experience is extremely maturing and fruitful, often with astonishing results. At the same time, opportunities for this kind of experience are quite limited and may be very costly. Generally, this experience is recommended to students who are mature, independent, and therefore ready for such a challenging undertaking.

THE STUDY ABROAD PROGRAM IN TREVISO (ITALY)

The Study Abroad Program is the most recent development offered by the Italian Studies division of Swinburne University of Technology. This program is based on the foundation of experiential learning theory, first explored by Dewey (1916, 1938) and then further developed by a number of other researchers (e.g., Bruner, 1961; Rogers, 1980; Kolb, 1984; Fayed, 1995). The term *experiential learning* refers to a particular learning process triggered by a number of activities beyond the classroom, in which students have the opportunity to acquire new skills through different types of structured or semi-structured experience.

An out-of-country experience offers students the opportunity for experiential learning overseas, enabling them to explore and experience directly some aspects of their studies. Previous research (Kwok, Arpan, & Folks, 1994; Turley & Shannon, 1999; Hutchings, Jackson, & McEllister, 2002) has shown that out-of-country experiences are highly valued by students, who have an opportunity to experience first-hand much of what they learn in class. These research studies refer to programs that have been designed either to improve the acquisition and appreciation of a foreign language or to provide students with a direct, hands-on experience in a different business culture.

Treviso was chosen as the city for our Study Abroad Program because of several factors. First, in 2001, Swinburne University of Technology, along with some of the other universities in Australia, received some very generous funding from Fondazione Cassamarca, a prestigious Italian financial organization based in Treviso. The president of Fondazione Cassamarca, Dr. De Poli, has true commitment and passion for the Italian culture. Fondazione Cassamarca has also recently financially supported the opening of a university in Treviso, which gives young students the opportunity to study in their own city. The university in Treviso has a Faculty of International Business, and English is offered as a compulsory language. Swinburne University of Technology and the university at Treviso complement each other and offer reciprocal benefits to students who travel between institutions. Moreover, Treviso and the surrounding region is a very productive, rich area of Italy that developed over the last 20 years into one of the most dynamic and profitable business areas in the whole country. An agreement between the two universities was signed which, among other things, facilitates the exchange of students and lecturers.

Methodology

In 2002 the first group of 40 students and two lecturers from Swinburne University of Technology visited Treviso for a four-week course of study. The program was designed to provide students with a wide variety of activities which would link Italian language, business knowledge, and immersion into the Italian culture and provide some leisure time. The curriculum was slightly modified to make the topics suit an environment in which students were required to interact in Italian all day. Students were also required to undertake small research projects and interviews which involved them directly with the local community.

Aim

A very important component of the Treviso Study Abroad Program is to expose students to the Italian language and Italy's cultural environment while providing them with hands-on experiences with the Italian business culture.

Outcomes

The students participating in the Treviso Study Abroad Program were surveyed before and after the program in order to rate their perceptions of the benefits of the program. A total 34 students completed surveys prior to the beginning of the Treviso Study Abroad Program, and 38 students completed surveys at the end of the program (the survey was not compulsory). Before their journey to Treviso, the students were asked to rank the benefits that they perceived that they would obtain from undertaking the Treviso Study Abroad program. Upon their return, they were asked once again to rank the benefits that they perceived they had obtained from the program. The reasons that the students listed as the most important for going to Treviso before undertaking the program, are as follows, rated in order of importance:

1. To greatly extend my competence in Italian
2. To experience Italian society
3. To expand my career opportunities
4. To gain a competitive advantage in my future career
5. To enhance my self-confidence and communication skills

At the end of the program, the students believed that the Treviso Study Abroad Program had provided the following benefits:

1. Contact with Italian society
2. Experience with a different way of life
3. Enhanced command of the Italian language
4. Experience traveling overseas
5. Learning not only in theory, but in practice

In general terms, the results of the surveys indicate that the students' expectations of the study abroad program were met and that they achieved their most important expectations, (i.e., improving their linguistic competence and experiencing the Italian way of life).

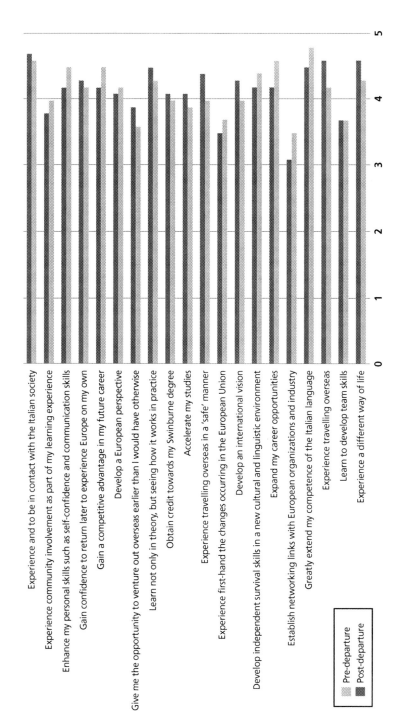

Figure 4.2. Mean rating score: Pre- and post-departure.

104

The survey revealed that prior to their departure, students had high expectations about greatly extending their competence of the Italian language. A language test designed to ascertain the linguistic improvement of the students participating in the Treviso Study Abroad Program was conducted before and after the program, and each student's individual improvement was measured. The language test involved a variety of reading, writing, listening, and speaking activities. The tests revealed that, during the four weeks spent in Treviso, there was a marked improvement in the students' oral fluency and in their communicative competence, particularly in the language used in everyday interpersonal interactions, which included the usage of idiomatic expressions. The students' language skills had improved to the extent that the Beginner students who had been to Treviso were advised by staff to join the Advanced class in order to provide them with the appropriate challenge and maintain their motivation towards further studies. The Advanced group, who also showed an improvement beyond the abilities of their colleagues who had not gone to Treviso, were provided with extra challenges in and outside class in order to maintain their level of language fluency and enthusiasm. A permanent solution to address this unexpected side issue of the Treviso Study Abroad Program is under discussion.

Overall, the experience can be summarized in the words of one of the enthusiastic students who undertook the Treviso Study Abroad Program: "The trip changed my perspective on my studies as now I feel a lot more involved when discussing different aspects of Italy and its people. The trip has made the things I'm learning now and what I've learnt in the past a lot more personal as I can relate them to my own experiences."

In addition to study abroad, a range of enhancement activities which use educational technology have been introduced into the program

CREATING THE RESOURCES
FOR THE INTERNATIONAL PROFILE

Technological Educational Strategies

During the last two years, online educational strategies are among the activities created and implemented in order to improve the learning resources for our students in the Languages and International Business section. Using flexible delivery and technological strategies, Swinburne University's aim is (a) to stimulate students' interest in expanding their horizons; (b) to increase new options and opportunities for teaching, learning, and practicing language; and (c) to promote students' understanding of cultural diversity. Swinburne University has a university-wide policy on learning and teaching which promotes the use of a flexible, learner-centered, self-paced approach through the use of a range of technological strategies. Evidence of the wide-reaching educational implications of Web-based systems is found in a number of articles (e.g., Wach, 2002; Gardner, Sheridan, & White, 2002; McDowell, 2002; Kuntz, 2003). A very useful resource incorporated directly into the teaching curriculum of the Italian Studies major is a multimedia CD-ROM which was compiled by Swinburn University staff to allow students to expand their knowledge of business Italian. This resource, entitled *A Business Italian Interactive Resource*, is part of students' study of a subject called "Introductory Business Italian." This CD-ROM contains a number of units that deal with topics pertinent to business practices in Italy. The units are in Italian, and the topics range from making contact with personnel of Italian companies to the format of correspondence and telephone communication in the business context. Each unit has a number of activities which use listening, reading, speaking, and writing skills. This tool not only presents relevant vocabulary but also provides added language practice in second language skills. A further development which supports student learning is a Web site (available via the online communication platform Blackboard) called "Italy through Melbourne." All students at Swinburne University of Technology who are enrolled in language, culture, and European subjects have access. The original aim was to bring together students of Italian language and culture with the Italian community in Melbourne in order to make their learning more relevant. This would extend their contact with the Italian language and culture outside the classroom, thus providing a more interesting and exciting learning environment. However, this aim has now been extended to include easy access to Italian Web sites that provide links to interesting, unusual, and generally stimulating articles and news about Italian culture and business.

Educational Outcomes

The strategies described above not only allow acquisition of information but also reinforce students' second language proficiency within a realistic Italian context. Students are thus immersed in the linguistic and cultural environment of the country whose commercial practices they are studying. It is generally a very powerful medium for providing important, useful, and enjoyable information to students. Work on the content of the Web page is continuing, as there is a constant need to add and update the material and check Web addresses regularly since they are often subject to change. The management of these systems can also be reviewed by gauging student responses. "Course Statistics," a feature of the Blackboard system, provides figures on the usage of the Web page. Anecdotal feedback from students can form a worthy basis for research into the effectiveness of these different forms of educational technology.

Cross-Disciplinary and Interdisciplinary Synergies

In addition to the use of technology, visitors from Europe are invited to join our classes to discuss their work. The Italian and European Studies programs at Swinburne University of Technology are designed to create synergies with professionals who come from diverse business environments in order to provide students (and colleagues) with expertise developed in contexts different from the traditional academic environment. The intention is to develop and emphasize interdisciplinary links and to assess the practical value of this inter-communication from the perspective of international management education. The practical aspects of this interdisciplinary exercise are (a) that it increases the professional opportunities of students and lecturers at an international level and (b) that it is particularly geared towards training future professionals capable of living and successfully working in transnational environments.

It is important to stress that international visiting guests generally bring a global perspective into the teaching program of the university in a way which adds value to the international business curriculum. A guest speaker addressing the influence of the Euro on the economies of Europe will unavoidably trace a parallel with American and/or Japanese trade and economic relations—not only in terms of comparison, but also because the audience will be interested in understanding economic differences. In so doing, the guest will provide a unique international perspective on the topic. These experts have the prerogative of creating debates that go beyond the usual teaching parameters, and a visiting expert working "offshore" may sometimes feel more prone to expose himself/herself to challenging discussions. Interesting discussions always occur when a speaker challenges opinions and theories and addresses the empirical aspects of issues such as the competition policy of the European Union, Third World aid policies and the cancellation of debts, pharmaceutical and drug policies in the genetics era, and ethical management in organizational life. Visiting researchers, academics, and experts speaking about these topics are very often confronted with challenging questions and expectations from students.

Educational Outcomes

In 2002 an interesting group of speakers was invited to address students of European Business Studies at Swinburne University. Their contributions tackled such issues as Italian–Australian trade relations (Gobbo, 2002) in an attempt to identify new markets and potential trade relationships. The economist Bresolin (2002) reconstructed the EU integration process, paying particular attention to the influence of political decisions on economy and business. The importance of political issues in Australian–EU relations was reinforced by Anderson (2002), who specifically addressed political questions in trade and economy. These issues found a most appropriate context in a seminar on the Euro and its impact on the EU economy, which was given at Swinburne University of Technology by the President of the *Banco di Roma* (Scialla, 2002). These speakers addressed some important topical issues and created a favorable discourse on the internationalization of academic curricula. The educational outcomes are easy to see. The seminars initiated by staff in Italian and European Studies provided the opportunity for students (and academics) to test their own knowledge and compare their data with those proposed by the visiting experts.

The staff of Italian and European Studies is perfectly aware of the risks of failure of any business teaching curriculum that neglects the importance of the international dimension of business and economy. According to Ferraro (2002, p. 7), "research has shown that failures in the overseas business settings most frequently result from an inability to understand and adapt to foreign ways of thinking and acting rather than from technical or professional incompetence." As Crane maintains, "The world is changing. In many ways, it is returning to an earlier, more complex time when cultures, languages, religions, and history were of key importance" (2000, p. *ix*). For whom or what were they important? They were fundamental to the very social and economic order of the past, in the same way as they are fundamental to the order of the 21st century, which Zinn (2002, p. 8) prefers to call the "tertiary civilization."

The implications of this type of academic activity for educational managers and teachers are numerous and varied, and the returns from educational investments in the form of guest speakers and visiting practitioners are high compared to the small costs involved.

CONCLUSION

A number of concerns have been addressed at Swinburne University of Technology by an approach to management education that builds on the work of Kwok et al. (1994). The approaches to teaching and learning that have combined the resources of academic staff and other experts from language and cultural studies with those from the business studies disciplines have been a successful response to the need for (a) the improvement of the international profile of business students; (b) the practical elaboration of theoretical and empirical data regarding the teaching of international subjects, (c) the challenges stemming from globalization and/or internationalization of business practice, and (d) the training of business professionals capable of speaking a second language and capable of being culturally sensitive to different world locations.

The model of an integrated approach to business education that embraces languages and cultural studies in addition to more traditional business subjects provides other educators and practitioners with an example that is based on best practice. Studies in teaching and learning have shown that immersion in other cultures is a highly successful approach to the development of language and cultural sensitivity. When combined with work experience, study abroad, and creative applications of educational technology, the benefits of this program are magnified. Additional benefits derive from the provision of a forum for international experts and business practitioners who can discuss their experiences and encourage the entrepreneurs of the future.

New approaches to business management education must combine relevant teaching and learning across disciplines in innovative ways. Creative collaborative efforts and greater flexibility in delivery methods of programs are essential components of a more relevant style of management education in a worldwide marketplace.

NOTE

1. The term *synolic* is derived from the Greek word *synolos*, meaning complete or all together (Moratis and van Baalen (2002, 161)).

REFERENCES

Abboushi, S., Lackman, C., & Peace, A. G. (1999). An international marketing curriculum: Development and analysis. *Journal of Teaching in International Business, 11*(2), 1–19.

Albers-Miller, N. D., Prenshaw, P. J., & Straughan, R. D. (1999). Student perception of study abroad programs: A survey of US colleges and universities. *Marketing Education Review, 9*(1), 29–36.

Albers-Miller, N. D., Sigerstadt, T. D., & Straughan, R. D. (2000). Internationalization of the undergraduate curriculum: Insight from recruiters. *Journal of Teaching in International Business, 11*(4), 55–80.

Anderson, A. (2002). Australian/EU relations: Trade, investment and political issues. School of Business Research Report Series. Swinburne, Australia: Swinburne University of Technology.

Arthur, W., Jr., & Bennett, W., Jr. (1995). The international assignee: The relative importance of factors perceived to contribute to success. *Personnel Psychology, 48*(1), 99–114.

Beamer, L. (1992). Learning intercultural competence. *Journal of Business Communication, 29*(3), 285–303.

Beamish, P. K., & Calof, J. L. (1989). International business education: A corporate view. *Journal of International Business Studies, 20*(3), 553–564.

Bresolin, F. (2002). European Union integration. School of Business Research Report Series. Swinburne, Australia: Swinburne University of Technology.

Bruner, J. S. (1961). The act of discovery. *Harvard Educational Review, 31*(1), 21–31.

Cavusgil, T. (1994). *Internationalisation of business education and research opportunities in international business.* [Occasional chapter 2/1994]. Centre for International Management and Commerce. Nepean, Australia: University of Western Sydney.

Crane, R. (Ed.). (2000). *European business cultures.* Essex, England: Pearson Education.

Deutschman, A. (1991, July 29). The trouble with MBAs. *Fortune,* 67–78.

Dewey, J. (1916). *Democracy and Education,* New York: Macmillan.

Dewey, J. (1938). *Experience and Education,* New York: Macmillan.

Domke-Damonte, D. (2001, Winter). Language learning and international business, *SAM Advanced Management Journal,* 35–40.

Fayed, R. (1995). Effective action learning and competitive advantage. Sydney: International Marketing Institute of Australia.

Ferraro, G. P. (2002). *The cultural dimension of international business* (4th ed.). Upper Saddle River, New Jersey: Prentice Hall.

Fugate, D. L., & Jefferson, R. W. (2001, January–February). Preparing for globalization: Do we need structural change for our academic programs? *Journal of Education for Business,* 160–166.

Gardner, L., Sheridan, D., & White, D. (2002). A Web-based learning and assessment system to support flexible education. *Journal of Computer Assisted Learning, 18,* 125–126.

Gobbo, J. (2002). Italian/Australian trade: Present trends and the potential: Some observations from recent visits to Italy. School of Business Research Report Series. Swinburne, Australia: Swinburne University of Technology.

Green, D. J., & Scott, J. C. (1996). The status of international business communication courses in schools accredited by the American Assembly of Collegiate Schools of Business. *Delta Pi Epsilon Journal, 38*(1), 43–62.

Hall, E. T. (1959). *The silent language of business.* Garden City, NJ: Doubleday.

Hall, E. T. (1976). *Beyond Culture.* New York: Anchor Press.

Hofstede, G. (1980). *Culture's consequences: International differences in work related values.* Beverley Hills, CA: Sage Publications.

Hofstede, G. (1990). *Marketing and culture* (Working chapter 90–006). Maastricht, the Netherlands: University of Limburg.

Hofstede, G. (1991). *Cultures and organizations: Software of the mind.* London: McGraw-Hill.

Hutchings, K., Jackson, P., & McEllister, R. (2002). Exploiting the links between theory and practice: Developing students' cross-cultural understanding through an international study tour to China. *Higher Education Research & Development, 21*(1), 55–72.

Javalgi, R., Vogelsang-Coombs, V., Lawson, D. A., & White, D. S. (1997). Designing an international business curriculum: A market-driven approach. *Journal of Teaching in International Business, 9*(2), 31–48.

Kahal, E. S. (1998). The internationalisation of business education in the United Kingdom: Contemporary trends and future developments. *Journal of Teaching in International Business, 10*(1), 1–14.

Kaynak, E., & Kucukemiroglu, O. (1997). Program and curriculum development in international marketing in an emerging economy: Issues and strategies. *Journal of Teaching in International Business, 9*(1), 51–70.

Kolb, D. A. (1984). *Experiential learning: Experience and the source of learning and development.* Englewood Cliffs, NJ: Prentice Hall.

Kuhne, R. J. (1990). Comparative analysis of U.S. doctoral programs in international business. *Journal of Teaching in International Business, 1*(3/4), 85–99.

Kuntz, K. (2003, May/June). Pathfinders: Helping students find paths to information. *Multimedia Schools, 10*(3), 12, 4.

Kwok, C. C. Y., Arpan, J., & Folks, W. R., Jr. (1994). A global survey of international business education in the 1990s. *Journal of International Business Studies, 25*(3), 605–619.

Larson, C. E. (1991). Globalization of business curriculum and international marketing: Symbiotic or authentic? *Journal of Teaching in International Business, 3*(2), 19–27.

Lascu, D. N., & Kenman, L. F. (2000). International business-related perceptions and preferences of future global managers: An empirical evaluation and implications for teaching international business. *Journal of Teaching in International Business, 11*(4), 81–98.

Lorange, P. (2003). Global responsibility: Business education and business schools: Roles in promoting a global perspective. *Corporate Governance, 3*(3), 126–135.

Lundstrom, W. J., & White, D. S. (1997). A gap analysis of professional and academic perceptions of the importance of international marketing curriculum content and research areas. *Journal of Marketing Education, 19*(2), 16–25.

Lundstrom, W. J., White, D. S., & Schuster, C. P. (1996). Internationalizing the marketing curriculum: The professional marketer's perspective. *Journal of Marketing Education, 18*(2), 5–16.

Martin, J., & Chaney, L. (1992). Determination of content for a collegiate course in intercultural business communication by three delphi panels. *Journal of Business Communication, 29*(3), 267–283.

McDowell, L. (2002). Electronic information resources in undergraduate education: An exploratory study of opportunities for student learning and independence. *British Journal of Educational Technology, 33*(3), 255–266.

Mockler, R. J., Chao, C., & Dologite D. G. (1996). A comparative study of business education programs in China and Russia. *Journal of Teaching in International Business, 8*(2), 19–38.

Moratis, L. T., & van Baalen, P. J. (2002). The radicalisation of the multiversity: The case of the networked business school. *The International Journal of Education Management, 16*(4), 160–168.

Nash, B. A. (1997). Internationalizing the business school: Responding to the customer's needs. *Journal of Teaching in International Business, 9*(1), 73–85.

Osman-Gani, A. M., & Ser Toh, T. (1997). Market-driven paradigm for developing internationally-oriented business curriculum: A Pacific Rim viewpoint. *Journal of Teaching in International Business, 9*(1), 1–14.

Rogers, C. R. (1980). *A Way of Being.* Boston: Houghton Mifflin.

Scherer, R. F., Beaton, S. T., Fall Ainina, M., & Meyer J. F. (2003) *Internationalizing the business curriculum: A field guide.* Euclid, OH: Williams Custom Publishing.

Scialla, M. (2002). The impact of the Euro on the economy of Europe: An analysis, with a particular focus on the economy of Italy. School of Business Research Report Series. Swinburne, Australia: Swinburne University of Technology.

Siaya, L., Porcelli, M., & Green, M. (2002, September). One year later: Attitudes about internationalization since September 11. *American Council on Education.*

Teck-Meng, T., Low Aik-Meng, A. P., & Liang, T. W. (1997). Internationalization of MBA program in Asia–Pacific: Looking beyond business study missions. *Journal of Teaching in International Business, 9*(1), 15–31.

Tesar, G., & Moini, A. H. (1998). Globalization of faculty, students, and programs: An approach. *Journal of Teaching in International Business, 9*(4), 85–104.

Tropenaars, F. (1993). *Riding the waves of culture: Understanding cultural diversity in business.* London: Nicholas Brealy.

Turley, L. W., & Shannon, J. R. (1999). The international marketing curriculum: Views from students. *Journal of Marketing Education, 21*(3), 175–180.

Victor, D. (1992). *International business communication.* New York: HarperCollins.

Vielba, C. A., & Edelshain, D. J. (1997). Are business schools meeting the challenge of international communication? *Journal of Management Development, 16*(2), 80–92.

Vogelsang-Coombs, V., White, S. D., & Mickovsky, J. (1996). Internationalizing business education: Curriculum design and power politics. *Business & the Contemporary World, 1*, 103–118.

Wach, H. M. (2002). How I arrived on the Web: A history teacher's tale. *History Teacher, 36*(1), 75–88.

White, D. S., & Griffith, D. A. (1998). International perspective: Graduate international business education in the United States: Comparisons and suggestions. *Journal of Education for Business, 74*(2), 103–115.

Zinn, K. G. (2002). *Zukunftswissen: Die Nächsten zehn Jahre im Blick der Politischen Ökonomie.* Hamburg: VSA-Verlag.

section II

CYBERSPACE PERSPECTIVES

CHAPTER 5

GLOBAL REALITY WITH VIRTUAL TEAMS

Lessons from the Globally Distant Multicultural Teams Project[1]

Joyce Osland, Allan Bird, Christian Scholz, Martha Maznevski,
Jeanne McNett, Mark Mendenhall, Volker Stein,
and Doris Weyer

ABSTRACT

Globally Distant Multicultural Teams (GDMT) is an experiential pedagogy that prepares students to work in virtual teams in global organizations. European and American professors created a virtual workplace in which their students completed a team project assignment via the Internet. In this chapter, we describe the creation, pedagogical foundation, and implementation of the GDMT Project. Our evaluation of the project includes feedback from the students, professors, and three external researchers who audited the project. We discuss team effectiveness in terms of team processes, cultural differences, and use of technology, and we close with a summary of student and faculty lessons and recommendations.

The Cutting Edge of International Management Education, pages 115–141
115

You have no choice but to operate in a world shaped by globalization and the information revolution. There are two options: Adapt or die.... You need to plan the way a fire department plans. It cannot anticipate fires, so it has to shape a flexible organization that is capable of responding to unpredictable events.

—Andy Grove, CEO of Intel, (*Fortune*, 1996)

I hear and I forget.
I see and I remember.
I do and I understand.

—Confucius

As educators we cannot know what the future holds for our students, but we can shape educational experiences to mirror this reality and develop in students the capability to respond to such unpredictability. This chapter reflects on our four-year journey of constructing an experience focusing on operating in a world shaped by globalization and the information revolution. Because the most effective learning comes from doing, the students work together across universities and countries to complete a project. We designed the experience carefully to help the students develop a global mindset and virtual team skills, and we have studied the project and revised it over the years to increase its learning impact. We begin here by describing the nature of globalization and the type of mindset and skills needed to live in an increasingly complex environment, followed by a brief discussion of our pedagogical foundation. We then outline the project itself. Next, we analyze our own observations to determine the predictors of team effectiveness in terms of team processes, intercultural effectiveness, and use of technology. We close with a summary of lessons learned by the students and by the faculty, including recommendations for others on the same journey. Our purpose here is to present a triangulation of the perceptions of the professors, students, and external observers regarding the efficacy and the implications of the Globally Distant Multicultural Teams (GDMT) Project.

GLOBALIZATION AND THE GLOBAL MINDSET

A foundation of understanding globalization is accepting that business borders and national borders in a global economy are not synonymous (Adler, 2002; Ohmae, 1990, 1995; Roberts, Kossek, & Ozeki, 1998; Salk & Brannen, 2000). *Global* does not simply mean *geographic reach* in terms of business operations. It also means *cultural reach* in terms of people and *intellectual reach* in terms of the development of a global mindset. Having a global mindset means having the ability to develop and interpret criteria for personal and business performance that are not dependent on the assumptions of a single country, culture, or context; and to implement those criteria appropriately in different countries, cultures, and contexts (Maznevski & Lane, 2003).[2] It requires a sufficient degree of cognitive complexity to make sense of globalization and an increasingly complex environment characterized by the following factors (Lane, Maznevski, Mendenhall, & McNett, 2004).

- *Multiplicity* across a range of dimensions
- *Interdependence* among a host of stakeholders and socio-cultural, political, economic, and environmental systems
- *Ambiguity* in terms of understanding causal relationships, interpreting cues and signals, identifying appropriate actions, and pursuing plausible goals
- *Flux* in terms of quickly-transitioning systems, shifting values, and emergent patterns of organizational structure and behavior.

Companies are increasingly coming to recognize that the way to address complexity is through attention to process management. In particular, managers find it necessary to focus on four processes (Lane, et al., 2004):

- *Collaborating:* Working with others in relationships characterized by community, flexibility, respect, trust, and mutual accountability.
- *Discovering:* Learning and creating transformational processes that lead to new ways of seeing and acting, which in turn lead to the creation of new knowledge, actions, and things.
- *Architecting:* The mindful design of processes that align, balance and synchronize organizational behavior.
- *Systems thinking:* Seeing and/or discovering the inter-relationship between components and levels in a complex system and anticipating consequences of changes in and to the system.

Students who develop these skills in the context of global complexity will be better suited to adapt to and succeed in our changing business world.

We chose to develop these skills in a virtual team project because of the growing importance of virtual teams in the business world and in education (Krämer, 2000; Seufert, 2000). Virtual teams are defined as remotely situated individuals affiliated with a common organization, purpose, or project who work interdependently across space, time and organizational boundaries and who communicate and coordinate via electronic communication.[3] Today many managers work closely with people whom they rarely meet face-to-face. The reality is that globalization cannot happen without people collaborating via technology. Embedding globalization skills and developing a global mindset in a virtual team project provides an added benefit—opportunities to practice virtual communication and team skills.

THE PEDAGOGICAL CHALLENGE

In the opinion of senior executives and MBA critics, one of the main failings of business schools is that graduates enter the workforce conceptually well-grounded, but without possession of specific "soft" skills—such as written, oral, and interpersonal communication skills—and the ability to work well in a team environment, etc. (Jenkins & Reizenstein, 1984; Mintzberg & Gosling, 2002; Mintzberg, 2004; Porter & McKibbin, 1988). We agree that conceptual development is incomplete without skill development, and we architected this experience accordingly.

It is, of course, possible to introduce students to the skills needed to work successfully in a global virtual team through lectures, reading assignments, videos, cases, and class discussion. One can teach cross-cultural interaction skills with these formats. In fact, these are the usual ways skill categories are taught in business schools around the world. But skills, by definition, can only be developed through practice. All of the above teaching formats, though highly useful, are only truly effective when they can be tied to the actual experience of working in a virtual team with team members from varying cultures.

The GDMT Project was designed to be a vehicle that provides students with an opportunity to recognize the need for—and to practice—skills that relate to global virtual team productivity. For example, it is one thing to understand conceptually that global time differences can influence productivity. The impact of this reality on productivity, trust, and stress levels only hits home when students have to organize virtual team meetings that everyone can attend. When students must negotiate, disrupt regular lifestyles and even sleeping habits, sacrifice personal preferences, and deal with stubborn colleagues, they develop skills and a deep-level understanding of working in a global virtual team far beyond a simple understanding of how academic scholars describe the phenomenon.

In this project, our faculty role was two-fold: first, to architect a challenging global learning experience that would meet the outlined objectives, and second, to serve as consultants to the students on an as-needed basis. An underlying goal was to coach students to "learn how to learn" from this experience, since continual learning and reflection are crucial skills in the rapidly changing world of international business.

At a meta-level, we saw a further challenge. As international business professors, we know we need to adapt to globalization and learn many of the same things our students do. We have to develop new ways of working together ourselves. We used the opportunity of this project to focus on our own learning—as reflected in this chapter, for example—as well as that of the students. The initiators of the GDMT Project came to the realization that we needed to adopt the same process approach and use the same sorts of strategies that global companies were using. If we were to educate our students to work in a global environment, then we needed to model that environment and the related processes. As faculty at different institutions, we could collaborate within our network to develop a rudimentary structure somewhat comparable to a small global company. We also needed to architect new types of experiences for our students. Doing this would require that we do some discovering ourselves; that is, that we learn to see and think in new ways. Finally, we needed to think in terms of both organizational/institutional and technological systems. Since our universities had different approaches to projects, coursework, and student learning, we needed to take into account those different systems as we designed our own system. We also came to appreciate that some of the same technologies available to global companies to help them accomplish their objectives were available to us and could be used to accomplish our goals. With our learning objectives and pedagogical foundation in hand, we set out to design an important learning experience.

THE GDMT PROJECT DESIGN

The GDMT Project experience is a joint effort of geographically distant universities to provide students with an innovative, international learning experience modeled on the virtual collaborations found in international organizations. The idea evolved in part from the national Web-based teamwork projects in German universities, such as the virtual HRM education that integrated students and company managers in the same learning environment (Scholz, Hoecker, & Scholz, 1998). The original GDMT Project was initiated in the fall of 1999 by three professors, each at a different university (Allan Bird at California Polytechnic State University, Mark Mendenhall at the University of Tennessee, Chattanooga, and Chris Scholz at the University of Saarland, Germany, assisted by Volker Stein.)

As in multinational corporations, teams composed of members from different cultures and countries completed a task that was primarily conducted and coordinated via the Internet. The first run of the project involved 77 students, with a mix of graduate and undergraduates. In fall 2000, the project was repeated (with Allan Bird now at the University of Missouri–St. Louis) and was expanded to include Chris Scholz's students at the University of Vienna, with the assistance of Doris Weyer. The total number of students involved grew to 90. To better understand the pedagogical and socio-cultural aspects of the project, three researchers (Jeanne McNett, Martha Maznevski, and Joyce Osland) were invited to function as "anthropologists" who observed and evaluated but did not participate in the year 2000 project. They monitored the communications of both students and faculty and surveyed[4] the students. We incorporated their feedback, along with other innovations, into the project design in 2001. In fall 2002, we added two other universities, one in Finland and the other in the Netherlands. In spring 2003, the length of the GDMT Project was shortened, and the team assignments were adjusted due to academic calendar issues among the three original participating professors.

We approached the GDMT Project from a "scholarship of teaching" orientation (Boyer, 1990), so that we could study and assess our results and subsequently make improvements each year. These analyses, coupled with experience from four runs of the GDMT Project, provide the foundation for this chapter. Although we include information and observations from all years, this chapter focuses on the lessons learned from GDMT 2000 because that was the most intensively examined year. The conclusions and recommendations from that examination were incorporated into the program design for future years.

Project Description

The group project was completed over approximately three weeks by groups of six to eight students. During the project period, students worked together primarily using e-mail, chat rooms, and other electronic forms. On rare occasions, groups spoke together over the telephone. As described in each section below, we designed the assignment to highlight the important characteristics of globalization and virtual teams in the real world so that students would experience and learn from the dynamics.

The assignment was to prepare a report or develop a Web site comparing a product, service, or organizational feature across countries. For example, one group analyzed differing marketing approaches and consumer attitudes related to soft drinks in Germany and the United States. We assigned a comparative task so that distributed team composition was critical to the task rather than an artifact of the project. We gave students a list of examples of acceptable projects:

- Write an analysis of a potential product development idea, examining whether a product that is successful in one culture would be successful in another culture.
- Create an idea for a managerial innovation for an existing company that operates both in the United State and in Germany.
- Analyze an actual case history of a product's success or failure across cultures.

To foster creativity, students were allowed to suggest other types of topics, as long as they were in keeping with the spirit of the assignment. Other than imposing a standard form of citation, students received no other instructions, such as page limits, etc.[5]

The teams' final products were graded by all participating professors and constituted a significant portion of the students' final grade (between 25% and 33%, depending on the instructor). The grading criteria were

- The quality of analysis on the issue (structure, theoretical content, methodological strength, etc.)
- The quality of the presentation (sections, table of contents, page numbers, grammar, etc.)
- The quality of the recommendations and implications (for practitioners and further research)

The teams had to produce an acceptable product in a short time frame, mirroring real-life demands for performance under pressure.

Team Formation

In designing the project experience, we sought to make the project as comparable as possible to what students might experience in a global company setting. Rather than assigning students to teams, they had to take the initiative to be hired on by a team leader. Before the project began, students went online and completed an "employee profile." These profiles included demographic and background information, photographs, and information about preferences in terms of work responsibilities (analysis, editing, etc.) and work skills (Web design, layout, etc.). Finally, each student submitted a project proposal—his or her recommendation about what a team could tackle. In this way, all students had to grapple with the assignment and sell their ideas.

One week prior to the start of the project, the faculty selected team leaders based on two criteria: the attractiveness of their project proposals and the need for proportional representation among the participating schools (e.g., nine teams, with three team leaders from each of the three schools). These team leaders were then charged with the responsibility of sorting through the profiles and recruiting students onto their team and observing group composition requirements based on the number of students participating at each university. Their instructions were as follows.

When forming your teams apply the following group composition requirements: Three to four Missouri members, one to two Tennessee members, one to two German members, and two Austrian members. Your responsibility as team leader is to recruit members, but potential team members may approach you and seek to join the team. Form a complete team by October

31. Next, inform Volker Stein of your project topic and team members so he can list you on the Web site. Then, contact Mark Mendenhall and provide him with a list of your team members and their e-mail addresses. He will arrange for a team e-mail list for your use.

Simultaneously, the professors announced the names of the team leaders and their project choices to the remaining students, who were then free to petition for membership in a given team. In essence, students worked through a corporate-style job-posting system. Since all students were required to be on a team, it was incumbent on them to find work as much as it was the responsibility of team leaders to staff the project teams. This was a "first come, first served" process with bi-directional initiatives from team leaders and students. Fully-formed team rosters were immediately posted on the GDMT Web site, so all participants were able to see which teams were still available. Once formed, teams were given full autonomy regarding how they structured their work and developed their team norms.

THE GDMT WEB SITE AND COMMUNICATION

To facilitate the flow of both information and feedback, the exercise was designed as an Internet course in which all information was posted on one central Web site. The faculty served as consultants on the projects, offering advice or intervening only as called upon by students. Student questions to the faculty were posted and answered on the Web site, which meant all students had access to faculty feedback on team issues. Individual professors had their own coaching style, and no effort was made to standardize this aspect of the project. For example, one professor began class sessions by asking, "How's it going?" he encouraged students to share practices that were effective as well as suggestions on how to solve problems. Only when the class was at a loss would he intervene and ask questions that would lead the students to a solution for their team problems.

The teams were asked to keep a log file of any communication among the team that took place outside the Web site, so that the external observers could use these records for anthropological analysis. The GDMT faculty had no access to these records. The faculty agreed to restrict themselves to using the same range of technology as the students so their interaction would also be available for evaluation by the external researchers. In other words, the professors relied primarily upon e-mails except when time-sensitive matters had to be resolved via telephone.

STUDENT PREPARATION

We sought to give a realistic job preview with regard to the project as a whole, cautioning students that the workload would be heavy because of the compressed time given to complete the project. We also pointed out that, in addition to cultural differences, geographical distance would impact the flow of communication, leading to delays in coordination and difficulties in sequencing their work.

   While information about the project was the same for students at all schools, there were differences among the faculty with respect to individual teaching styles, the content of the courses, and their approaches to learning. For example, Allan Bird and Chris Scholz each used the exercise as part of a course on international management, whereas Mark Mendenhall used it in conjunction with a course on innovation management. Although this provided some design challenges, it mirrored the differing conditions and expectations of employees in a global company. Because of these differences, we minimized the amount of instruction we gave in our respective classes regarding working in virtual teams. Prior to the GDMT Project, we gave students general, rudimentary advice regarding the need to establish group norms and identify group roles. Again, although perhaps not ideal, this is in line with the general depth and rigor of training virtual team members receive in the "real world." Also, we posted articles about virtual team skills in the Library Forum on the GDMT Web site so that students could review them during the project (e.g., Cohen & Gibson, 1999; Maznevski & Chudoba, 2000).

Faculty Evaluation Process

   Each faculty member graded and rank ordered projects separately (see criteria above under "Project Assignment"), resulting in three grades for each project. The faculty members then compared the three grades and discussed discrepancies until a consensus grade emerged for each team.

Pedagogical Development

   On a meta-level, the professors were engaged in an activity nearly identical to that of the students. In our case, the project that required completion was the organizing of the learning experience and the grading of the final projects. Our time pressures came from the need to have each stage ready for students and to meet varying grade submission dates on top of our other career demands. Like the students, we confronted cultural and individual style issues that required adaptation or resolution. We too had to reconcile different member perspectives about how an effective team functioned. The same technology issues that students faced either helped or impeded our progress. And finally, we too had an opportunity to become aware of our own skills, strengths, and weaknesses for working in a multicultural virtual team. Thus, modeling virtual team behavior for students (although we make no claim to perfection) was part of the pedagogical rationale for our course design. We shared observations on our own virtual team experience with students in class, but we made no attempt to formally link our lessons to the student experience.

PREDICTING TEAM EFFECTIVENESS

When we reflect on both the students' and our own experience with the GDMT Project, we see that team process matters, culture matters, and technology matters in both the quality of project output and the quality of the learning experience. We will describe what happened in each area and explore its impact.

TEAM MATTERS

In recent years increasing numbers of scholars have focused on competencies and effectiveness in the relatively new organizational form of virtual teams (e.g., Armstrong & Cole, 1995; Byrne, Brandt, & Port, 1993; Coyle & Schnarr, 1995; Davidow & Malone, 1992; Druskat & Wheeler, 2003; Duarte & Snyder, 2001; Furst, Blackburn, & Rosen, 1999, Gibson & Cohen, 2003; Hedberg, Dahlgren, Hanssen, & Olve, 1997; Kirkman, Rosen, Gibson, Tesluk, & McPherson, 2002; Montoya-Weiss, Massey, & Song, 2001; Rennecker, 1999; Scholz, 1998; Scholz & Stein, 2003; Townsend, DeMarie, & Hendrickson, 1998). Scholz (2000) has noted that in many ways, the prerequisites for team success do not differ substantially between virtual teams and traditional teams. However, the contextual variable of geographic distance increases the degree of difficulty in achieving the prerequisite conditions for team productivity in virtual teams. Additionally, in the case of global virtual teams, the variable of cross-cultural differences between team members combines with that of geographic distance to further constrain the potential for team success. According to research, the list of competencies needed for virtual teams are as follows:

- the mutual understanding of an almost symbiotic coexistence and reaching a feeling of co-destiny (e.g., Davidow & Malone, 1992; Scholz, 2000)
- Shared vision and shared goals (e.g., Coyle & Schnarr, 1995: Scholz, 2000)
- Fairness and trust (e.g., Cohen & Gibson, 1999; Fuehrer & Ashkanasy, 1999; Handy, 1995; Scholz, 2000; Welles, 1993)
- Ability to develop a culture of virtuality with shared values such as strict customer orientation, focus on technology, and a feeling for polychronicity (Hall & Hall, 1990; Scholz, 2000)

The experiential nature of the GDMT Project gave students a deeper understanding of the challenges of virtual teams and a chance to focus on some of the skills that are a prerequisite to successful virtual teams that are listed above. In particular, we noticed situations dealing with individual and team relationship development, project management, participation, leadership, and trust.

Relationships

As people who went through adolescence and early adulthood without the Internet, we (the professors) found the students' social construction of distance-relationships fascinating. Though they hadn't met any of their team members other than the one or two at their own university, the students fleshed out fairly sophisticated impressions of those teammates. They began with the "employee profiles," then added to and revised their impressions based on e-mail and chat room exchanges. By the end of the project they described teammates in some detail, especially in terms of reliability, work ethic, depth of analytical ability, and social role within a team. When face-to-face relationships were impossible, the students learned to substitute many virtual indicators to construct detailed pictures of their working relationships.

Individuals' relationships with the teams also developed over time. People enter new teams as individuals and, depending on various contingencies, generally come to see themselves as team members in a gradual way. Regardless of country of origin, we observed the same behavior in our students. It often took students a week or so to change their perspective on the project. Many students initially approached the project as they would any class assignment or group project, focusing on what needed to be done to earn a good grade. While that focus did not fade, it was frequently overshadowed by an appreciation of the complexity of the process they were being asked to manage. The group took on overtones of an "enterprise." In the same way that members of a global company project become immersed in the task, students began to immerse themselves in the project and the activities of their team. For example, in the beginning, individual students—especially leaders—would often try to keep track of the whole project and become involved in every activity. This is typical behavior of high-achieving students who focus on earning a good evaluation. When the complex reality hit, however, they could focus only on their own part, with the leaders managing the integration—behaviors more typical of real world virtual teams. This was satisfactory only in the teams that had developed good working relationships.

We found that most project teams behaved in similar ways in the early phases of the project—by beginning to build relationships. Initial team formation was usually followed immediately by socializing. A member in one team offered this advice to future participants: "Plan for a long warm-up phase." Teams that sought to avoid socializing, preferring instead to get right down to the task, invariably ran into morale and cooperation difficulties later in the project. Those team members were unable to develop the kind of relationships that brought them together as a team rather than a group of individual students.

Project Management

In parallel with lessons on relationships, the project also highlighted issues of project management. We found that students managed the project in problem-oriented ways throughout most of its duration. That is, completion of the final report was viewed as the central problem that had to be solved. Information gathering, analysis, writing, editing and so forth were subsidiary problems that had to be addressed in order to solve the central problem. Teams that produced high quality projects coordinated these elements well and managed the processes explicitly and carefully, with all members contributing information and meeting deadlines. Teams often downplayed or ignored distance, time and culture at first, but then addressed them as critical constraints that members had to address if the team was to be successful.

To facilitate project management, we advised the teams to establish group norms or agree on common rules that everyone would follow. For instance, one team set a rule of replying to any e-mail within 24 hours. This meant that every member had to check e-mails at least once a day. Other examples of rules were firm task lists and set time schedules and deadlines. In instances where students did not comply with agreed upon norms—for example, missing an important meeting—penalties varied across groups. In one or two teams, for example, members who missed their first deadline for a task were "put on probation" with an understanding that missing any subsequent deadline might lead to dismissal from the team.

Students learned how to incorporate communications technology into the project management process in sophisticated ways. The teams' initial concern was that everybody should know how to work with the different software applications used by the group. Tech-savvy students tended to assume that others were equally proficient. When this assumption proved inaccurate, they frequently became frustrated. It was not unusual to see some groups set up an event such as a full-group chat, only to discover at the appointed hour that not everyone knew how to use a chat room. Over time, though, students began to think and behave in complex, net-centric ways. They developed strategies for coordinating work at a distance, such as setting up shared workspace on the Web, and passing work from one time zone to the other to make progress overnight.

As part of the debriefing process and the survey, students were asked what advice they would give to future participants regarding project management processes. For example, one student advised: "If you don't schedule the pieces in advance, you won't produce anything worthwhile. The coordination issues are so difficult, you need to make sure that at least everyone is playing from the same playbook to start with." Another said, "Keep talking about how the group will work. The decisions you set up at the beginning may not be realistic. If you do not keep talking about them, you will have chaos. Better to replace them with something that works."

Participation

The most frequent process recommendations were about participation—simply "make sure everyone communicates frequently." Teams experimented with a variety of tactics for eliciting participation from others. For example, some teams required participation through explicitly agreed-upon norms and sanctions. Others assigned a role to someone on the team to manage the participation, and that person would track participation and contact people directly to encourage contributions. We saw no correlation between a specific mechanism and actual participation; rather, the patterns for each group seemed to be emergent and dependent on the team members' commitment (which could of course be influenced by leadership or other factors).

Contrary to our observations, students stressed that the cultural differences in participation that arose and required attention from the team were rarely seen as an obstacle. For example, one student wrote: "Culture is not a big issue; neither should it be forgotten or ignored." At that time, we concluded that, in our roles as international management scholars, we (the professors) are hypersensitive to the influence of culture and that our position of comparing across all teams rather than being immersed in one gives us a different perspective on cultural influence from that of the students. We will explore culture further in the next section

Leadership

One particularly striking feature was the strong consensus across teams and over the years that team leaders were extremely crucial to a quality end product. The leader style they employed could vary, but leadership had to be visibly present and come across as confident or self-assured. As a member of one team warned, "If the team leader shows little capability at decision-making, elect another immediately." In virtual teams, the leader plays a critical role in ensuring that relationships are well developed, managing the project process, and encouraging and setting the tone for participation. It seems that in virtual teams there are fewer substitutes for leadership than in face-to-face teams.

Trust

Relationships, project management, participation, and leadership are aspects of team membership that are influenced by trust. The central challenges of trust for the GDMT students involved sorting out how to develop trust at a distance and between cultures as well as to what extent to accept dependency, (i.e., vulnerability to others whom one has never met and knows only through electronic exchanges). Vulnerability was not a minor consideration given that their project grade, and ultimately their course grade, was partially in the hands of others. Some groups tended to rely on mechanisms and techniques acceptable for developing trust within their own culture in face-to-face encounters. For example, members would share information about their project-related capabilities in research, editing and so forth, with the expectation that team members would not take advantage of this information, but reciprocate with honest disclosure about their own capabilities. In a related vein, some team leaders would allocate tasks within the group, imposing few if any monitoring mechanisms and relying on the good will and commitment of team members. This approach appeared to work until there was friction within the group. At that point, tempers would flare; then the group would either settle for a grudging coexistence or take the time to consciously work on developing or reestablishing trust. When teams experienced problems, they usually concerned (a) disagreement over topic choices, (b) how to structure the work, (c) lack of responsiveness from team members who came to be seen as "missing in action," (d) failure to meet deadlines, and (e) failure to produce work of acceptable quality.

Culture Matters

Not surprisingly, cultural issues took longer to emerge and struck at underlying core understandings of the process and project. For example, late in the project, it was not unusual to find teams that were grappling with the following fundamental questions, determined in large part by cultural expectations: What is research? What is quality? What is participation? What is teamwork? What is academic honesty? What is an appropriate format? On occasion, some teams explored these issues at length. More frequently, however, the questions surfaced at a point in the project when time was scarce and the demands of completing the report pushed these unanswered questions to the side.

Content analysis of the e-mails and survey answers indicate that major cultural differences among the students centered on four issues:[6]

- Work attitudes and approach. While the German students expressed a concern for defining the joint work structure and schedules, the United States students sought clarification about the task and the process. Both the German and Austrian students demonstrated a greater emphasis on empirical data as the source of truth and expressed the concern "Can we get the data?" Compared to the Europeans, some of the Americans tended to do their work at the last minute.
- Differing views of plagiarism. While plagiarism was clearly not sanctioned by people in any country, slightly different definitions about what was inside and outside the acceptable boundary created conflict in some teams
- A preference for different styles of team leadership. The general preference across cultures was for participative leadership. For some United States students, however, time pressure legitimized autocratic leader behavior, which may relate to expediency ("It's due—you decide").
- A preference for differing levels of inclusion (e-mail communication to the entire team versus a subgroup). Sociograms of team communications indicated an unequal degree of communication among members in the form of subgroups from the same universities. The United States students were more active e-mailers and included more "small talk" than the Europeans.

Some of these observations could also reflect (a) differences in age, (b) undergraduate versus graduate student rank, and (c) full-time versus part-time student status. For the students, communication presented a greater difficulty than cultural differences. Communicating frequently with all team members was advice often recommended to other teams.

The cultural differences manifested in the professor's e-mails related to

- Power distance and status-oriented communication. The Europeans' behavior indicated higher power distance than that of the Americans. For example, the Europeans addressed the German senior professor more formally by his title and with more deference.
- Disclosure of weakness. The American professors (as well as the students) were more likely to acknowledge areas of weakness ("This is not my forte") with regard to team tasks.

Such differences did not affect the professors' working relationships. Only when they discussed fundamental questions, such as definitions of team effectiveness and evaluation standards in grading projects, did cultural expectations play a significant role. For example, a central concern of United States students was social loafing by some group members who fail to carry their share of the work. One of the United States professors addressed this issue by using peer evaluation forms that students shared with their fellow teammates before submitting their report; these evaluations were factored into the students' project grades so that individual effort was fairly rewarded. The United States professor assumed that the introduction of a peer evaluation form would be uncontroversial, though he imagined there might be some discussion about what the specific form and process should be. In Germany, however, the notion of peer evaluation that might actually affect one's grade in the course was viewed as odd, if not downright questionable, from an ethical standpoint.

All cross-cultural endeavors have the potential to teach greater cultural understanding or, if the experience is negative, to contribute to negative stereotypes or misattributions. We saw some evidence of both results, which prompted the professors to pay more attention to possible negative stereotypes. One strategy they adopted was to ask the class how the projects were going; this brief in-class check allowed students to express and test their impressions. For instance, if a student reported a negative experience with an individual from a different nationality or university, other students were likely to chime in and say something like, "Really? We haven't observed that. In fact, we saw just the opposite behavior." Exploring the reasons behind such discrepancies was a "teachable moment."

Technology Matters

Although technology is crucial for the success and performance of virtual teams in multinational firms, and in fact enables these teams in the first place (e.g., Axel, 1996; Geber, 1995; Hartzler & Henry, 1998), using technology wisely to support relationship building, project management, participation, and leadership is more important than focusing on the latest or most complex technology (Maznevski & Chudoba, 2000). Technological support is clearly important in educational efforts like the GDMT Project. From the outset, we sought to provide adequate technical support, but we believed that technology complexity should not become a central feature of the project. Although some teams relied on chat rooms and one or two teams carried out conference calls, for the most part, the teams relied upon e-mails and e-mail lists to communicate with one another and complete the assignment. This was the easiest way to cope with time zone differences between United States and Europe. In some teams, e-mail usage was complemented by live Internet chats at least once a week to elicit immediate responses and jointly make decisions in a time-efficient way. The open discussion boards on the project Web site were seldom used. According to students, these boards did not facilitate effective group discussions. They did, however, serve as a platform for distress calls during the team building stage when team members seemed to be "missing in action." In urgent cases, Web messaging and phone calls were used to ensure that mails were read in time.

Students reported different levels of technological knowledge and expertise coming into the course. The Austrian students who were enrolled in a Web-based distance learning program had already developed the skills required for the GDMT Project, while virtual skill levels varied more in the United States and German universities. Teams that had one or more members with greater technological sophistication were often inclined to use more complex technology, which sometimes resulted in an increase in the technical skills of other team members. However, the more sophisticated technologies did not appear to give those teams an advantage in terms of completing the project in advance of deadlines or in achieving a higher level of quality in the final product.

Neither the frequency of use nor the type of technology (telephone, conference calls, e-mail, chat rooms, fax) that students chose to use predicted the quality of team output. However, teams that used technology appropriately to facilitate team processes (relationship building, project management, participation, leadership) did produce better projects and higher satisfaction. For example, online chats were helpful when teams were forming relationships and making important, initial decisions, since all members could express opinions and react in real time to new suggestions. E-mail was more suitable for simple information gathering. To the extent that a team matched the appropriate technology to the tasks or processes it faced at different times, the use of technology improved the quality of their output.

We expected, based on cross-cultural research on attitudes in general and on information technology research in particular (Boudreau, Lock, Robey & Straud, 1998; Smith & Strand, 2003), that attitudes toward technology would be culturally influenced. However, we did not observe any cultural differences in this area. We suggest two explanations. First, the project parameters were very clearly defined and the amount of time devoted to the project was quite short. Culture is more likely to influence attitudes and behavior in an evident way over longer periods of time and in situations without clear expectations (Maznevski, Gibson & Kirkman, in press). Second, all of these students have been exposed to global information and communications technology systems for many years and have participated in the development of the Internet age. North America and Western Europe have developed similar platforms and approaches to Web use. Norms about the use of technology developed in this context may have overridden cultural differences. When we conduct end-of-project debriefings, we caution students against making generalizations from the GDMT experience and against assuming that culture does not make a difference; it may matter in future projects with different parameters, with people from other parts of the world, or with older generations.

Basically, technology seemed to serve two functions in the GDMT Project. On one hand, it was an enabler that helped the teams accomplish their tasks. On the other hand, it was a driver, urging some team members to learn new skills so they could keep up with fellow team members and compete with other teams. Technology can allow equal access to information and resources, which can increase transparency in teams (Jassawalla & Sashittal, 1999), but this only holds true if all members have the skill to use the technology. In these virtual teams, the technologically skilled students were at an advantage and saw themselves as superior to students with less skill. In educational projects like this, the students' commitment to using a broad range of technology is very important. The function of the teaching faculty—as well as executives—is to design and implement technological supports for knowledge transfer and encourage its use.

STUDENT LESSONS

Over the course of the project, students had many experiences that provided fertile ground for learning—about the nature of virtual teams, about how others work, and about how they themselves work. Though some insights were acquired along the way, much of the higher-order learning took place during the post-project debriefings that each instructor conducted. The debriefing process was based on the professors' own pedagogical style, strengths, and course objectives without an attempt to standardize their efforts. In one of the International Management courses, the debriefing was centered on the challenges of working in multicultural virtual teams—communication aspects, task/structure/accountability aspects, and technological aspects. The general debriefing focused on what students thought they did well, where they thought they could improve, what they would do differently in the future, and what advice they would have for future students undertaking this project. The motive behind the last question was to help them focus on what they'd learned; their responses were not formally transmitted to future students, except by way of professor comments in the classroom.

The students varied widely in terms of international exposure and managerial experience. For example, the Missouri undergraduates had the least international and managerial experience due to their age and geographical location. The Tennessee MBAs and the Austrian students had more work and managerial experience. As a group, the Austrian students had the most GDMT Project-related technological expertise, perhaps because they were enrolled in a distance-learning program. This diversity resulted in different learning challenges for different individuals, but we saw no evidence indicating that some groups learned more or enjoyed the experience more than others.

The purpose of the GDMT Project was to give students real experiences that would lead to the development of skills that could be used in global companies in the future. The skills students acquired varied as a consequence of the abilities of the individual student and his or her particular project team experience. However, the survey responses to a question concerning what they had learned can be categorized into three types of increased skill development.

- *Interpersonal Skills.* Many students expressed a belief that the project helped them to identify weaknesses in their interpersonal skills with regard to communicating clearly and effectively, motivating others; coping with, or exercising, power and influence within a group; and finally, skillfully and maturely resolving conflict. In each of these areas, students indicated improvement in ability.
- *Technical Skills.* A second category of skill development involved technology. At the end of the project, students reported higher levels of technical skill with regard to comprehensive, effective Internet searches, Web page development, use of groupware and electronic communication in general. For some students, the GDMT Project

was their first serious effort at using electronic media to carry out group work.

- *Management Skills.* Students reported that they had developed their skills in project management, team building and leadership. In many instances, students felt they had little or no prior experience in doing these things. All of the students had taken at least a basic course in organizational behavior and management. These courses, however, had not provided opportunities to put into practice what they learned. Students felt that the GDMT Project gave them the opportunity and forced them to accept the responsibility of actually managing, as opposed to talking about it.

A critical aspect of management skills challenges had to do with administrative issues. The administrative issues that students reported were described as surface-level issues that often appeared to be easily solved. Differing time zones, for example, presented a challenge to real time exchanges among team members. However, an acceptable meeting time—late in the day for Europeans, early in the day for North Americans—usually could be established. Some surface-level administrative issues such as the meaning and usage of words appeared to be culture-driven. Though all electronic communication was in English, from time to time European and North American students discovered that their words had varying connotations. For instance, one group studying television commercials found it necessary to clarify the difference between "commercial" and "advertisement."

FACULTY LESSONS

Perhaps the greatest lesson we have learned as faculty from the GDMT experience is that the project, for a time during the semester, allows the faculty member to educate students from a managerial role rather than from the traditional faculty role. In the real world, managers cannot step into virtual teams and make unilateral decisions effectively; the external manager must coach the virtual team leader and offer encouragement without offering pat answers to the team's questions. The external manager must also evaluate the team's productivity and assist the team members as best as he/she can. In the end, however, it is all in the team's hands. Once the students realized that this assignment was qualitatively different from sitting in a classroom/lecture setting, and that the faculty members expected them to solve their own problems and would not step in and kick a student out of the group or give detailed answers as to how to go about solving a thorny problem, the teams became autonomous and self-reliant. It was refreshing to sit back and watch students learn for themselves, within their own team contexts, and to provide support and encouragement for that learning.

Another learning "take-away" for the faculty members was the necessity for communicating to students that the GDMT project is an opportunity to learn and grow, that it would not be easy, and that it would be frustrating at times. Sugarcoating the assignment would only set the students up for failure. It was important to point to previous learning experiences of past students as examples of reasons why the project was worthwhile. It also helped to emphasize that this assignment was not a simulation or role-play; the students would be working in real virtual teams and could leverage that experience in job interviews. Indeed, several students referred to their GDMT experiences in job interviews and credited the sharing of their GDMT experience in getting job offers. For example, one past student wrote to her professor the following e-mail after the 2000 GDMT Project:

> I just wanted to let you know that I got an excellent job at Motorola as a project administrator. The biggest factor that helped me get this job was the GDMT experience. I guess it wasn't that bad after all, although sometimes I really wanted to kill you for making me the team leader (especially after several all-nighters). The job is in Warsaw, Poland. We're implementing a new telecommunications system for the Warsaw police. The reason why the GDMT experience was so important is that I have to work with people from Arizona and Germany in virtual teams. Although they do visit Warsaw sometimes, most of the time we have to depend on e-mail to get things done.

Comments such as this one have provided a strong sense of face validity to the students involved in subsequent GDMT Projects and have justified the rationale for the project's existence in the eyes of the students.

Most of the professors require students to write a self-analysis of their experience in working with their global virtual team; thus, they must turn in a team product and then analyze how their behavior in the team contributed to success of the team's process and product. Students analyze how well they applied principles of virtual team effectiveness themselves in an actual virtual team situation, discuss what they could have done better and what they did well, and describe how they would approach things differently the next time. This assignment induces self-insight and self-awareness around specific competencies, something that multiple-choice and essay-type exams cannot accomplish. To use Kolb's (1984) learning mode terminology, the follow-on assignment takes students through the entire learning cycle. The first stage, the concrete experience, is succeeded by the other stages in Kolb's learning cycle—reflective observation (What did you observe during the experience?); abstract conceptualization (How does your experience relate to the literature on virtual teams? What generalizations can you make about virtual teams?); and, finally, active experimentation (What did you learn and what would you do differently next time?). Students have predispositions toward different learning styles that may cause them to prefer or emphasize some stages in this learning cycle more than others. Kolb maintains that all stages are essential for optimal learning (1984), an argument for including individual student analyses after the team finishes its work.[7] A post-project survey included as a course requirement, similar to the one created by the project anthropologists, can also be used to help students reflect on and assess their learning.

The presence of the project anthropologists opened up new avenues of learning for the instructors and had two interesting effects. First, having colleagues looking over our shoulders freed us to concentrate on the exercise itself rather than evaluation. Second, after the exercise was concluded, we had an opportunity to experience a debriefing very similar to the students' debriefing. The project anthropologists' observations as independent evaluators helped us discover insights and lessons that would have been difficult to uncover by ourselves. For instance, we were unaware of how much some of us contextualized information in our e-mails to one another. In contrast to our students, who tended to propose or even impose a decision, with or without a supporting rationale, we were more likely to begin by acknowledging the different perspectives of instructors with different concerns, propose alternative actions to their pros and cons, and seek input on decisions. We did not realize that we were doing this until the project anthropologists brought it to our attention and helped us recognize our tacit knowledge about communicating in multicultural virtual teams. As a result, we were better equipped to teach our students when they needed to provide more context and lay the groundwork for decision making in their e-mails. Due to their training and their access to student communications, the project anthropologists helped us to better understand the team process issues that occurred during the project and, as a result, we became better coaches to the students.

In addition to recommendations for improving the project, the project anthropologists' report, based on their analysis of all the available artifacts—projects, communication records, and survey data—gave us the assurance that students were in fact learning what we wanted them to learn. At that time, we were moving in the direction of making the project even more complex and realistic, but the external evaluation indicated that the current level of complexity was sufficient to achieve our learning objectives.

There are a couple of "fit" issues that need to be carefully managed in order for the GDMT to be successful. First, there must be a conceptual fit between GDMT and the content of the course it is part of, and between the content of the other courses as well. While this may seem an obvious requirement, in reality it is subtler than it appears. For example, two of the courses involved in GDMT 2000 were international management courses. One was an innovation in business course, and the Austrian students were assigned this project as part of their general coursework in a totally virtual business degree program. The course project then had to be carefully crafted to conceptually fit into the content of each course, yet work together conceptually across all the courses as well.

The second fit regards the nature of the project and the personalities of the course instructors. This is, in our opinion, a critical variable to the success of the project. Simply running a project like this because it is a good learning experience for students is probably a mistake. The instructors must all believe deeply that subjecting students to a real experience, with all of its unforeseen obstacles, is not only a good thing to do, but is also a fun, important, and wise thing to do as well. The instructors must be committed to the extra time and effort involved in setting up the project and working through their own dynamics as a team, possibly changing their teaching styles for the duration of the project. In short, if the faculty members do not believe in the efficacy of the project, do not have a vision of what it can produce in students, and do not commit their own efforts, the students will not engage emotionally and will not enter the project with an implicit understanding that "this looks scary, but it will be a good learning experience." In effect, each instructor has to be willing to say, truthfully: "This project will be hard; you will hate me. After it is over, you will thank me." There is a Rubicon regarding this project that must be crossed by faculty members. We question whether an instructor can reap the full benefit of the exercise without a deep sense that this is the right thing to do.

The instructors and participants in the project must also feel comfortable with the long term and more personal effects of the GDMT experience. As in company virtual teams, boundaries between personal and work life may become blurred for everyone involved. It has not been uncommon for team members to stay in contact with one another for several months and years to come after the project ends. In one case, a German student traveled to Tennessee to visit a student the summer after the program. In another instance a California student hosted several German and California team members for a weekend reunion. On the other hand, one United States student developed a very negative stereotype about Germans based on an experience with one teammate. The instructor had to engage in extensive personal coaching to help the student learn to see his own role in creating the destructive dynamic and to learn not generalize from one incident to a culture. Without this extra coaching, the student would have learned lessons that countered the project's objectives, rather than met them.

In short, because the GDMT Project is not a simulation but real life, an instructor must recognize and accept that there will be outcomes and impacts that extend well beyond the walls of the classroom and the borders of the curriculum.

CONCLUSION

We live in age of increasing globalization—an age of heightened complexity. In order to function effectively in this new world, students need to acquire the knowledge and skills necessary to manage complexity. Our experience with the GDMT Project over the past four years has led us to conclude that it is a powerful mechanism for doing so. While we can lecture students about what is required, to borrow the words of Sophocles, "One must learn by doing the thing; for though you think you know it, you have no certainty until you try." The GDMT Project represents a real world virtual experience that gives students the opportunity to try.

NOTES

1. This chapter is based on a symposium, "Globally Distant Multicultural Teams: Intercultural Teaching in Times of Virtuality" (winner of the Best Symposium Award, Management Education Division, 2001), presented at the Academy of Management meeting in Washington, DC, 2001.

2. The global mindset construct is built upon two components (Boyacigiller, Beechler, Taylor, & Levy, 2004). The first is *cosmopolitanism*, which is defined as the intellectual and esthetic openness toward divergent cultural experiences, the search for contrasts rather than uniformity, and cultural competence. It is an orientation toward the outside world, rather than a parochial view. The second component is *cognitive complexity*, the ability to generate several competing interpretations of events and their interactive effects. People who are more cognitively complex use and perceive more constructs or dimensions when they describe a domain and see a greater number of links among these different constructs.

3. This definition is based on various sources: www.asq.org/info/glossary/v.html accessed January 20, 2004; Lipnack & Stamps, 2000; and Duarte & Snyder, 2001.

4. The survey consisted of four sections: culture, teaching, technology, and a team climate survey. The culture section examined cultural stereotypes and learning and the benefits and challenges of working on a multicultural team. Students described a critical incident in which culture played a role and a created a sociogram showing whom they felt closest to and interacted with most frequently on their team. The teaching portion of the survey measured self-reported learning in interpersonal, managerial and technological skills. The technology portion asked participants what type of technology they used to accomplish six basic team tasks, such as scheduling meetings, assigning tasks, gathering information, reporting problems, solving problems, and achieving social goals. The team climate survey examined how well their teams set objectives and worked together to achieve

them. Of a total population of 90 students, we received 43 responses, mostly from Austria and Missouri. Therefore, the responses were representative of all the different teams but not sufficiently representative of each university; they were, however, a valuable contribution to the other data points in this descriptive case study.

5.   In subsequent years, we provided more structure, including suggested page length, an executive summary, and assigned topics and team composition.

6.   The e-mail communications were examined for patterns of intercultural communication styles (Gudykunst & Ting-Toomey, 1988; Ting-Toomey, 1999) and cultural value dimensions (Kluckhohn & Strodtbeck, 1961; Hofstede, 1980; Hampden-Turner & Trompenaars, 1993; Schwartz, 1992). However, few differences were evident in the e-mails.

7.   For a European view on learning styles, see Barmeyer, C. I. (2000). *Interkulturelles Management und Lernstile*. Frankfurt–New York: Campus.

REFERENCES

Armstrong, D. J., & Cole, P. (1995). Managing distance and differences in geographically distributed work groups. In S. R. Jackson & M. N. Ruderman (Eds.), *Diversity in work teams. Research paradigms for a changing workplace* (pp. 187–216). Washington, DC: APA Books.

Axel, H. (1996). Company experiences with global teams. *HR Executive Review, 4*(2), 3–18.

Boyacigiller, N., Beechler, S., Taylor, S., & Levy, O. (2004). The crucial but illusive global mindset. In H. Lane, M. Maznevski, M. Mendenhall, and J. McNett (Eds.), *Handbook of global management*. Oxford: Blackwell.

Boyer, E. J. (1990). *Scholarship reconsidered: Priorities of the professoriate*. Princeton, NJ: The Carnegie Foundation for the Advancement of Teaching.

Byrne, J., Brandt, R., & Port, O. (1993, February 8). The virtual corporation. *Business Week*, 98–102.

Cohen, S., & Gibson, C. (1999). Mutual understanding, integration and trust: Creating conditions for virtual team effectiveness. Unpublished manuscript.

Coyle, J., & Schnarr, N. (1995). The soft-side challenges of the "virtual corporation." *Human Resource Planning, 18*(1), 41–42.

Davidow, W. H., & Malone, M. S. (1992). *The virtual corporation: Structuring and revitalizing the corporation for the 21st century*. New York: Harper Business.

Druskat, V. U., & Wheeler, J. V. (2003). Managing from the boundary: The effective leadership of self-managing work teams. *Academy of Management Journal, 46*, 435–457.

Duarte, D. L., & Snyder, N. T. (2001). *Mastering virtual teams. Strategies, tools, and techniques that succeed.* (2nd ed.). San Francisco: Jossey-Bass.

Fuehrer, E. C., & Ashkanasy, N. M. (1999). Communicating trust in the inter-organizational virtual organization. Paper presented at the 1999 Annual Meeting of the Academy of Management, Chicago, IL.

Furst, S., Blackburn, R., & Rosen, B. (1999). Virtual teams: A proposed agenda. Paper presented at the 1999 Annual Meeting of the Academy of Management, Chicago, IL.

Geber, B. (1995). Virtual teams. *Training, 32*(4), 36–40.

Gibson, C., & Cohen, S. (Eds.). (2003). *Virtual teams that work: Creating the conditions for effectiveness.* San Francisco: Jossey-Bass.

Gudykunst, W. B., & Ting-Toomey, S. (1988). *Culture and interpersonal communication.* Newbury Park, CA: Sage.

Hall, E. T., & Hall, M. R. (1990). *Understanding cultural differences: Keys to success in West Germany, France and the United States.* Yarmouth: Intercultural Press.

Hampden-Turner, C., & Trompenaars, A. (1993). *The seven cultures of capitalism: Value systems for creating wealth in the United States, Japan, Germany, France, Britain, Sweden, and the Netherlands.* New York: Doubleday.

Handy, C. (1995). Trust and virtual organization: How do you manage people whom you do not see? *Harvard Business Review, 73*(3), 40–50.

Hartzler, M., & Henry, J. E. (1998). *Tools for virtual teams: A team fitness companion.* Milwaukee, WI: ASQC Quality Press.

Hedberg, B., Dahlgren, G., Hansson, J., & Olve, N.-G. (1997). *Virtual organizations and beyond. Discover imaginary systems.* Chichester, England: Wiley.

Hofstede, G. H. (1980). *Culture's consequences: International differences in work-related values.* Beverly Hills, CA: Sage.

Jassawalla, A. R., & Sashittal, H. C. (1999). Building collaborative cross-functional new product teams. *Academy of Management Executive, 13*(3), 50–63.

Jenkins, R. L., & Reizenstein, R. C. (1984). Insights into the MBA: Its contents, output, and relevance. *Selections, 2,* 19–24.

Kirkman, B., Rosen, B., Gibson, C., Tesluk, P., & McPherson, S. (2002). Five challenges to virtual team success: Lessons from Sabre, Inc. *Academy of Management Executive, 16*(3), 67–79.

Kluckhohn, F., & Strodtbeck, F. (1961). *Variations in value orientations.* Evanston, IL: Row, Peterson.

Kolb, D. (1984). *Experiential learning: Experience as the source of learning and development.* Upper Saddle River, NJ: Prentice Hall.

Krämer, B. J. (2000). Forming federated virtual university through course broker middleware LearnTEC 2000. *Schriftenreihe der Karlsruher Kongreß- und Ausstellungs-GmbH. 1,* 137–148.

Lane, H., Maznevski, M., Mendenhall, M., & McNett, J. (2004). *Handbook of global management.* Oxford: Blackwell.

Leavitt, H. J. (1989). Educating our MBAs: On teaching what we haven't taught. *California Management Review, 31*(3), 38–50.

Lipnack, J., & Stamps, J. (2000). *Virtual teams: People working across boundaries with technology.* (2nd ed.). New York: Wiley.

Maznevski, M. L., & Chudoba, K. M. (2000). Bridging space over time: Global virtual team dynamics and effectiveness. *Organization Science, 11*(5), 473–492.

Maznevski, M. L., Gibson, C. B., & Kirkman, B. L. (in press). When does culture matter? In K. Leung, (Ed.), *New directions in cross-cultural research* (Vol. 1, JIBS). New York: Macmillan Research Series.

Maznevski, M. L., & Lane, H. W. (2003). Shaping the global mindset: Designing educational experiences for effective global thinking and action. In N. A. Boyacigiller, R. A. Goodman, & M. E. Philips (Eds.), *Crossing cultures: Insights from master teachers* (pp. 343–371). New York: Routledge.

Mintzberg, H. (2004). *Developing managers, not MBAs: A hard look at the soft practice of managing.* Upper Saddle River, NJ: Prentice Hall.

Mintzberg, H., & Gosling, J. R. (2002). Reality programming for MBAs. *Strategy and Business, 26*(1), 28–31.

Montoya-Weiss, M. M., Massey, A. P., & Song, M. (2001). Getting it together: Temporal coordination and conflict management in global virtual teams. *Academy of Management Journal, 44,* 1251–1262.

Ohmae, K. (1990). *The borderless work: Power and strategy in the interlinked economy.* New York: Free Press.

Ohmae, K. (1995). *The end of the nation state.* New York: Free Press.

Porter, L. W., & McKibbin, L. E. (1988). *Management and education development: Drift or thrust into the 21st century.* New York: McGraw-Hill.

Rennecker, J. (1999, August). Overlap and interplay: Cultural structuring of work and communication in one virtual work group. Paper presented at the 1999 Annual Meeting of the Academy of Management, Chicago, IL.

Scholz, C. (1998). *Towards the virtual corporation: A complex move along three axes.* Arbeitspapier Nr. 62 des Lehrstuhls für Betriebswirtschaftslehre, insbesondere Organisation, Personal- und Informationsmanagement an der Universität des Saarlandes, Saarbrücken.

Scholz, C. (2000). *Strategische organisation. Multiperspektivität und virtualität.* (2nd ed.). Landsberg/Lech: Moderne industrie.

Scholz, C., Hoecker, G., & Scholz, S. (1998). Ein interaktives seminar im Internet. Zukunftsorientiertes Personalmanagement. *CoPers, 6*(2), 18–23.

Scholz, C., & Stein, V. (2003, June 4–6). International virtual teams (IVTs): A triple "mission impossible"? In M. J. Morley, D. Cross, P. C. Flood, C. Gubbins, N. Heraty, & H. Sheikh (Eds.). *Exploring the mosaic, developing the discipline.* [CD-Rom]. Full Proceedings of the 7th Conference on International Human Resource Management, University of Limerick, Ireland. Dublin: Interesource Group

Schwartz, S. H. (1992). Universals in the content and structure of values: Theoretical advances and empirical tests in 20 countries. *Advances in Experimental Social Psychology, 25,* 1–65.

Seufert, S. (2000). *Education/distant learning in the NA.* (December 12, 2000) Retrieved July 15, 2003, from www.netacademy.org/netacademy/netacademy.nsf/pages/education_research.html

Ting-Toomey, S. (1999). *Communicating across cultures.* New York: Guilford.

Townsend, A. M., DeMarie, S. M., & Hendrickson, A. R. (1998). Virtual teams: Technology and the workplace of the future. *Academy of Management Executive, 12*(3), 17–29.

Welles, E. O. (1993, August). Virtual realities (*Inc.* cover story). *Inc.,* 50–58.

CHAPTER 6

INTERNATIONAL ONLINE WORKPLACES

A Perspective for Management Education

Kirk St. Amant

INTRODUCTION

The spread of globalization means that today's managers are increasingly interacting with employees, clients, and co-workers in other parts of the world. In many cases, this interaction takes place via online media such as e-mail, corporate intranet sites, or online bulletin boards. Communicating with persons from other cultures, however, can be a far more intricate process than many individuals might think—a process that is more complicated when done via online media. For these reasons, management education needs to provide students with the training required to successfully supervise international virtual teams, or work groups comprised of international individuals who interact exclusively through online media.

This chapter examines how instructors can use online materials to familiarize students with factors that can affect the management of international virtual teams. The chapter begins with an overview of developments that

The Cutting Edge of International Management Education, pages 143–165
Copyright © 2004 by Information Age Publishing
All rights of reproduction in any form reserved.

contribute to the use of such teams. Next, the chapter presents a framework for understanding the management of communication in such teams. This framework is then followed by a series of Internet-based exercises that management educators can use to familiarize students with the ways that factors of culture and media can affect interactions in international virtual teams. This approach provides readers with information and a methodology they can use to prepare students for management situations involving factors of culture and online media.

OFFSHORING: A NEW MANAGEMENT PARADIGM

In the past five years, global Internet access has grown dramatically, especially in developing nations. The governments of India and China, for example, have adopted strategies to increase online access. As a result, India has become a leading offshoring location in software and information technology (IT) production ("When India Wires Up," 2000). The number of Chinese Internet users grew from 2.1 million in 1999 ("Wired China," 2000) to nearly 60 million by the end of 2002 ("Section IV Survey Results," 2003). In Africa, the United Nations and private companies such as Hewlett-Packard have undertaken initiatives that would increase online access both in specific nations and to the continent in general ("Tapping in to Africa," 2000; Kalia, 2001). In Latin America, Global Crossings Ltd. has completed a project that uses fiber optics to give "multinational companies the ability to communicate with Latin America as efficiently as with any other region" ("Tying Latin America Together," 2001). And in Eastern Europe, the number of individuals going online is expected to climb from 17% to 27% by 2006 ("IDC Research: Net Usage Up," 2003).

This increased global access has prompted many companies to explore different production methods involving online communication technologies. Perhaps one of the most interesting of these approaches is *offshoring*, a process in which organizations use online media to exchange information and electronic products (e.g., software) with employees located in other countries. The primary benefit of this process is easy access to labor forces in other countries—namely developing nations that have highly skilled technical workers who can provide services at a fraction of what they would cost in more industrialized countries. Online media allow these international workers to exchange information directly and quickly with one another and with the company sponsoring a project. This speed and directness related to international online exchanges also means that different parts of an overall process can be performed simultaneously in different locations, and that electronic products (e.g., software) can be forwarded from one location/time zone to another in a manner that would allow work to continue without pause.

The ideal result of such processes is a quality product that can be completed more quickly and at a fraction of the cost it would have taken to produce domestically. These benefits have inspired both private companies and municipal governments to use offshoring for everything from computer programming and IT work to accounting practices and the staffing of call centers ("New Geography," 2003; "Relocating the Back Office," 2003; "Lost in Translation," 2003). Moreover, trends in information technology and in demographics indicate that offshoring practices will increase in coming years. For a more detailed discussion of this topic, see Drucker (2001) "The Next Society: A Survey of the Near Future," and Lui and Chan (2003) "Inexperienced Software Team and Global Software Team."

For managers, these trends create new situations related to supervising project development and overseeing employee activities. In some cases, managers might find themselves working with conventional/onsite work groups, but using online media to outsource parts of a project to individuals in different nations. In other cases, managers might be supervising entirely virtual teams made up of international employees who meet and exchange information exclusively though online media.

The key to success in both cases is communication, for ineffective exchanges of information could result in overseas employees performing a process incorrectly, and the results of miscommunications might not be noticed until a later point in the overall process. Moreover, the fact that the manager and the overseas employee are separated by geographical space and marked time differences means that more direct methods of checking employee progress (e.g., stopping by an employee's office or having an informal chat) are not available. Thus, the management of international virtual teams involves not only traditional supervisory approaches, but also requires managers to oversee the process through which information is exchanged.

The management of communication can be a daunting process when done in a traditional work environment. It is made increasingly complex when factors of culture and aspects of online media are added to the mix. For example, international individuals can have different levels of proficiency in the language used to exchange information, and this proficiency factor can affect the quality of the work produced by international virtual teams. Additionally, cultural groups can have different expectations of how information should be presented and interpreted—both verbally and visually.

These differences, in turn, can lead to miscommunication or confusion when individuals from different cultures interact via more traditional media. As Bliss (2001) explains:

In Japanese, for example, it is typically considered rude to point out to the listener or reader what a person should do or believe. Yet academic English often demands an overt statement about what the reader should do or believe [a thesis statement] followed by evidence that supports the writer's claim. (p. 17)

These situations are further complicated by the restrictions online media can impose on the overall communication process (Ma, 1996; Artemeva, 1998). For example, researchers in computer-mediated communication (CMC) note that many online media (e.g., e-mail, chats, and online bulletin boards) reduce communication to typed text and restrict the identity of individuals to usernames or e-mail addresses (Hiltz & Turoff, 1993). In so doing, these media remove many of the non-verbal cues individuals use to establish the status of individuals involved in an exchange (Sproull & Kiesler, 1986; Hiltz & Turoff, 1993; Kiesler et al., 1984). Both of these factors have led to problems when individuals from the same culture interact online (in essence, confusion arose over who was in charge of a given process).

From the perspective of cross-cultural communication, this lack of obvious status can become even more complicated. The problem is that some cultural groups have different perceptions of how the status of individuals involved in an interaction affects the way in which information should be presented. That is, some cultures view the status of the individuals involved in an exchange as a key piece of information individuals need to know in order to present information and voice opinions. (That is not to say that status is not an important factor in all cultures; rather, how status affects the way in which individuals are expected to present information differs from culture to culture.) Without such status information, individuals from some cultures might be hesitant to participate in online exchanges, for they would fear reprisal for adopting incorrect behavior in relation to authority figures. The result would be silence, or unwillingness to present ideas, a behavior that has been observed in conventional cross-cultural interactions where the status of participants was unknown (Ng & Van Dyne, 2001).

Such reticence, however, means that crucial information or opinions might not be presented in international online situations where the status of participants is unknown. International virtual teams could, in turn, find themselves operating with missing or incomplete information that could lead to costly results. Individuals who manage these teams therefore need to be aware of how these factors of culture and medium can affect the exchange of information both among co-workers and with managers if they are to help the team operate effectively.

ADDRESSING CULTURE AND MEDIA
IN MANAGEMENT CLASSES

Offshoring practices complicate the task of management educators, for they now find themselves in the position of having to teach students how to work effectively within the constructs of a new production paradigm. Addressing factors of management, media, and culture, however, can be a complicated and daunting task. For this reason, exercises that examine these factors and that are easy to incorporate into a variety of classroom contexts can help reduce instructor workload while enhancing student learning. The purpose of this chapter is to provide instructors with both these kinds of exercises and with a framework for integrating them into different management classes.

The educational objectives of the exercises presented in this chapter are twofold. The first educational objective involves heightening student awareness of how culture can affect discourse in online teams. The ultimate learning objective for students then becomes gaining a foundational understanding of how aspects of culture and media can affect information exchange in international virtual teams. The second educational objective of these exercises is to provide students with an opportunity to experience how factors of culture can affect online communication. The learning objective for students in this case is to use their knowledge of culture and media to analyze different kinds of information exchanges in order to develop "best practices" for managing communication in international virtual teams.

To help educators achieve these objectives, the remainder of this chapter is structured in the following way. First, the chapter presents a framework for teaching students how to view the management of international virtual teams in terms of two key parts—interaction and design. The chapter then presents a series of educational exercises that fits into this two-part framework. The presentation of these exercises begins with a conceptual overview that introduces readers to concepts that can affect communication in international virtual teams. This conceptual information, in turn, can serve as the foundation for a brief introductory lecture on those particular ideas or topics. These conceptual parts are then followed by exercises that have students examine how a particular topic might affect information exchange in international virtual teams.

In using these exercises, instructors could begin with an introductory lecture on a particular cultural communication concept (the lecture to be based on ideas presented in the "Conceptual Overview" sections of the chapter). Students would then discuss how they would address (manage) that concept in a conventional workplace situation involving employees from other cultures. Next, students could work in teams, and each team would devise a management strategy that would be presented to the entire class. All students (and the instructor) could then discuss and critique these presentations and try to come to a consensus on what would constitute best practices in relation to a particular culture and communication concept.

Once students establish these best practices, they can perform the related Internet-based exercise in order to compare how the practices they devised might require modification when applied to online interactions. Once students complete the exercise, they would engage in a class discussion of what they had observed, and then work together—either in groups or as a class—to develop strategies for addressing a particular cultural concept when managing international virtual teams. Through this mix of information and application, students can gain a more complete understanding of the complexities of communication in such teams.

INTERACTION AND DESIGN: A TWO-PART FRAMEWORK

Communication in international virtual teams involves two different aspects—interaction and design. *Interaction* is the direct exchange of information between or among individuals. As a result, it often involves a back-and-forth process in which concepts are discussed and ideas are critiqued. Such processes relate to verbal presentations of information and would include online media such as e-mails, online chats, or online bulletin boards. The key cultural factors related to interaction would include the language used in the exchange (i.e., the level of proficiency participants have in that language) and expectations of how information should be presented (e.g., what is the best way to present negative news or honest criticism).

As a result, interaction is closely linked to the concept of *translation*, or how different linguistic and cultural groups prefer to present ideas in a given situation. That is, translation involves more than just converting words in one language into words in a different language. Rather, translators review what is said in the original item (or the source) in order to determine what meaning one wishes to convey with those words. The translator then needs to determine how that same concept should best be presented in another language (the target language).

In some cases, cultures could differ on the best way to present the same meaning, and the style/structure of the resulting translation might seem quite different from the original source. For example, many Americans use the phrase "excuse me" to indicate to a shop owner that they wish to have his or her attention. For many French speakers in France, however, the preferred method of conveying that particular meaning in that same context would be "Excusez-moi de vouz déranger, mais. . . ." ("Excuse me for bothering you, but....") (Platt, 1998, p. 32). This difference in the expected or the preferred format for conveying meaning also applies to exchanges in which individuals from different cultures use the same language to interact. Research indicates that people tend to favor their native culture's format for presenting information, even when that information is presented in a different language (Ulijn, 1996).

Design involves the visual display of information via online media such as Web sites, and it generally relates to one-way presentations of information. That is, one individual displays information online for others to use (e.g., a Web page that displays corporate policies) or one shares information with others and interacts though an online interface (e.g., the portal that individuals use to access an online chat). The idea is that individuals use design materials as a foundation for interaction—they either discuss the information presented via a design aspect or interact through an interface that is a design aspect.

The design part of communication, in turn, is closely linked to the concept of *localization*, often abbreviated as L10N (meaning that there are ten letters between the *L* and the *N* in the word *localization*). The idea is that cultural groups have different preferences related to the visual presentation of information (e.g., format, layout, and kinds of images used in a presentation). Additionally, some cultural groups may be in areas that have limited technical capabilities, meaning that information can only be accessed or used if it conforms to the available technology standard. Faxes, for example, might be of limited use in regions that have few reliable telephone lines. Localization, in turn, is a process in which one attempts to convert materials designed for one cultural group into items that meet the expectations of a different cultural group. In essence, one uses localization to make materials more acceptable and accessible to different cultural audiences. Such a conversion increases the chances that materials will be interpreted and used as intended.

Interaction and design are therefore both essential aspects of effective communication in international virtual teams, for they govern different factors related to how individuals exchange information. For this reason, managers need to be aware of how both factors can affect the overall communication process. The remaining sections of this chapter provide information and exercises instructors can use to familiarize students with how both interaction and design aspects can affect communication in international virtual teams.

INTERACTION EXERCISES

Conceptual Overview

The interaction aspect of international virtual teams involves two key parts—language and rhetoric. In the case of language, the challenge involves making sure that there is a common language all participants can use to exchange information. One particular problem related to language can be technology; that is, some individuals could assume that linguistic ability is not particularly important, for certain computer programs can act as translators that transfer meaning from one language to another. Unfortunately, most machine translation programs are ill-equipped to deal with many of the subtleties related to conveying meaning across languages. As a result, these programs often make a poor substitute for humans who can speak a language well. For this reason, managers need to make sure that all of the individuals who will participate in a virtual online team can communicate proficiently and effectively in the same language.

Even when a common language is found, new and unanticipated problems can arise related to rhetoric, or the way in which information is presented. That is, cultural groups often have use different methods to express the same meaning or ideas. These methods, in turn, affect how information is presented and how it is perceived. Moreover, failure to meet a particular culture's rhetorical expectations can inadvertently result in confusion or offense. Additionally, research indicates that individuals tend to evaluate presentations in other languages according to the rhetorical expectations of their native culture (Ulijn, 1996).

In the rhetoric of some cultures (e.g., China), for example, it can be considered impolite or offensive to voice the concept of "no" directly. As a result, individuals from these cultures will often use a different rhetorical structure to convey the idea that they are unable to do a particular thing. In many cases, that structure takes the form of the expression, "We will need to do more research" or "We will need to get back to you on that issue" (Hu & Grove, 1999). The intended meaning is "No, I cannot do what you are asking." For individuals not familiar with such an indirect rhetorical style, however, the meaning of these expressions might be taken literally. As a result, counterparts from other cultures might misunderstand the meaning conveyed by, "We will need to get back to you on that," and wait for a response (an incorrect interpretation of what the speaker intended). Frustration could then occur, and valuable time could be lost waiting for a response that never comes.

Online media can complicate factors of language and rhetoric in a number of ways. First, individuals working in an online medium tend to make more spelling and grammar mistakes and to be more tolerant of such mistakes (Gutzman, 2001). In some cases, this pattern involves incomplete sentences or poorly structured communiqués. These communication patterns are problematic because they can allow individuals with a limited proficiency in a language to fall through the cracks. That is, in most conventional interactions, factors such as spelling and grammar errors, the frequent use of incomplete sentences, and awkwardly structured presentations can all serve as cues that an individual has a limited proficiency in the language being used. By making these cues more permissible, online media mitigate aspects that could be used to identify linguistic limitations. As a result, the linguistic limitations of individuals who are interacting online might not be realized until problems related to comprehension occur.

Also, as noted earlier, many online media reduce interactions to typing, and in so doing, remove characteristics such as foreign/non-native accents from an exchange. This removal of accents, combined with more permissive grammar and spelling standards, might cause individuals involved in international online interactions to forget that they are communicating with someone from a different cultural and linguistic background—one that might use a different rhetorical approach to convey ideas. This oversight could lead to a misinterpretation of the information presented by certain individuals (a failure to understand the meaning behind the rhetoric). Similarly, the fact that online media allow users to interact directly and immediately with persons in other parts of the world could lead one to forget that he or she is interacting with an individual from a different culture because the immediacy of the exchange obscures the cultural background of the individual. Again, the result would be an oversight that could lead to a misinterpretation based on different cultural preferences related to rhetoric.

The exercises in these sections teach students about the complexities related to verbal communication in online exchanges. Through these exercises, students learn the importance of linguistic proficiency and the importance of understanding how rhetorical differences can affect interactions in international virtual teams. Such knowledge could be important to the managers in the following ways:

- It helps them understand the importance of both language proficiency and technical skills related to the successful functioning of international virtual offices. As a result, managers can devise requirements for language proficiency that would be used in selecting employees for participation in such teams.
- It can help them analyze international online interactions to determine how cultural rhetorical differences result in miscommunication in online exchanges.

- It allows them to use their knowledge of culture, rhetoric, and online media to anticipate potential areas of miscommunication in international virtual teams and then develop communication protocols to avoid such problems.

By understanding these factors, managers can better select individuals for participation in international virtual teams. They can also gain a better understanding of why language proficiency is a key factor to successful communication in these teams.

The first exercise presented in this section addresses the issue of language by revealing the limitations of machine (computer-based) translation in relation to international virtual teams. The remaining two exercises place students in sample situations that allow them to explore how different rhetorical expectations can lead to interesting situations in international online exchanges.

Exercise 1: Examining Machine Translation

The purpose of this exercise is to familiarize students with the limitations of machine (computer-based) translation. In this exercise, students first access a free online translation program, such a babelfish (located online at babel.altavista.com). Students then type in a phrase such as "What's up?" and have the program translate it from English into another language (e.g., French). Once the translation appears, students use the same program to translate that French expression back into English to see what the expression means. In the case of "What's up?", the resulting French translation might be something like "Qu'est vers le haut?" that, when translated back into English becomes "What is upwards?" Students can repeat this back-and-forth translation process three to five times with different phrases in order to see how the program presents their original idea in another language.

In the next part of the exercise, the class would discuss the results of its experimentation with machine translation. During this discussion, the instructor should ask the students to consider how machine translation could cause problems when used as a substitute for actual language proficiency. Next, the instructor should ask students to consider why language proficiency might be as important as technical or professional competence when selecting individuals for international virtual teams. The class could then work together to try to devise a standard for evaluating the language proficiency of individuals before including them in such teams. The development of such a standard could become the foundation for a class research project (e.g., a short paper on what factors to consider when determining language proficiency).

Though this process, students would

- Discover the limitations of machine translation
- Examine the importance of linguistic proficiency in relation to the functioning of international virtual teams
- Explore the balance between linguistic and technical skills when selecting individuals to participate in international virtual teams
- Consider prospective standards that could be use to test the linguistic proficiency of individuals interested in participating in international virtual teams.

By understanding such concepts, students can better determine which individuals should participate in international virtual teams.

The objective of the next two exercises is to have students from two different cultures interact via online media in a "back-and-forth" process. To perform these exercises, instructors first need to form a partnership with individuals teaching in other countries. Instructors can use certain strategies to locate overseas partners. For example, individuals can contact their institution's international studies/studies abroad office to identify overseas schools with which their college or university already shares a bond. The instructor can then contact this "sister school" in order to find a counterpart who would be interested in participating in such exercises. In other cases, instructors can review management journals or review the membership lists of professional organizations in order to identify persons who teach at overseas institutions. The instructor could then contact these individuals to see if they would be interested in participating in one or more online exercises. Once an international teaching counterpart is found, the partners must

- Make sure that all participants must have a common language in which they can interact effectively/proficiently.
- Agree upon a standard medium (e.g., e-mail, online chats, and online bulletin boards) for interacting and establish a minimum technology requirement (e.g., minimum modem speed and monitor resolution) needed to participate in the exchange.

As these exercises do not require individuals to interact via real-time (synchronous) online media, time differences should not inhibit the kind of international partners with whom individuals can work.

Once international teaching partners have addressed these factors, they can then use certain exercises to examine how cultural factors might affect international online interactions. These exercises follow similar approaches used by researchers such as Ulijn, Lincke, and Karakaya (2001), Verckens,

DeRycker, and Davis (1998), and Vogel et al. (2001). It should be noted that since these exercises involve students and not actual professionals/employees, they might not be an exact reflection of communication in international virtual teams. However, through the opportunity to interact with counterparts from different cultures, these exercises provide students with a foundation for understanding how cultural rhetorical expectations can affect the presentation and the perception of information in an online exchange.

Exercise 2: Examining Culture and Rhetoric

The purpose of this exercise is to teach students how rhetorical expectations can affect online cross-cultural exchanges that take place in the same language. To achieve this end, the following exercise examines cultural perspectives of a particular presentation factor—ostentation, or showy behavior. This selection is based on the fact that past research reveals participants in online exchanges often use showy displays of their knowledge and abilities to establish their online credibility (Baym, 1997; Warnick, 1998). What is considered an acceptable level of ostentatious behavior (versus expected humility) can, however, vary from culture to culture (Hu & Grove, 1999). This exercise examines how cultural perspectives of ostentation can affect online discourse.

Students begin the first task by drafting an e-mail in which they present themselves to persons from the "other" culture. In their messages, students should present or discuss their backgrounds, accomplishments, and experiences. Recipients of this e-mail (persons from the other culture) would then review this message and

- Evaluate the message for style
- Create a list of ways the message could be stylistically improved
- Explain why such changes should be made
- Provide examples of ways to improve the message

After this initial evaluation, the recipients of these messages would present their assessments (complete with actual examples) to their classmates.

The instructor supervising the exchange would then collect the responses generated by the students and send them to the counterpart in the other culture. The counterpart would present these collected responses to his or her class, and the class would discuss how the original analysis they had performed and the comments they had received identify certain rhetorical differences related to cross-cultural communication in online media. The class could also discuss writing strategies and tips one could use to create more effective style for the other cultural audience participating in the exchange. Instructors could conclude the overall exercise by explaining how this activity illustrates the unpredictability managers could encounter when supervising the communication of international virtual teams. Through this exercise, students

- Learn how cultural rhetorical expectations can transcend linguistic barriers
- Explore the ways in which cultural expectations can affect the presentation and the interpretation of online messages
- Formulate ideas for how to address different cultural rhetorical expectations in online messages

Students can use this new level of understanding to temper the way in which they review, react, and respond to online messages from individuals from other cultures. The exercise also helps students gain a level of heightened cultural awareness they can use to review and revise their own online messages before sending them off to international recipients.

Exercise 3: Examining the Concept of Face in Relation to Rhetoric

The purpose of this exercise is to examine how different perspectives of *face* (public appearance) affect the rhetorical styles used by different cultural groups (Lustig & Koester, 1999). To achieve this end, the following exercise examines how interpretations of face affect the ways in which different cultures convey criticism or related bad news (Artemeva, 1998).

In this exercise, instructors would first divide both sets of students into groups of two or three, and the instructors would then tell each group that it would be interacting with a specific partner group from the other culture. The instructors would then tell these groups that their partner group in the other culture sold them a faulty product, and each group must now draft an e-mail message in which they convey their displeasure to that international partner while also taking steps to make sure that their international partner will replace the product. Each set of international partners, however, would be asked to comment on a different situation and a different kind of product. For example, one partner group might comment on faulty computer chips while another might comment on a tainted shipment of grain. Each group would then send this e-mail to its international partner for review.

Instructors would then ask the recipients of these messages to identify what the senders (the international partners) are trying to get them (the recipients) to do and to comment on how effective such messages would be in getting recipients to perform that task. The recipients of these messages would also provide a list of suggestions for how to better present criticism and requests according to their cultural norms. These analyses and related examples would then be shared among students from the same culture.

The instructors overseeing this exercise can collect these comments and suggestions and send them to their partner instructors who would share these responses and suggestions to his or her own class. These responses can then be used as a foundation for discussions in which students identify cross-cultural problem areas related to presenting negative or critical information.

The purpose of such an exercise is to teach prospective managers the importance of face in international business relationships. In many international situations, if one causes another to loose face, then the relationship between the two parties is ended. As a result, managers could accidentally foil international business relationships by inadvertently jeopardizing the face of an overseas counterpart. In many cases, this face-threatening behavior often relates to the presentation of criticism or displeasure, which different cultures believe must be done in different ways to avoid costing someone face (Lustig & Koester, 1999). Thus, this exercise helps prospective managers learn about the concept of face, and the exercise helps them gain an understanding of how they should choose their words wisely when expressing criticism or displeasure in international virtual teams. Through this exercise, students

- Learn the importance of face in relation to the rhetorical styles used by different cultures
- Examine how to revise messages to address different cultural perceptions of face
- Realize how different cultural perspectives of face can affect discourse in international virtual teams

By understanding these factors, students can develop communication guidelines or protocols that set standards for how to convey certain kinds of information in international virtual teams. In so doing, they can improve the exchange of information in these teams.

DESIGN ASPECTS OF ONLINE COMMUNICATION

Conceptual Overview

The design aspects of cross-cultural communication involve two concepts—acceptance and access. Acceptance is based on the idea that cultural groups have different expectations of how one should present visual materials. Failure to address these expectations, in turn, can result in images that offend or layouts that confuse. Such factors could either deter individuals from using online materials or could prevent them from using those materials in the intended manner. In these situations, communication breaks down, and the success of the entire team is jeopardized.

Several different factors can affect the acceptance of design aspects. For example, Horton (1993, 1994) and Forslund (1996) both comment on how different expectations of how women should be depicted in images (e.g., dress, task performed, etc.) can result in cross-cultural miscommunication. In such cases, key materials—such as healthcare instructions—might be ignored because they contain pictures that display women "immodestly" by the standards of a particular culture. Similarly, Horton (1993, 1994) notes how cultural associations for different hand gestures could cause problems as what is an acceptable gesture to one culture could be an offensive gesture in a different culture. For example, the open palm many Americans use to indicate "stop" is a highly offensive gesture in the Greek culture. Different cultural associations related to color can also result in communication mishaps. A blue ribbon, for example, indicates "first place" or "best" in the United States, but represents "second place" in the United Kingdom. Moreover, both Horton (1993) and Gillette (1999) note how different cultural expectations of what traits an object should have can result in confusion when identifying items. For example, using an image of a mailbox to indicate "e-mail" can cause communication problems depending on what a mailbox looks like in a particular culture.

The second major concept—access—relates to the idea that individuals working in different parts of the world could be operating under different kinds of technology constraints. These constraints could include the reliability and the carrying capacity of telephone lines, the speed of microprocessors, and the resolution of monitors. Such factors are important, for they can affect how individuals in other regions access, use, and perceive online information. Gillette (1999), for example, notes that persons in different cultures might have different connection speeds for accessing online materials. This difference can affect how easy (or how difficult) it is for individuals to access and re-access online information. In some cases, the preference is to print online materials for review in order to save on the costs related to maintaining an Internet connection (which can be billed at the rate of an international telephone call in some developing nations). In such cases, if certain online information does not print out (as with frames) as it appears in an online display (in black and white vs. color), or is too costly to print out (contains too many graphics that require too much ink), the quality of the information individuals receive could be compromised. In other cases, employees in other countries might be using older monitors with low resolutions to view online materials. Differences in resolution can affect the ease with which individuals can recognize online images and can affect the interpretation of related information.

The exercises presented in this section introduce students to the different acceptance and access factors that can affect communication in international virtual teams. In so doing, these exercises introduce students to design factors that managers should consider when sharing information with such teams. The focus of these exercises is on analyzing online materials designed for persons from other cultures. Because these interactions focus on materials and not on people, they involve aspects of visual design, layout, and image use which allow students to overcome language barriers when examining international items. As a result, these exercises allow students to review a broad range of materials related to many different cultural groups. These exercises also teach students that effective cross-cultural communication encompasses more than language alone, and the exercises can help students develop strategies for creating effective design materials for different cultural groups.

The insights resulting from such experiences can provide students with a perspective on how design aspects can affect information exchange in international virtual teams. Such a perspective, in turn, could be important to the management of international virtual teams in two ways:

• Managers could review online interfaces to determine if their design might cause communication problems for employees from different cultures. Managers could then remove or revise these problem aspects in order to enhance communication within the overall team.
• Managers would have different mechanisms/strategies they could use for creating design materials that meet the communication expectations and constraints of individuals involved in international online teams. In so doing, managers would increase the chances that employees could access, understand, and use those materials as is intended.

The first two exercises in this section allow students to examine the acceptance aspects related to design factors. The third and final exercise provides students with the opportunity to explore how access factors affect information exchange in international virtual teams. Through this approach, students gain a more complete perspective of the complexities and the nuances related to managing communication in international virtual teams.

Exercise 1: Identifying Expectations

The first exercise introduces students to the idea that a cultural group could have a particular set of expectations related to visual design. In this exercise, students work individually, and all students are asked to review three to five Web sites designed by individuals from a particular culture (a culture other than the students' own). While students may review different Web sites, all sites must be designed for the same cultural audience. That is, the entire class might be asked to locate three to five sites designed for a French audience. (See Appendix for a list of sties that can be used for this exercise.)

When reviewing these sites, students would look for patterns or consistencies in how individuals from that culture present information visually. In this approach, students would use the first Web site they examine as the foundation for a checklist of design features they observe on the site (e.g., "This site contains the following design features . . ."). Students would then review a different site and compare the data on their initial checklist to what they observe on that second site. The objective would be to see what design elements are repeated and what elements are new (not observed previously). Students would then modify their initial checklist to note what factors were repeated and what factors were new. This review, compare, and modify process would be repeated for each of the remaining sites the student examines.

Once the process is completed, students would use their findings to create a final design checklist of the "most commonly occurring" features they observed. Students would then engage in a group discussion in which they present and compare the checklists that resulted from this process. Through such a discussion, students would

- Explore how particular patterns were repeated throughout all sites
- Discuss why these patterns might be important and how they could affect the way in which members of that culture perceive and use Web sites
- Create an overall checklist on how to design online materials for individuals from that particular cultural group
- Examine how the process used in this exercise could serve as a methodology for creating online materials for employees working in international virtual teams

Through this overall process, students learn how cultural factors can affect communication in international virtual teams and could explore steps managers could take to address these factors.

Exercise 2: Comparing Cultures

The purpose of this exercise is to teach students that different cultural groups can have varying expectations related to the design of online materials. Whereas Exercise 1 had all students review the same culture and create a checklist, Exercise 2 has students compare the design expectations of different cultures in relation to a similar topic or product. In this exercise, students work in groups of two or three, and the instructor would assign each group a particular culture to analyze (e.g., France, Brazil, China,). Once the instructor has assigned these cultures, all groups would then go to the international site or world site a particular company uses to present information to different cultures, for these world sites provide access to the Web sites the same company has designed for different cultural audiences. Good sites to use for this project would include the Sony global site located at www.sony.net or the Mercedes-Benz global site located at www.mercedes-benz.com.

Each group would review the site for its related culture and create a checklist for how one should design Web sites for that particular cultural audience. Groups would next present their checklist and findings—complete with examples from the related Web site—to the class, and students would discuss how cultural audiences seem to differ in their expectations of Web site design.

After this discussion, the same groups would review a second world site that was designed for the same culture they researched originally, but that related to a different product or topic. In this second review, groups would compare their observations to the checklists they had developed earlier. The purpose of this comparison would be to identify re-occurring design factors in order to determine what aspects might reflect a cultural preference in overall Web site design and what aspects seem to differ according to company and product.

After this second round of review, groups would present their findings to the class and discuss what design features were repeated and what aspects were new. In this discussion, students would note aspects that seem to indicate a cultural preference in design, and what factors seemed to change based on the product or topic related to a site. The class would discuss both how cultural groups seemed to have different online design preferences and how the members of a particular culture seem to prefer a certain consistency of design within the medium of a Web site. Through such this overall process, students

- Learn how cultural groups can have differing expectations about how to present information online
- Learn how differences in cultural expectations can affect the ways in which one uses online media to convey information about the same topic to different cultural groups
- Examine how certain cultural design preferences seem to transcend the product or the topic related to a Web site

- Examine how certain aspects of Web design can differ according to topic or product within a culture
- Learn a methodology they can use to analyze the expectations different cultural groups associate with the display of online information

Through such a process, students learn that similar content does not always mean similar design used to present that information. Through such an understanding, students learn how the managers of international virtual teams might need to use a variety of designs when sharing information with the members of such teams.

Exercise 3: Technology and Access

The purpose of this exercise is to familiarize students with how technological limitations in different regions can affect information exchange in international virtual teams. For this exercise, the instructor should begin by discussing how different regions operate under different technology limitations that can affect how individuals access and view online information. The instructor can also explain how, in some areas, online access can be expensive as it is sometimes billed by the minute and at the rate of an international telephone call. For this reason, the speed with which one can access online materials affects what pages will be used and re-used by individuals from certain cultures. The instructor should also note that, due to these access issues, individuals in some cultures will print out important Web pages in order to reduce the time they need to spend online (Gillette, 1999). Additionally, individuals in different nations have different kinds of monitors with different degrees of resolution (clarity), a factor that can affect the way in which a Web page appears on a given monitor.

All of these factors affect the access different members of international virtual teams may have to online information. In some cases, technology restrictions may be so great that persons either cannot access information or cannot view it as is intended. In both cases, the results are a lack of communication that can affect the workings of international virtual teams. For this reason, managers need to consider technology limitations when developing online materials to share with such teams.

After the instructor presents this overview, he or she would have students access certain "high profile" business pages designed for more "high tech" audiences (e.g., msnbc.com, microsoft.com, amazon.com). Next, the instructor should have students download these pages at different modem speeds (e.g., 33.6K, 56K, and 126K) while timing the length of each download. To put the exercise into context, the instructor can tell students they are paying $10 per minute for this access, and that they need to calculate how much money was spent finding a specific kind of information on a particular Web site. The instructor can then ask students to review these same pages at different monitor resolutions (e.g., 640×480 pixels, 1024×768 pixels, and 1280×1024 pixels) and then print the site splash (initial) page for a site at each of these resolutions.

Once students complete these tasks, they would discuss the different experiences—and frustrations—they encountered while performing these activities. The class would then discuss how individuals might design a Web site that "high-speed access" cultures would find interesting (and thus usable) but that would also be accessible and usable to more "low-speed access" cultures. Students could also be asked to write a short (one to two page) reflection paper in which they explore whether it is worth the effort to design low-speed access Web sites for relatively low-tech (poorer) cultures with smaller consumer bases, or if companies should instead focus on designing flashy, high-speed access Web pages for users from more affluent cultures. Such reflection can help students understand how design choices related to online materials could have interesting ethical implications. Students can also brainstorm guidelines for determining what information an organization really does need to present, via online media, to international employees. Through this exercise and related discussion, students

- Learn how technology factors can affect information exchange in international virtual teams
- Learn how certain technology factors can affect online information exchange in different ways
- Examine options for addressing technology factors when working with international virtual teams
- Develop plans for how to address technology limitations when working with international virtual teams

By understanding such concepts, students can better plan how to disseminate online information to employees in virtual teams and how to best use international employees based on factors related to online access.

CONCLUSION

Online communication technologies are making the world a smaller place. As a result, managers will need to develop skills for using online media to interact effectively with employees from different cultures. This chapter examined different Internet-based teaching exercises that management instructors can use to familiarize students with the complexities of managing international virtual teams. Through such exercises, management students learn about cultural communication expectations and about how online media can affect cross-cultural interactions. Such experiences can provide students with the knowledge needed to succeed as managers in the global workplace of the future.

APPENDIX

The following Web sites provide access to a wide range of online materials designed for members of specific cultural groups. For this reason, instructors may wish to use or to review these sites when having students do the design exercises presented in this chapter.

- Foreign Embassies of Washington, DC
  http://www.embassy.org/embassies/index.html
  This site provides access to nation-specific Web sites of foreign/non-United States embassies located in Washington, DC.

- International Monetary Fund—Country Information
  http://www.imf.org/external/country/index.htm
  This site contains information on certain countries; some of the country information pages contain links to that country's banking and financial institutions and government organizations.

- Mercedes-Benz Corporate Web site
  http://www.mercedes-benz.com
  This site provides access to culture-specific Web sites for the various nations in which Mercedes-Benz automobiles are sold.

- Permanent Missions to the United Nations
  http://www.un.int/missions/webs.html
  This site provides access to the nation-specific Web sites of countries with permanent missions to the United Nations in New York.

- Sony Corporation's Global Headquarters Web site
  http://www.sony.net
  This site provides access to culture-specific Web sites for the various nations in which the Sony Corporation markets its products.

- The U.S. Commercial Services–Country Commercial Guides
  http://www.usatrade.gov/website/ccg.nsf
  This site provides access to country- and culture-specific commercial guides that contain information on certain nations; see the "US and Country Contacts" link in the listing for each country.

REFERENCES

Artemeva, N. (1998). The writing consultant as cultural interpreter: Bridging cultural perspectives on the genre of the periodic engineering report. *Technical Communication Quarterly, 7,* 285–299.

Baym, N. K. (1997). Interpreting soap operas and creating community: Inside an electronic fan culture. In S. Kiesler (Ed.), *Culture of the Internet* (pp. 103–120). Mahwah, NJ: Lawrence Erlbaum Associates.

Bliss, A. (2001). Rhetorical structures for multilingual and multicultural students. In C. G. Panetta (Ed.), *Contrastive rhetoric revisited and redefined* (pp. 15–30). Mahwah, NJ: Lawrence Erlbaum Associates.

Drucker, P. (2001, November 1). The next society: A survey of the near future. *The Economist,* 3–5.

Forslund, C. J. (1996). Analyzing pictorial messages across cultures. In D. C. Andrews (Ed.), *International Dimensions of Technical Communication* (pp. 45–58). Arlington, VA: Society for Technical Communication.

Gillette, D. (1999, December). Web design for international audiences. *Intercom,* 15–17.

Gutzman, A. (2001, May 11). And Now for Some Bad Grammar. *Manage the Ecommerce Business.* Retrieved January 22, 2004, from http://ecommerce.internet.com/how/biz/print/0,,10365_764531,00.html

Hiltz, S. R., & Turoff, M. (1993). *The network nation: Human communication via computer networks.* Cambridge, MA: MIT Press.

Horton, W. (1993). The almost universal language: Graphics for international documents. *Technical Communication, 40,* 682–693.

Horton, W. (1994). The icon book: Visual symbols for computer systems and documentation. New York: John Wiley & Sons.

Hu, W., & Grove, C. (1999). *Encountering the Chinese: A guide for Americans.* Yarmouth, ME: Intercultural Press.

IDC Research: Net Usage Up in Central and Eastern Europe. (2003, February 19). *NUA Internet Surveys.* Retrieved June 22, 2003, from http://www.nua.com/surveys/index.cgi?f=VS&art_id=905358723&rel=true

Kalia, K. (2001, July/August). Bridging global digital divides. *Silicon Alley Reporter,* 52–54.

Kiesler, S. et al. (1984). Social psychological aspects of computer-mediated communication. *American Psychologist, 39,* 1123–1134.

Lost in Translation. (2003, November 27). *The Economist.* Retrieved December 20, 2003, from http://www.economist.com/displayStory.cfm?Story_id=2248308

Lui, K. M., & Chan, K. C. C. (2003). Inexperienced software team and global software team. In A. Gunasekaran, O. Khalil, and S. M. Rahman (Eds.), *Knowledge and Information Technology Management: Human and Social Perspectives* (pp. 305–323). Hershey, PA: Idea Group.

Lustig, M. W., & Koester, J. (1999). *Intercultural competence: Interpersonal communication across cultures* (3rd ed.). New York: Longman.

Ma, R. (1996). Computer-mediated conversations as a new dimension of intercultural communication between East Asian and North American college students. In S. Herring (Ed.), *Computer-Mediated Communication: Linguistic, Social and Cross-Cultural Perspectives* (pp. 173–186). Amsterdam: John Benjamins.

New geography of the IT industry. (2003, July 17). *The Economist.* Retrieved December 20, 2003, from http://www.economist.com/display-story.cfm?story_id=S%27%29HH%2EQA%5B%21%

Ng, K. Y., & Van Dyne, L. (2001). Culture and minority influence: Effects on persuasion and originality. In C. K. W. De Dreu & N. K. De Vries (Eds.), *Group consensus and minority influence: Implications for innovation* (pp. 284–306). Malden, MA: Blackwell.

Platt, P. (1998). *French or foe? Getting the most out of visiting, living, and working in France* (2nd ed.). Cincinnati, OH: C. J. Krehbiel Company.

Relocating the Back Office. (2003, December 11). *The Economist.* Retrieved December 20, 2003, from http://www.economist.com/displaystory.cfm?story_id=2282381

Section IV Survey Results. (2003, January). *Semiannual Report on the Development of China's Internet.* Retrieved June 22, 2003, from http://www.cnnic.net.cn/develst/2003-1e/444.shtml

Sproull, L., & Kiesler, S. (1986). Reducing social context cues: Electronic mail in organizational communication. *Management Science, 32,* 1492–1512.

Tapping in to Africa. (2000, September 9–15). *The Economist,* 49.

Tying Latin American together. (2001, Summer). *NYSE Magazine,* 9.

Ulijn, J. M. (1996). Translating the culture of technical documents: Some experimental evidence. In D. C. Andrews (Ed.), *International dimensions of technical communication* (pp. 69–86). Arlington, VA: Society for Technical Communication.

Ulijn, J. M., Lincke, A., & Karakaya, Y. (2001). Non-face-to-face international business negotiation: How is national culture reflected in this medium? *IEEE Transactions on Professional Communication, 44,* 126–137.

Verckens, J. P., De Rycker, T., & Davis, K. (1998). The experience of sameness in differences: A course in international business writing. In S. Niemeier, C. P. Campbell, & R. Dirven (Eds.), *The cultural context in business communication* (pp. 247–261). Philadelphia, PA: John Benjamins.

Vogel, Douglas R. et al. (2001). Exploratory research on the role of national and professional cultures in a distributed learning project. *IEEE Transactions on Professional Communication, 44,* 114–125.

Warnick, B. (1998). Rhetorical criticism of public discourse on the Internet: Theoretical implications. *Rhetoric Society Quarterly, 28,* 73–84.

When India Wires Up. (2000, July 22–28). *The Economist,* 39–40.

Wired China. (2000, July 22–28). *The Economist,* 24–28.

CHAPTER 7

AT A DISTANCE

Learning About Cross-Cultural Virtual Teams in an International Management Course

Mikael Søndergaard, Marta B. Calás, and Paul F. Donnelly

ABSTRACT

In this chapter, we narrate our experiences designing and teaching an international management course which was technologically enhanced to include cross-cultural interactions between the United States and Denmark. Our rationale—that issues regarding globalization have accelerated the need to bring together through virtual means people from different cultures to engage in collaborative performance at a distance—is addressed in the context of theoretical concerns regarding cultural differences. We discuss the theoretical premises on which we based the course, illustrate the three core distance activities that we designed for these purposes, evaluate the general outcome in light of our objectives, and assess their value for others engaged in teaching courses such as ours. At the end, we link our experiences to broader issues pertaining to distance-education in today's university environments.

The Cutting Edge of International Management Education, pages 167–200
Copyright © 2004 by Information Age Publishing
167

INTRODUCTION: GLOBALIZATION, TECHNOLOGICAL HYPE, AND TIME-SPACE COMPRESSION

Among the most typical assertions about globalization these days are those that equate information technologies with a woven world of distant encounters and instant connections (e.g., Yergin & Stanislaw, 1998). In these views, people between and within organizations and nations become connected in such a way that they end up configuring a boundaryless and mobile economy, full of complexities which are difficult, if not impossible, to control from any one point or institution.

Several other discourses of globalization assert a need to prepare students for the information-based jobs of the global village (Dimitriades & Kamberelis, 1997; Fulton, 1998; Miller, 1995; Molnar, 1997; Secretary's Commission on Achieving Necessary Skills, (1991), to make sure that they become capable of dealing with "a world increasingly constituted by and through rapidly developing technological apparatuses" (Dimitriades & Kamberelis, 1997, p. 138). Still others believe that the global citizen will need to develop a better sense of interconnections between cultural, social, technological, economic, and representational phenomena, for the global culture is an on-going and complex contest between sameness and difference which is often technologically produced and mediated (Appadurai, 1990).

While not without criticism (Altbach, 2000; Brender, 2001; Wesley-Smith, 2003), issues of globalization have indeed accelerated interest in bringing together through information technologies people from different cultures who, for whatever reason, may need to engage in collaborative performance at a distance (Adam, Awerbuch, Slonim, Wegner, & Yesha, 1997; Drexler, Larson, Cogliser, Sullivan, & Watson, et al., 2000; Efendioglu & Murray, 2000; Johnson, 1999; Lelong & Fearnley-Sander, 1999; Osland, Bird, Maznevski, McNett, & Mendenhall, et al., this volume; Rice, 1996). It has also become clearer that technological mediation has the potential to exacerbate language and cultural issues (e.g., Wesley-Smith, 2003). No surprise, then, that the use of information technology and its intersection with cultural issues in international business activities and pedagogy is gaining increased attention (American Society for Training & Development, 2003; Huff, 2001; Klein & Partridge, 2003; Sitze, 2002; Wheeler, 1998).

In particular, as virtual teams have become more prevalent among transnational organizations, both the academic and the more popular literatures on multicultural teams increasingly address technological mediation and its cultural implications (e.g., Daly, 1996; Day, Dosa, & Jorgensen, 1995; Laroche, 2001; Lazear, 1999; McCain, 1996; Myers, 1992; Neale & Mindel, 1992; Singelis, 2000). For example, Kiser (1999) describes a situation at Royal Dutch Shell where English was the agreed upon virtual teams' common language and, therefore, assumptions were made about the ease in communication. Yet, Dutch team members felt that their United States colleagues were talking in code, especially when colloquialisms were used. The United States team members, on the other hand, argued that their Dutch counterparts had a preference for structure, wanting excessive details about the process, how it would work, and who would make decisions.

Other writers support Shell's experiences. For example, Hiltz and Wellman (1997) note that computer-mediated communication "seems good for giving and receiving information, opinions and suggestions; [but that] it is less suited for communicating agreement and disagreement; and it is worst for social-emotional tasks involving conflict and negotiation" (p. 45). Others, such as Cellich (2001), consider that international business negotiations over the Internet should be made on a selective basis and, ideally, as a preamble to arrangements for actual face-to-face negotiations, while Andres (2002) reports results that indicate team productivity to be superior in face-to-face settings rather than videoconferencing settings. In fact, Shell and ABB, among others, have found that traveling to meet face-to-face is still a necessary element for a virtual team's success.

As this brief discussion illustrates, there are very concrete intersections between the practical, the pedagogical, and the theoretical regarding technological mediation under globalization that could be integrated as content in international management courses. These arguments come alive, beyond the hype, in the microcosm of our own academic work as international management professors. New technologies for our everyday work and, in particular, the teaching environment, stress—experientially and concretely—the complex relationships that ensue because of technological mediation between different actors.

We, as scholars living and working in universities around the world, collaborate now with one another more readily than ever before, given the time-space compression (Harvey, 1989, p. 240 ff.) of our academic milieu. Concurrently, the transnational management literature through which we teach provides ready-to-hand insights into the workings of business corporations, where the interaction and integration of important organizational units located throughout the globe is represented as a business imperative. Yet, more often than not, our students are located in a classroom, in a particular course, in a university, within a country. Students constantly face the contradictions between the international/global arguments in our courses and their lack of lived experience with such arguments. At the same time, they are often caught between current ubiquitous portrayals of distance learning as education anywhere, any time, any place and the constraints of their experiences as bounded in time and space.

This chapter addresses these issues through a narrative of our experiences: designing and teaching an international management course which was technologically enhanced to facilitate cross-cultural teamwork at a distance between the United States and Denmark. The rationale which we followed was based on our own personal experiences as "connected academics"; the contradictions experienced by our students regarding their relationships to distance-based and computer-mediated activities in their own local educational contexts; and reports from the international management literature regarding virtual business activities. In our view, it was by explicitly articulating these intersections in the concrete context of classroom activities that students would be able to experience the advantages and limitations pertaining to distance and virtual information and communication, as well as to practice with the possibilities of their new identities as global citizens.

However, since we started to consider several years ago ways to use technology in our international management courses, our primary concern was conceptual issues regarding cultural differences. And, as may be gleaned through the paragraphs that follow, we found ourselves supporting the uses of information technologies in the instructional process neither as an unavoidable reality in the context of globalization nor as the latest tool for international business problem-solving. In fact, we were not even concerned with debates around distance-education, which were then not as prevalent as they are today. Rather, we found ourselves eventually involved in these debates while trying to do something perhaps more modest from a technological perspective and more complicated from a theoretical perspective. As we saw it then, the technology was simply a means to enhance experiences of cultural differences that are difficult to obtain within conventional classrooms. Since then, we have learned much more.

In the rest of the chapter, we discuss first the theoretical provenance of our activities. Second, we describe three exercises that we designed and how we used them in our courses in two different semesters. In each instance, we discuss our results and evaluate the more general outcome of these activities in light of our theoretical objectives. We also assess their value for others engaged in teaching courses such as ours. Finally, we link our experiences to broader issues pertaining to distance education in today's university environments.

DEFYING CROSS-CULTURAL COMPARISONS: INCOMMENSURABILITY, HYBRIDIZATION, AND COMMON INTERESTS

Encountering Incommensurability

As we started to design technologically mediated exercises, our primary interest stemmed from the theoretical positions we take in our courses regarding cross-cultural differences. Our interests also stemmed from difficulties that we had encountered trying to provide experiential knowledge about these differences. Specifically, most courses that consider cross-cultural issues often assume the possibility of cultural comparisons. However, this assumption has been thoroughly challenged through concepts of cultural incommensurability from both inside and outside the organizational literatures (e.g., Adler, 1984; Boyacigiller & Adler, 1991; Clifford, 1986, Czarniawska, 1998; Geertz, 1983; Hofstede, 1980; 1993; Kaghan & Phillips, 1998; Kuhn, 1970; Laurent, 1983; Redding, 1994; Taylor, 1985). That is, *to compare* implies that the issues under comparison can translate into one another, or that they can be evaluated in relation to a neutral standard. Said differently, *cross-cultural* often assumes equivalence across cultures. Yet, differences may be incommensurable when they belong to different systems of understanding or, to use a much-abused term, when they belong to different paradigms. Further, to say *cross-cultural comparisons* is also to conceal the fact that there are no neutral standards for comparison since all standards are cultural creations. To say *standard* is to depict the normalizing premises of some cultures but not of others. To say *standard* is also to promote cultural universalism.

Therefore, despite assumptions of sensitivity to the uniqueness of different cultures, cross-cultural arguments often promote uncritical cultural universalism as they search for generalizable frames for comparison and understanding. Adler (1997), among other critics of universalism, cautions that cross-cultural miscommunication frequently results from the lack of cultural self-awareness (the ignorance associated with not knowing one's own cultural conditioning) and subconscious cultural blinders (the lack of conscious attention to specific cultural assumptions) (Hofstede, 2001). Lack of cultural self-awareness often provokes *projected similarity*, meaning the belief that people are more similar to one's self than they actually are. Such beliefs may bring about inappropriate behaviors that exacerbate further misinterpretations by all members in the situation.

Critiques of cultural universalism appear, as well, in the globalization literature. In this case, the critiques are directed to those who equate globalization with expectations of cultural homogenization. For instance, Barber (1995) argues that there are clear tensions between Western homogenization and the fragmentation promoted by a multiplicity of other cultural and religious understandings, which undermine the possibility of a common global democratic future. Similarly, Sinclair, Jacka, and Cunningham (1996) show that despite the apparent influence of Western television the world over, audiences receive and respond differently to these influences along regional lines. In fact, these media may encourage new regional differences, supported by common cultural, linguistic, and historical connections.

Thinking Hybridization

In short, assumptions of cultural homogenization (or Westernization, or Americanization) under premises of globalization are often greatly exaggerated. These assumptions may also stem from simplifications of more complex processes, including lack of attention to the appearance of newer cultural formations brought about by increasing contacts between world societies, which go unrecognized through conventional analyses focusing on static cultural differences or similarities. Known as *cultural hybridization*, this latter perspective posits the emergence of cultural forms and identities that are "something else" than whatever existed before (Pieterse, 1995). These arguments extend beyond discussions of cultural divergence versus convergence in earlier international management debates (e.g., Kerr, 1983), for as noticed by Schneider & Barsoux (2003, pp. 113-114), there is continued divergence of management practices despite increased internationalization since 1980.

The emergence of hybrid cultural forms and identities in any society is better understood as processes of hybridization, as active components of cultural change. These may happen through casual encounters of different human activities, such as when traditional crafts in a society introduce some changes in design inspired by contacts with members of another society. Similarly, social movements (as much as intentional and unintentional appropriations and resignifications of particular social, economic and political forces and symbols) transform and reconfigure, on an ongoing basis, whatever was there before (e.g., Bhabha, 1994; Escobar, 1995; García-Canclini, 1990).

Under conventional cross-cultural premises, these changes would be erroneously read as cultural evolution assumed to be occurring over long periods of time. In fact, descriptions of cultural change (i.e., fast or slow) are often used to classify societies for comparative purposes into problematic value-laden terms such as "modern" or "traditional," whereby the former (often associated with industrialized societies) is represented as more prone to rapid change than the latter (often, but not necessarily, associated with non-industrialized societies). This is an issue of particular relevance in United States classrooms, for assumptions are often made as if the United States is the arbiter of modernization and innovation and, therefore, as if levels of modernization should be judged according to each country's standing in an (imaginary) scale in reference to the United States.

Classificatory terms of this type already tilt the odds regarding who gets to know whom and in whose terms. Almost by definition, modern societies would be less likely to be known by traditional societies, for they are more prone to undergo fast changes, while the opposite would be true for traditional societies, whose almost static way of being is represented as easily knowable. Expectations of this type further create hierarchies regarding types of knowledge, as well as who is the known and who is the knowing subject. That is, the modern, including implicitly the society where the classificatory scheme was created, is privileged over traditional ways of understanding.

Nonetheless, even in the unlikely case that in the past societies could be differentiated according to their pace of cultural change, under premises of globalization, there is no reason to expect that at present cultural change in any society in the world would be evolutionary. Rather, the exponential increase in contacts between all societies (no need to use invidious comparisons), whose traditions of all kinds have now become currency in circulation throughout the global marketplace, would defy expectations of eventual stability of one or another transformed cultural form, or the appearance of settled cultural identities. These contacts include the actual migration of people as well as increased traveling and newer modes of communication, including information technologies, which bring acceleration of cultural hybridization as an ongoing process of cultural (trans)formation.

From the perspective of cultural hybridization, therefore, the theoretical premises that support cross-cultural comparisons represent an unreflective, static, and outmoded way of thinking. That is, the notion of cross-cultural comparisons has always tended to leave out or deprecate certain traditions given the cultural blinders located within its own premises; at present they also leave out the actual processes of cultural transformation that better represent the contemporary world.

Forging Common Interests

Finally, recent cultural theorizations, which in principle accept formulations of cultural incommensurability as well as hybridization, have been concerned with the excessive focus on differences forwarded by these formulations at the expense of noticing possible relational practices between and within members of different societies. These concerns address the aftermath, to put it metaphorically, of thinking at the edge of borderlands. Said differently, the arguments that sustain cultural incommensurability emphasize that which cannot be comprehended as societies face each other, which is also a way to establish a boundary against comprehending that which could be common to both. The arguments that sustain cultural hybridization, on the other hand, emphasize comprehending what is emerging, what is constantly becoming, which puts a boundary against comprehending what is still there—the traces that may have been left behind. In either case, a question remains: Is there a place where members of different societies can still find something in common? (e.g., Esteva & Prakash, 1998).

The metaphor of borderlands, a common ground rather than a dividing line, has been mobilized by several authors to represent a space where societies could encounter each other, whether in their historical differences or in their newly found common causes (Anzaldúa, 1987; Michaelsen & Johnson, 1997; Saldívar, 1997). These views focus on ways to create new linkages among people, and on a space to articulate their particular interests while confronting the forces brought about by globalization—that is, forces that do not benefit all people nor attend to all human interests. These views focus on both cultural commonalities and differences not as *givens* but as circumstances that can be mobilized to construct new common grounds (e.g., consider the World Social Forum as response to the World Economic Forum). These views emphasize local circumstances, what is particular to each place, in the face of what is global, such as what the majority of the people in the world may experience as part of global economic expansion at the expense of their own local interest. These are, indeed, critical views that bring up issues of power relations so often concealed by the apparently benign cross-cultural rubric.

Mohanty (2003) expresses similar arguments, under the concept of common interests, in terms of what they mean for the pedagogical context. In her words:

> My recurring question is how pedagogies can supplement, consolidate or resist the dominant logic of globalization. How do students learn about the inequities among women and men around the world? ... I look to create pedagogies that allow students to see the complexities, singularities and interconnections between communities ... such that power, privilege, agency and dissent can be made visible and engaged with. (p. 523)

From Theoretical Loftiness to the Everydayness of Classrooms

The discussion above undergirds many issues that we, as instructors of contemporary international management courses, hope to be able to translate into the fundamentals of our courses. Past experiences have taught us that most students who enter our courses, either as upper division undergraduates or MBA students, expect to deal with cross-cultural comparisons in a fairly straightforward manner. More often than not they assume that cultures are easy to compare, as if they exist in a fairly static and well-bounded condition, within a hierarchical scale normed through levels of development or in measurable multidimensional spaces representing cultural distance and/or cultural clusters. Thus, our challenge is to be able to introduce other possible, more processual, and critical modes of thinking while easing the transition between students' original expectations and the unexpected complications of the topic.

The fundamental complexity of these issues creates specific challenges for international management courses. More practical concerns repeatedly become the center of attention; for instance, how to communicate across cultures or how to make decisions that take into account cultural differences—even if incommensurability is conceptually acknowledged. Unstated assumptions behind these practical concerns hide many facts of incommensurability, for it is more comfortable and feasible for students to assume that differences could be resolved through mutual understanding than to address the reality that such understandings may never be possible. In particular, there is clear reluctance to address power relations that may be concealed under apparent common grounds, despite the fact that agreements may often be based on common interests of groups with little cultural commonalities, which face, nonetheless, a temporary necessity to bind together in the borderlands. Consider, for example, the collapse in November 2003 of the WTO meetings in Cancun, under the pressure of a newly formed, and precariously sustained, grouping of an NGO and 21 developing nations, whose common interests hinged mostly on issues around agricultural subsidies.

Resistance to addressing critical issues beyond cultural differences may appear perhaps more frequently in professional education courses taught under conventional instructional formats. For instance, classroom instruction within a specific country and with students who belong mostly to that country are not conducive to address the problematics of cross-cultural comparisons. The situation is not much better in classrooms that include international exchange students. These students often hold in common the fact that they come on exchange assuming more advanced professional knowledge outside their own countries, and usually they are a diverse minority who must face the locals in an on-going basis. Such a situation does not lead easily to classroom discussions where incommensurable cultural issues would be vented or critically questioned, even if they may often be the subtext of apparently more benign cultural interactions. Further, classroom-based cross-cultural simulations used within a single country, even in the best-case scenarios—e.g., Bafá-Bafá (Shirts, 1977) and Randömia Balloon Factory (Grove & Hallowell, 2001)—fare not much better. They are contrived situations of short duration, and there is little external validity on which to rely when it comes to learning the difficulties that may ensue in actual cross-cultural interactions.

Thus, in a more general sense, the activities we designed were intended to deepen students' understanding of cultural differences through actual multicultural encounters while attempting to overcome the limitations described above. The mediation by technology in our original intent was the bridge toward fulfilling this objective. This mediation would provide concrete experiences giving local meanings to abstract concepts of globalization. It would also be the space where incommensurability, hybridization, and common interest become the norm against expectations of simple cultural similarities and differences.

In other words, we wanted to produce a reflective knowledge-creating environment that would represent, in form and content, the complex world of which our students were to become a part upon graduation, and to enhance at the same time their critical thinking skills about such a world. While we were also interested in exposing our students to the difficulties of working in virtual teams through computer-mediated engagements, that was not our central objective, but rather a way to insert or enhance cross-cultural complexities in the assumed commonalties.

DEVELOPING CROSS-CULTURAL TEAMWORK AT A DISTANCE

No Virtual Beginning

The immediate situation that prompted the creation of these activities had few virtual components. The two first authors had known each other for several years and had maintained e-mail correspondence over time. We shared a mutual interest in international management and in cultural issues, and often taught similar courses in our respective institutions, which are business schools in public universities in the United States northeast and, at the time, in southern Denmark. As a reflective point to our arguments, we each came originally from very different cultural backgrounds and live in different cultural environments. Experiences with each other as friends and colleagues had, no doubt, influenced our conviction that it was necessary to address cross-cultural complexities in our courses beyond conventional treatments in our management textbooks and other course materials. At the same time, our long-term relationship contributed to our willingness to risk experimenting with these activities, for we had developed a high level of face-to-face trust long before any virtual engagement. The third author was a member of the instructional staff at the United States institution working with the second author also for several years, and shared similar experiences, including being a non-United States national teaching international courses at a United States university.

In 1997, during an informal gathering at a professional conference in the United States, we discussed possibilities for combining our common interests in cross-cultural issues and cognition into a teaching experience that could be run jointly through electronic means. At the time we each had already engaged in within-country computer-mediated activities with our students and were ready to go the next step, extending these activities into cross-nation exercises. Content-wise, we both were teaching standard international management courses for upper-division students within the span of a semester, which more or less coincided in dates between February and May.

We taught these courses concurrently in the spring semester of 1998 and again in the spring semester of 2002. Our syllabi were sufficiently similar, and it was not difficult to find dates in which our courses could "come together at a distance." With the collaboration of the third author, we coordinated our course units such that at certain points in the semester our students would come together through electronic communication to either solve a case or participate in an experiential exercise. Table 7.1 summarizes details about the students, group design and communication and information technology used each year.

First Time—1998

Early in 1998 we finalized our syllabi and agreed to the formation of e-mail cross-national groups. It worked to our advantage that our classes had an identical number of students, which facilitated the organization of these groups as equivalent as possible, including trying to minimize the possibility of single-sex groups. Students in both countries were fairly homogeneous as representative of the majority population in their respective locations.

We deliberately chose a very simple communication tool, namely e-mail, since our concern was to use computers to support human-human interactions rather than human-computer interactions. As indicated, we did not

Table 7.1. Summary of Student Characteristics, Group Design and ICT Used, 1998 and 2002

Year courses were taught	1998		2002	
	Denmark	U.S.	Denmark	U.S.
Student characteristics:				
Number	36	36	68	39
National and ethnic/racial composition	All Danish nationals, non "ethnic"	All U.S. nationals white	1/3 Danish nationals; 2/3 eighteen other nationalities;	2/3 US nationals, white; 1/3 four other nationalities, plus "diverse" U.S. nationals
Sex composition	Almost even M/F	Almost even M/F	Almost even M/F	2/3M, 1/3F
Group designs:				
Pen-pals	First grouping[a]: 36 cross-national groups		No	
Small groups	Second grouping[b]: 12 cross-national groups		12 virtual groups[c]: Based on original groupings for other on-location projects in the Danish course—U.S. students were added to these groups	
Group size	6 students each (3 pen-pal U.S.–Denmark pairs per group)		8 or 9 students each (5 or 6 from Denmark; 3 or 4 from the U.S.)	
Information and communication technology				
Paired pen-pals	Email[d]	Private emails between members of each pair	Discussion boards[e]	No
Small groups	Group distribution lists—emails shared within each group			Each group could only access own discussion board (password protected)
All participants	Common distribution list—emails shared by all members of both courses		Common discussion board—common to all members of both courses	
Website	No		Each course had its own Website, but they were linked to each other	

[a] For the Islamic Headscarf case.

[b] For both the ABB and the BioTech exercises.

[c] For all three activities (Islamic Headscarf, ABB and BioTech).

[d] This set-up was intended to facilitate more informal and private discussions of the cases or exercises first in pairs, and then to foster student participation in reaching group level decisions before posting solutions to the "all participants" common list. Both the group distribution lists and the common distribution list served as collaborative spaces to support sharing different perspectives on the issues presented in the case or exercises. Instructors and their teaching assistants had access to all email communications, except for those between pen-pals, and students were informed from the start about our "presence".

[e] Instructors and teaching assistants had full access to all communications on the boards, and students were informed from the start about this fact.

think of the technology as the center of attention but as a simple tool through which our students would easily interact with each other.

There were three levels of communication. The first level was the link between student pairs (pen-pals), which was private between themselves. The second level was through each cross-national group distribution list, which was shared by the students within each group only. Finally, the third level was shared by all the students in both countries through the common distribution list. As members of the e-mail lists we, instructors and teaching assistants, were able to monitor the decision-making exchanges, and later in class "on location" provide feedback about these processes.

To get used to the media and to each other, once students were paired at the very outset of the semester, they were invited by their instructor to start communicating on an informal basis with her or his pen-pal. This occurred even before the distribution lists were created. Students also had some opportunities to practice with the lists before the first exercise (a case) was posted.

Second Time—2002

In 2002 we did not use the pen-pal approach; instead, we organized the students in virtual teams from the start of the semester. This time we decided to use Web-based discussion boards rather than e-mail because they allowed for threaded discussions.

The creation of these teams was also different from the original approach in 1998. Specifically, the Denmark class was expected to produce group papers and case analyses throughout the semester as part of their course. These groups were organized according to preferred (for them) paper topics, and they self-selected to participate in one group or another. When the United States students became part of these groups, the Danish groups already had a common history. The United States students were an add-on for specific purposes (i.e., the three virtual team activities) throughout the semester.

As we will discuss later, while compared to 1998, these different group arrangements may have contributed to different dynamics during the virtual activities, and other differences in the student populations might have contributed as well. The Denmark class was almost double the size of the United States class and, therefore, the groups were not only larger but also more unbalanced in terms of number of students from each side. Both classes were also more diverse than the 1998 classes. Further, because of the way the Denmark groups had been structured on a self-selection basis, we had less control over the diversity of each group, including gender, ethnicity, and nationality. At the end, the United States instructor decided to assign her students to the Denmark groups at random. This action may have contributed even further to certain group dynamics since the Denmark students may have felt more "in control of their fate" than the United States students.

The Three Activities

In both 1998 and 2002 we used the same basic activities, structured in levels of increasing difficulty as described below. The first activity, the discussion of a case ("The Islamic Headscarf") occurring in France and addressing highly sensitive cultural issues, happened fairly early in the semester, and was introduced suddenly with a relatively short deadline for completion and posting on the general list or board. This was followed by two other exercises. One exercise was presented in mid-semester and consisted of a set of situations depicting different moments in the trajectory of ABB, from its creation through merger of a Swedish company and a Swiss company to current issues in the life of the company. The other exercise, run almost at the end of the academic year, was a decision-making simulation (BioTech), which considered ethical issues in China. All these activities pertained to specific subjects within our syllabi: Culture; Organizing for transnational management; and Ethics in international environments. Cross-cultural issues were embedded within all these subjects and enhanced, in our view, through the virtual interactions between our students.

Incommensurability or Hybridization?
The Islamic Headscarf

This first activity consisted of a mini-case adapted from the case "The Controversy Over the Islamic Headscarf: Women's Rights and Cultural Sensibilities" (Phatak, 1997, pp. 166-170). An abridgment of the case as it appeared in this textbook was discussed first in each class in the United States and Denmark. Afterwards, students were asked to communicate with their partners in the other country to discuss the questions we posed to them and to report the outcome of such discussions in the following class meeting. In 1998 the discussion took place between pen-pals only, while in 2002 it was the first try-out of the discussion boards.

Briefly, the case pertains to an actual situation that happened in France in September 1994 when the national minister of education issued a directive that banned headscarves from classrooms. In October, police were called in to prevent 22 Muslim girls from entering their school wearing their headscarves. Polls had shown that a majority of the French supported the education minister's decree. The actual controversy included a general perception that the headscarf was a threat to secularism and the separation of religion and state. There was also concern that it would divide Muslim and non-Muslim students, that it would introduce religious influences into the public school, and that it would place undue strain on other students to conform to Islam's dress or moral code. Another claim was that the headscarf constituted a violation of women's human rights despite the fact that the students involved wanted to wear it.

The case, inspired by this issue, illustrates a situation where a fully westernized Iranian Muslim woman, Taraneh, who emigrated to France years before because of religious fundamentalism in her own country, decided to move to the United States. Her decision was due to circumstances involving her daughter, who wears the headscarf to school, when the daughter becomes part of the controversy described above. The case ends when the woman starts working at a management position in a multinational company located in Texas. She had worked there some twenty years before while she was studying in the United States. The personnel manager of the company, a Texan male, describes for her how the company has grown since then and points out the friendly atmosphere of the workplace as well as the multicultural environment, for the company is a leader in the promotion of diversity.

In our view, this case was interesting for our purposes but it was also full of cultural stereotypes regarding the actors in the situation and their particular locations. Thus, we decided to further complicate the situation by adding the following to set the stage for case discussion:

> Consider that this is happening now, at this point in time: You are the personnel manager depicted at the end of the case. Now, you have been transferred to the French subsidiary of the company, and you want to bring Taraneh back to France with you since you think she'll help your approach as personnel manager in this subsidiary. The first situation you encounter is that some French managers in the company are objecting to the fact that several women workers, including secretaries, are observing the Islamic dress code. How would you handle this issue? What would you do? Explain the rationale for your answer using your course materials as well as your knowledge of facts behind this case.

While this first assignment could be considered a warm-up exercise to make the students comfortable with the technology and the time lags in communication, clearly the substance of the case was in itself important for issues of cross-cultural differences. The actual case situation occurred in a third country (France) that was a foreign location for both the United States and Denmark students in 1998. There were a few French students in the Denmark class in 2002, but this did not seem to affect the discussion, compared to 1998. The case also portrayed general circumstances that are subject to Western cultural stereotyping of women in Islam (Czarniawska & Calás, 1997).

Both times, not all students communicated with their counterparts, but those who did reported in class the similarities (a good deal) and differences (modest) in their opinions. Not surprisingly, the similarities referred to common (in the West) stereotypes concerning Islamic women. This offered an opportunity to discuss in class the formation of cultural stereotypes regarding migrant populations to Western countries and highlight the hybridization that occurs through cultural contacts, including whether Taraneh's assumed assimilation to Western norms could be perhaps a simplistic explanation. Would she be a "cultural translator" when back in France? Would the situation look different now than when she left France because of her daughter? Is a dress code necessarily a sign of oppression? Who defines what is a non-oppressed woman?

The assumed modest differences, however, provided an even richer discussion since students in Denmark were more aware of the conditions in France than were the United States students, and more experienced with immigrant situations than their United States counterparts. To a certain extent, the discussion became the occasion to remark the fundamental differences in the experiences and expectations of both groups that may have been masked under the common focus on the women in this case. In Denmark, the issue itself was of importance in the immediate local milieu while in the United States the argument seemed quite "foreign." This was not surprising in 1998 given that very few United States students would have had any experience with issues of dressing preferences under stereotypical notions of "American tolerance for difference." Yet it is surprising that United States students reacted in a similar way in 2002, given the focus on Islamic dressing brought about by the events of 9/11, the war in Afghanistan, and the very public arguments associating certain immigrants with terrorist activities.

Altogether, students in Denmark were willing to consider the special circumstances of French institutions under French regulations and the multiplicity of issues brought about within this workplace. In other words, these students saw the situation as quite complex, and not easily resolved, for it included political as well as religious issues in addition to labor and management issues. Students in the United States, on the other hand, were fairly adamant about the need for a universal solution based on "diversity training," no matter the location or the actors involved. For them the situation was a managerial problem that the United States manager would be able to solve mostly by himself, often ignoring even the possible mediation by Taraneh. It was the students' own divergent attitudes toward the nature of the problem, as they voiced their own incommensurable premises, that provided a glaring example of the difficulties behind notions of "cross-cultural comparisons" which served as the basis for debriefing at each location.

It is important to remark that in 1998 we had not put much emphasis on the technological mediation used to discuss the case. The focus was the classroom discussion on each location since for this case we had allowed interactions between our students to occur almost on a voluntary basis. We used their self-reports as the basis for discussion. In 2002 this exercise was the try-out for the threaded discussions on the boards, and we were able to read what was happening as the discussions went on. Both times we found that student participation was less than we had expected. Still, we expected that those students who had been involved in the interactions would encourage those who had not to become involved in the future, once they reported in class "how much fun they had doing it." Unfortunately, as we will discuss later, this was not always the case.

Common Interests in the Borderlands? Asea Brown Boveri

In 1998 we assigned a case on Asea Brown Boveri (Simons & Bartlett, 1992) and introduced it to the students by mid-semester. This was the first time we were emphasizing "working in virtual groups" in the course, and we introduced the argument by remarking how much the company (ABB) both depended on, and developed, information and communication technologies for their own global operations. In a sense we were creating a situation in which students would experience ABB's notion of being "global and local," by becoming, themselves, "local and global" in order to discuss the case "at a distance."

Students were assigned to work on several questions for the case and discuss them within their own virtual groups through their own group's distribution list. Each group was also required to post their final answers on the general list to the questions a day before the next class meeting, at a specified time. It was important that all groups posted at the same time to prevent any one group from "gathering inspiration" from another group's responses. Time differences between Denmark and the United States made it difficult to schedule synchronous activities, and students started to understand the difference that time lags can make when working at a distance. While some complained about it, it also provided more realism to our activities. The case was discussed in each class (Denmark and United States) using the responses given by the groups.

ABB is perhaps the best representative of the logic of "being local worldwide" among transnational corporations. That in itself could have been an avenue for exploring cross-cultural differences at the core of company policy. However, the students became focused instead on the transnational and global organizational structures pertaining to this company and, in a sense, found there a common "safe ground" on which to allay any difference of opinions.

It should be noted that the topics we were discussing at the time in both locations involved organizing for international business and that the course materials in both our locations, with some exceptions (e.g., Schneider & Barsoux, 1997), were from United States-based texts and research. That is, the theoretical arguments pertaining to these topics are not "culturally-neutral" for the literature and research on transnational and global organizations have been mostly generated in the United States through this country's conceptualizations of organization theory.

Thus, while in appearance, students seemed to become culturally disconnected from the topic so that the discourse of "organization" became their common zone of engagement—their "borderlands for common interests. In fact, students from both sides were relying mostly on United States notions of organization theory to articulate their responses. The question of cultural imperialism of organizational theories could have been raised at this point, in particular when ABB adopted English as their lingua franca, but we did not do so at the time. As we will discuss, eventually the question of language also became an issue in our course, but at the point of this case we were unaware of it.

In 2002, ABB continued to be the focus of our transnational organization discussions. As a starting point we used this case, ABB -Transformers Denmark, (Søndergaard & Naumes, under review). It deals with a situation in Odense in which the local plant is about to be transferred to Thailand. We further reconfigured the exercise by extending it beyond the specifics of any written case, and bringing it to the present in time and space, for ABB's organizational structure was changing rapidly at the time, and it was worth it to experience the reality of such a situation.

That is, we created a set of activities that students on both sides would do together through research on the Web, including researching the very rich ABB Website. As previously indicated, this time the virtual teams had their own discussion boards, and it was possible to maintain threaded discussions. Throughout the length of the ABB exercise (close to a month after mid-semester) students would consult questions posted periodically on the "all participants" board by the instructors and discuss them on their own team's board. At certain pre-established times, each group would post its responses on the main board and, as before, these responses would serve as the basis for class discussions.

However, remembering the neglect of "culture" in 1998, this time we included pointed questions that would lead them to discuss some particular cultural aspects of ABB's organizational forms. For instance, we asked students to consider whether the company's original matrix organization would have been possible as a working organizational form for so many years if certain values (i.e., Nordic values) had not been so fully represented through the top management of the organization. This allowed us to extend the discussion of organizational theory as culturally laden by including other possible organizational arrangements that may represent historical, cultural, and institutionalized preferences in different societies (e.g., Ethnic Chinese Business Networks; Mexican Grupos, as well as Nordic and Anglo conceptualizations of organization). We emphasized the processual over the structural, and cultural change over permanence by addressing what may have been happening at the company's local levels (the assumed "being local worldwide") underneath assumed common global structuring.

Altogether, the design of our first two virtual activities did not differ much from the traditional mode of case teaching, except that the students were required to prepare and conduct class discussions through computer-mediated communications at a distance. This in itself was a valuable experience by illustrating the difficulties of accomplishing tasks in virtual teams, let alone experiencing cultural differences as part of their collaborations. However, it was the third exercise that presented them, and us, with perhaps the more valuable experiences.

The Return of Incommensurability beyond the Borderlands: BioTech China

This third assignment differed from the other two in that student preparation and learning took place via a simulation (rather than a case) in international ethics (Larsen & Rathcke, 1996), based on ethical dilemmas from real life situations. Existing research on the subject of business ethics in international contexts points to the difficulty of arriving at any universal ethical position (e.g., Barker & Cobb, 2000; Cohen, Pant, & Sharp, 1992; Payne, 1998; Stajkovic & Luthans, 1997; Vogel, 1992). Through "ethical dilemmas" we sought to further question the possibility of a unitary cultural system under conditions of globalization. This possibility was in fact already called into question by the prior cases and our debriefing of them, but it was in this exercise that the more dramatic results of our course occurred both in 1998 and in 2002, for the student's dynamics produced new content for debriefing.

The simulation is made up of a series of decision-making situations in which "bribery" figures prominently. These situations occur in the context of a fictive joint venture (BioTech) between a Danish company (BioDana) and a Chinese company (ChenTech). An expatriate manager, a Dane, on a three-year contract to manage the joint venture in China, is confronted with on-going ethical dilemmas, from arrival in China to everyday activities managing the venture. The dilemmas are arranged in levels of increasing complexity and seriousness of consequences, but in association to each other. They range from a request of grease payment for the expatriate to rent a car upon first arrival in China to the company auditor's suspicions of embezzlement by the expatriate, who then invites the expatriate to pay a bribe.

As we used it in this course, in the next to last unit of the semester, the actual simulation was divided into two parts. In the first part, a general description of the case (formation of the joint venture, sending an expatriate to China, etc.) was handed to the students in each "on location" course and assigned as homework for the following class meeting. Also, students were given the first five dilemmas that confronted the Danish manager, and were asked to choose within each virtual group the decisions (among available multiple choices) that each group would have made if they had to face these situations. They also were asked to write down what kind of consequences they expected from those choices.

It was important to have this first part done as homework. The students became fully familiar with the simulation and the details of the case, but also became aware by design of the simulation that their commitments to a particular course of action at one point would influence their range of choices in later situations. As before, the groups were required to post their responses to the "all participants" e-mail list or discussion board at a particular time prior to the following class meeting.

In 1998 the second part of the simulation occurred in synchronous fashion. We were able to arrange for a class period when both "on location" courses could meet in real-time in a way that was not too disruptive to each course despite the six hour time difference (mid-morning for United States; mid-afternoon for Denmark). During this class period the students received from the instructors, via e-mail, the additional seven ethical dilemmas. These were introduced consecutively by the instructors to the virtual groups, allowed to be discussed within groups for a few minutes, and followed by posting each group's choice to the "all participants" list. The students were also able to offer open-ended decisions (not in multiple choice options) as their responses.

The teaching assistants in each "on location" course moderated the physical situation and observed the students while they were embedded in the task. At the end of the class period the students were asked to fill out two questionnaires to record their experiences both for process and content of the simulation. Discussion and debriefing of the simulation and group experiences took place during the following class periods "on location." Regarding the results, our first surprise was that the responses given during the synchronous activity were consistently oriented toward universalism, while there was more variation and more cultural relativistic responses in the earlier asynchronous homework.

The second surprise might nonetheless explain the first. Some of the United States participants voiced that the level of interaction with their Denmark counterparts during the synchronous discussions was less than they would have liked, while others noted that their Denmark counterparts seemed to simply agree with them rather than engage in discussion. Many cultural stereotypes seemed to have emerged at that point regarding "the Danes." Yet, there were mediating language issues in this situation, in which the Denmark students would take longer to reply as they were making sure that they were communicating correctly in English. Consistent with this, United States students considered that their own personal opinions were reflected in the final results a great deal, while the Denmark students considered theirs to be less so. Such discussion clarified the results by reiterating a consistent preference for "universal solutions" on the part of United States students, which had already appeared in the "headscarf exercise" and possibly glossed over the "organizational universals" in the ABB discussions.

In 2002 we made some significant changes. Rather than using synchronous e-mail interactions, students in each location completed the second part in their "on location" groups (each country's subset of each virtual group) during their own class meetings. Results from these responses were tallied and posted as tables (Denmark and United States responses) on the all participants discussion boards. Students were asked to discuss the significance of these results in their virtual groups (through threaded discussions on their boards). Our questions were guided by arguments about the possibility of "global ethics," which was part of the course readings (Schneider & Barsoux, 1997), as well as the effects of national vs. transnational "codes of conduct" and regulations for multinational corporations. Further, we also wanted to highlight some more critical points regarding the position of countries in the world economy and how these economic differences affect different populations.

Discussions on the team boards were substantial. There was a higher level of engagement than in the previous ABB exercise, and it was clear that the topic of discussion could raise some heated debates. The tables posted on the common board showed that the Denmark side took once again a more cultural relativist approach toward the issues, often seen as social problems, while the United States side was bound to more universalist principles and managerial concerns. The debates that ensued often reflected surprise on the part of the students: That such differences could suddenly appear within groups that apparently had already taken for granted similarities among their members from the previous exercise was deemed unthinkable!

LESSONS FROM "A DISTANCE" IN THE "HERE AND NOW"

Below we offer some additional learnings that resulted from these activities. While some stem from our own reflections over experiences with the
course, others are based on the observations of the students by the teaching assistants and on the students' responses to informal questionnaires.
We should make clear that these results should not be taken as formal
research results of any kind. They are the product of a pedagogical exploration about what we thought was possible at the time. Moreover, we did
not design the course as a research project, and it was only in the process
of learning from the events that unfolded that we thought there was any
merit in sharing these experiences more formally with others.

Learning about Culture

As we reflect upon how activities and interactions evolved throughout
the semester on both occasions, it seems that we did succeed in configuring a situation in which student expectations for more conventional cross-
cultural "comparisons" always ended up in more complicated and difficult-
to-grasp cultural issues. From the Islamic Headscarf case to the BioTech
simulation, students were constantly challenged to abandon their comparative premises and to observe that which could not be so easily articulated.
As indicated, students were surprised to find out by the end of the BioTech
simulation that differences between the two sides remained.

As an illustration, the content of the first case lends itself to discussions
about hybridization and incommensurability, but the debriefing process,
which included the student inputs, became additional content to complicate the situation in an experiential manner. It was not that the Denmark
students were more "relativistic" and the United States students more "universalistic" (as an example of something that kept on creeping up in the
debriefing of all the activities). Rather, the point we made was that comparative notions such as "relativistic" and "universalistic" may conceal that the
label "relativism" could mean something different and not the opposite of
"universalism." Different systems of understanding may be hidden behind
these labels.

Specifically in this case, the "relativistic" arguments made by the Denmark students addressed very concrete knowledge of institutional, legal,
and historical conditions of immigration in France. In contrast, the "universalistic" premises of United States students were a reflection of prior
assumptions referring to United States management theories, which are
supposed to be based on universal principles. Students from each country
were paying attention to the case from very different perspectives and were

therefore repositioning the case within their own preferred (and different) understandings of what the case meant. To a certain extent, they were solving two different cases. As a further point, by debriefing the case in this manner, hybridization may also have happened when we explicitly voiced these theoretical arguments for both locations (how would the students on each side reappropriate and make sense of these arguments over their own prior understandings?). The possibility of incommensurability became, at the same time, a very concrete experiential fact.

Perhaps more interesting were the dynamics created by the students themselves, which were oftentimes unintended but powerfully relevant consequences of our planned activities. One such dynamic worth recalling pertains to language. As indicated above, all the activities plus both courses used English as their language of exchange. In 1998 both courses had a fairly homogeneous composition of students, in which the United States class was fully first-language English while the Denmark class was homogeneously Danish with good working knowledge of English. Issues regarding language appeared as a concern from the Denmark side in which they saw themselves at a disadvantage (for instance, when responding in synchronous activities, which took longer for them) vis-à-vis the United States side.

Things took a different turn in 2002. The Denmark class had 19 nationalities and 16 different languages. There were two native English speakers out of 68 students. In the United States class, one student had English as her second language, but English was the native language of the other 38, including all other international students. Thus, the interactions in English from the Denmark side were more difficult not only because of having to interact with the United States side, but also when working with each other in Denmark before posting responses to discuss with the United States side. Two of us, the original designers of the course, are not native English speakers. Thus, much of the arguments that we heard from our students truly "spoke" to some of our own experiences, and we were quite sympathetic. Perhaps for this same reason, we were unaware at first that something else was happening.

While our own pedagogical interests were reflected on the formal posting on the boards, the students were enacting their own set of "cultural concerns." In fact, discussion boards became very contentious grounds. Possibly one third of the groups were functioning "according to plan," while the rest had decided on other approaches. It was clear that only certain members of each group were participating, which meant that several members of each class did not seem interested in engaging with each other. But those who did participate were transforming the boards into new "borderlands."

It was the international students, both native and non-native English speakers, from both sides who engaged in consistent informal interactions.

They seemed quite comfortable using the technology informally, often using bits and pieces of their own native languages interspersed throughout the English lingua franca (hybridization in action!), and seemed to find it pleasant to create and maintain friendships this way. Interestingly, in most cases the cross-postings were between students of different nationalities who seemed to find on the boards the space to address their common interests as "the foreigners" in their local classrooms. New groups were formed for these purposes out of our original groupings as students shared freely the board passwords. Alliances were forged among strangers in cyberspace!

In retrospect we now see that the way the course "configured itself" in 2002 closely reflects the realities of a global society. The difficulties that we experienced when we thought that the situation was "out of control" are nothing but a reflection of "the real world" of virtual encounters under conditions of globalization. It is gratifying to know that these experiences are similar to other reports regarding virtual teams and recent literature about doing courses of a similar nature (e.g., Hamada & Scott, 2001; Pauleen, 2003; Schallert & Reed, 2003; Walker & Jeurissen, 2003).

The Culture of Technology/the Culture of the Technology

Perhaps the most important learning from these activities is something that we may have missed out of our impetus toward making our theoretical interests come alive through the "virtual teams." While there is no doubt that course activities created several situations in which to highlight issues of incommensurability, hybridization, and common interests, the one thing we did not consider was what type of cultural intervention we were making by bringing these different groups of students together. What kind of new cultural form is created by technological mediation in the context of globalization? What is the culture of technology? What is the culture of the technology? What kind of cultural form is the technology?

We were very wary of the hype about using technology in our classrooms given that many of these claims are based on untested assumptions (see Nissenbaum & Walker, 1998). We also had been involved in discussions about introducing technology in educational contexts, which promptly degenerated into the "nuts and bolts" of the technology at the expense of pedagogical aims (Barab, Thomas, & Merrill, 2001; Schutte, 1996). Thus, we were probably overly cautious, not allowing ourselves to be seduced by the technology, for we did not want to risk losing the objectives of our courses. And yet, for these very reasons, we may have missed bringing into the course the many cultural aspects that are due precisely to the technology.

For instance, the technology itself was and is created and used with a strong level of unidirectionality, dictated by the interests of the West (or more precisely the Triad) to the rest, even if we call it "global" (whose "common interests" are thus represented?). Noticing this is, as well, a way to call attention to the origins of the theories and the texts through which we are teaching "international," as recognized by Schneider & Barsoux (2003). Similarly, it was neither an accident nor just a matter of convenience that the lingua franca in our course was English. The majority of the traffic in the Internet is in English, and as more global interactions occur, and as more countries are added to courses like ours and others through distance education, the more likely it is that English will be given preference, since the major producers of "distance education" are based in Anglo countries (i.e., forced "commensurability"?) What may get lost in that picture?

As discussed above, however, the pace of the required work, as well as time-lags, all contribute to creating unexpected cross-cultural situations that need to be negotiated, often through means others than those "officially sanctioned." First, the fast pace of activities enabled by the technology as much as the shortening of the distance between the two groups (at least from our perspective) was resisted in more than one way by our own students, who often created their own pace and space in parallel to our expectations. That is, the technology can be used in many different forms, and appropriated by all for many different purposes and common interests. Second, this is also an argument in support of hybridization, in which contacts between populations create emerging cultural forms and identities that are more transient and less easily knowable than we often assume.

For example, there were probably new identities in formation, such as many different possibilities for notions of the "global citizen," represented throughout the playful and informal use of the discussion boards by international students as well as in their refusals of our requirements. This should also be noticed in regards to the "on location" composition of our classrooms, which in the short span of 4 years (1998-2002) changed from homogeneous to diverse, heralding the ethnoscapes of globalization in the local context, which so often escape from view (Appadurai, 1990). The students' preferred interactions illustrate the new borderlands, which recreate the global in the local and vice-versa.

It seems that there was indeed "a moose in our cyber-room" which we did not want to notice. This was a sorely missed opportunity but also a main learning point for the future.

Evaluating the virtual teams

In 1998 we decided to evaluate the students' experience with their virtual teams. For that purpose we used a brief questionnaire with open-ended questions, which we repeated in 2002. These were given to the students during the class meeting (in each country) after the last virtual team exercise (BioTech). Based on these responses it is possible to make some general observations about student perceptions and opinions. Table 7.2 summarizes their experiences.

As could be gleaned from Table 7.2, the perceptions from both groups did not always coincide. In general, Denmark students were more able to detect differences in their interactions with the United States students than the other way around, for United States students tended, perhaps unreflectively, to report more cooperation and agreement than was perhaps the case. This may also reflect a tendency towards conflict-avoidance, which is so ubiquitous in United States managerial literature, as well as assuming that more interactions meant better knowledge (on this point, see Schallert & Reed, 2003).

Technological difficulties were present as a concern on both occasions, and this was further compounded by time concerns. Despite the fact that students were more sophisticated in their use of technology in 2002 than they were in 1998, issues around it kept on surfacing. Preference for face-to-face communication could as well be related to these difficulties, but in 2002 there was also more general agreement that group results were better than if they had worked independently. The latter was exactly the opposite in 1998. Therefore, technological difficulties may hinder what otherwise could be a more generalized trend toward preference for teamwork.

This is a less acknowledged and more mundane issue in our experiences, which also points to other limitations faculty and students face when employing information technology in the curriculum. That is, no matter how sophisticated the task, there are technological limitations due to variations in hardware and software used on campus and by students. No surprise, then, that both the business and the instructional literature recommend to maintain technological-mediated interactions as technologically simple as possible (e-mail is a highly recommended approach) no matter how many "bells and whistles" one may consider possible (Solomon, 1998). Technological sophistication often becomes so much the center of attention that we forget the purpose for which we wanted to use it.

Table 7.2. Students Self-reported Experiences Working in Virtual Groups, 1998 and 2002

Year courses were taught	1998		2002	
	Denmark	*U.S.*	*Denmark*	*U.S.*
Like/dislike for technological mediation	Indifference and skepticism about technology's contribution to group results	More indifferent and skeptical; some frustration about problems with technology	General liking for the use of technology; concerns with technological problems; would prefer face-to-face communication	Some liking but also some skepticism; concerns with technological problems; would prefer face-to-face communication
Group dynamics	Cooperation as the norm; but similar results could be attained independently	Highly cooperative as the norm; but similar results could be attained independently	Some friction and saw greater differences of opinion; yet most students said their opinions were taken into account; group work was better than if they had worked on their own	Personal friction and differences of opinion about the task practically nonexistent; group work was better than if they had worked on their own
Cultural learning	"virtual teams" was better than a traditional "on location" learning situation to enlighten cross-cultural ethical dilemmas	"virtual teams" was better than a traditional "on location" learning situation to enlighten cross-cultural ethical dilemmas	Cultural differences were minimal following the ABB activities; differences become greater following the simulation	Cultural differences were minimal in all activities
Time/space concerns	Central concern—i.e., not enough time	Central concern—i.e., not enough time	Central concern—i.e., not enough time	Central concern—i.e., not enough time

CONCLUDING THOUGHTS

Today several issues stand at the center of evaluations about the benefits of distance education: (a) economic issues, including the identity of universities as educational institutions vs. profit-making ventures (Victor, 1999; Young, 2001); (b) pedagogical issues regarding course delivery and reception as well as learning outcomes and accreditation (Alavi, Yoo & Vogel, 1997; Webster & Hackley, 1997); (c) technological issues including both questions of adequate technologies for course delivery (Heerema & Rogers, 2001; Mirabito, 1996; Schank, 2001); and issues about access for particular populations (Ali, 1999; Gladieux & Swail, 1999; Grill, 1999; *International Labour Review,* 2001). Perhaps more importantly, there is still a paucity of quality research that could document some definitive answers for most of these issues (NEA, 2001; Trinkle, 1999).

While we are sitting on the fence in these debates, as they pertain to the elimination of the traditional university and its substitution by virtual universities, we do recognize the unique opportunity the Internet represents toward enhancing our efforts to assist students in constructing new knowledge and in reconstructing existing knowledge. We also recognize that virtual learning situations such as ours raise important questions regarding what we understand by *university*. Essentially, we had two professors and teaching assistants, from two separate, independent institutions in two different countries, collaborating on teaching an undergraduate course in international management. Each had a class of students physically located at each institution and met with them at the officially scheduled time. Yet, we created a third institution, located in cyberspace, where part of our separate courses came together at different points throughout the semester. This institution was neither the United States nor Denmark, nor their local educational institutions, but another institution that transcended the limits of space and time, one that enabled us as educators to collaborate in a way that had not been possible until very recently. Yet, the space we created is different from that generally trotted out in the literature we reviewed in that we have moved beyond merely thinking about transforming our individual bricks-and-mortar institutions into virtual campuses.

We, as individual professors, see advantages in continuing to offer courses within our institutional boundaries, while also working in the borderlands of cyberspace. This is especially pertinent for those of us teaching courses with an international component. We can more easily incorporate other ways of knowing into our cyberspace classrooms, ways that can potentially introduce colleagues and students from countries around the world to experiences that would otherwise be next to impossible without the available technology. Certain hybrid forms, which include both "on location" and "distance," seem to be taking the lead in reconfiguring our higher education institutions today towards those ends (e.g., Drexler et al., 2000; Hamada & Scott, 2001; Lelong & Fearnley-Sander, 1999; Osland et al., this volume). We consider our approaches as part of this trend—a trend that, in our view, represents best the global/local conditions in which we all live.

Under the premises of globalization, then, it is possible to reconsider instruction through these technologies as a blessing in disguise. That is, these instructional approaches may provide a way to debunk the orientation toward education as an end product with a more or less shortened "shelf-life" (as apologists of the marketization of education through "virtual learning" would lead us to believe) and towards an on-going hybridization process of learning to further our common interests despite our differences.

REFERENCES

Adam, N., Awerbuch, B., Slonim, J., Wegner, P., & Yesha, Y. (1997). Globalizing business, education, culture through the Internet. *Communications of the ACM, 40*(2), 115–121.

Adler, N. (1984). Understanding the ways of understanding: Cross-cultural management reviewed. In R. N. Farmer (Ed.), *Advances in international comparative management* (Vol. 1, pp. 31–67). Greenwich, CT: JAI Press.

Adler, N. (1997). *International dimensions of organizational behavior* (3rd ed.). Cincinnati, OH: South-Western.

Alavi, M., Yoo, Y., & Vogel, D. R. (1997). Using information technology to add value to management education. *Academy of Management Journal, 40*, 1310–1333.

Ali, A. J. (1999). Digital divide: A challenge that must be faced. *Advances in Competitiveness Research, 7*(1), i–ii.

Altbach, P. G. (2000). The crisis in multinational higher education: The convergence of multinational and distance education, its promise and challenge. *Change, 32(6), 29–31.*

American Society for Training & Development. *(2003). Online and corporate universities: Online and corporate universities take learning to the head of the class. T&D, 57(9),* 75–86.

Andres, H. P. (2002). A comparison of face-to-face and virtual software development teams. *Team Performance Management, 8(1/2), 39–48.*

Anzaldúa, G. (Ed.). (1987). *Borderlands/La Frontera: The new mestiza.* San Francisco, CA: Spinters/Aunt Lute.

Appadurai, A. (1990). Disjuncture and difference in the global cultural economy. *Public Culture, 2*(2), 1–24.

Barab, S. A., Thomas, M. K., & Merrill, H. (2001). Online learning: From information dissemination to fostering collaboration. *Journal of Interactive Learning Research, 12*(1), 105–143.

Barber, B. R. (1995). *Jihad vs. McWorld.* New York: Times Books.

Barker, T. S., & Cobb, S. L. (2000). A survey of ethics and cultural dimensions of MNCs. *Competitiveness Review, 10*(2), 123–131.

Bhabha, H. K. (1994). *The location of culture.* London: Routledge.

Boyacigiller, N. A., & Adler, N. J. (1991). The parochial dinosaur: Organizational science in a global context. *Academy of Management Review, 16,* 262–290.

Brender, A. (2001, March 30). Distance-education road show. *The Chronicle of Higher Education,* p. A43.

Cellich, C. (2001, January). FAQ frequently asked questions . . . About business negotiations on the Internet: Used effectively, e-mail and the web are good communication channels that business executives can use for negotiations. *International Trade Forum, 10–11.*

Clifford, J. (1986). Introduction: Partial truths. In J. Clifford & G. E. Marcus (Eds.), *Writing culture: The poetics and politics of ethnography* (pp. 1–26). Berkeley, CA: University of California Press.

Cohen, J. R., Pant, L. W., & Sharp, D. J. (1992). Cultural and socioeconomic constraints on international codes of ethics: Lessons from accounting. *Journal of Business Ethics, 11,* 687–700.

Czarniawska, B. (1998). Who is afraid of incommensurability? *Organization, 5,* 273–275.

Czarniawska, B., & Calás, M. B. 1997. Another country: Explaining gender discrimination with "culture." *Administrative Studies, 4,* 326–341.

Daly, C. B. (1996). Teamwork: Does diversity matter? *Harvard Business Review, 74*(3), 10–11.

Day, D., Dosa, M., & Jorgensen, C. (1995). The transfer of research information within and by multicultural teams. *Information Processing & Management, 31*(1), 89–100.

Dimitriades, G., & Kamberelis, G. (1997). Shifting terrains: Mapping education within a global landscape. *The Annals of the American Academy of Political and Social Science, 551,* 137–150.

Drexler, J., Jr., Larson, E., Cogliser, C., Sullivan, D., Watson, M., Miguel, M., Fu, P. P., Schalk, R., & Wang, X. (2000). *We're not just talking about it—we're doing it: A multi-media presentation of employing technology to facilitate learning and thinking critically about global business.* Symposium presented at the annual meeting of the Academy of Management, Toronto, Canada.

Efendioglu, A. M., & Murray, L. W. (2000). Education at a distance: Teaching executives in China. THE (Technological Horizons In Education) Journal, 27(6), 84–87.

Escobar, A. (1995). *Encountering development: The making and the unmaking of the Third World.* Princeton, NJ: Princeton University Press.

Esteva, G., & Prakash, M. D. (1998). *Grassroots post-modernism: Remaking the soil of cultures.* London: Zed.

Fulton, K. (1998). Learning in a digital age: Insights into the issues. *THE (Technological Horizons in Education) Journal, 25*(7), 60–63.

García-Canclini, N. (1995). *Culturas híbridas: Estrategias para entrar y salir de la modernidad.* México (D. F. Grijalbo, Trans.). [Hybrid cultures: Strategies for entering and leaving modernity.] Minneapolis, MN: University of Minnesota Press. (Original work published 1990)

Geertz, C. (1983). "From the native's point of view": On the nature of anthropological understanding. In *Local knowledge: Further essays in interpretive anthropology* (pp. 55–70). New York: Basic Books.

Gladieux, L. E., & Swail, W. S. (1999). The virtual university and educational opportunity: Issues of equity and access for the next generation. *Policy Perspectives.* Washington, DC: The College Board.

Grill, J. (1999). Access to learning: Rethinking the promise of distance education. *Adult Learning, 10(4), 32–36.*

Grove, C., & Hallowell, W. (2001). *Randömia Balloon Factory: A unique simulation for working across the cultural divide.* Yarmouth, ME: Intercultural Press.

Hamada, T., & Scott, K. (2001). Anthropology and international education via the Internet: A collaborative learning model. *The Journal of Electronic Publishing.* Retrieved February 9, 2004, from http://www.press.umich.edu/jep/06-01/hamada.html

Harvey, D. (1989). *The condition of postmodernity.* Oxford: Blackwell.

Heerema, D. L., & Rogers, R. L. (2001). Avoiding the quality/quantity trade-off in distance education. *THE (Technical Horizons in Education) Journal, 29(5),* 14–19.

Hiltz, S. R., & Wellman, B. 1997. Asynchronous learning networks as a virtual classroom. *Communications of the ACM, 40(9), 44–49.*

Hofstede, G. (1980). Motivation, leadership, and organization: Do American theories apply abroad? Organizational Dynamics, 9(1), 42–63.

Hofstede, G. (1993). *Cultural constraints in management theories. Academy of Management Executive, 7(1),* 81–94.

Hofstede, G. (2001). *Culture's consequences: Comparing values, behaviors, institutions, and organizations across nations.* London: Sage Publications.

Huff, T. E. (2001). Globalization and the Internet: Comparing the Middle Eastern and Malaysian experiences. *The Middle East Journal, 55,* 439–453.

International Labour Review. (2001). The digital divide: Employment and development implications (Introduction). *140(2),* 113–117.

Johnson, A. K. (1999). Globalization from below: Using the Internet to internationalize social work education. *Journal of Social Work Education, 35(3), 377–392.*

Kaghan, W., & Phillips, N. (1998). Building the Tower of Babel: Communities of practice and paradigmatic pluralism in organization studies. *Organization, 5,* 191–215.

Kerr, C. (1983). *The future of industrial societies: Convergence of continuing divergence.* Cambridge, MA: Harvard University Press.

Kiser, K. (1999). Working on world time. *Training, 36(3),* 28–34.

Klein, C., & Partridge, J. F. L. (2003). Transnational conversations: A Web pedagogy. *Academic Exchange Quarterly, 7(1),* 282–286.

Kuhn, T. S. (1970). *The structure of scientific revolutions* (2nd ed.). Chicago, IL: The University of Chicago Press.

Laroche, L. (2001). Teaming up. *CMA Management, 75(2),* 22–25.

Larsen, J., & Rathcke, T. (1996). *When in China. . . . BioTech China Ltd.* Odense, Denmark: University of Southern Denmark

Laurent, A. (1983). The cultural diversity of western conceptions of management. *International Studies of Management and Organization, 13* (1/2), 75–96.

Lazear, E. P. (1999). Globalisation and the market for team-mates. *Economic Journal,* *109*(454), 15–16.

Lelong, P., & Fearnley-Sander, M. (1999). E-mail communities: A story of collaboration between students in Australia and Indonesia. *The Social Studies, 90*(3), 114–120.

McCain, B. (1996). Multicultural team learning: An approach towards communication competency. *Management Decision, 34*(6), 65–68.

Michaelsen, S., & Johnson, D. E. (Eds.). (1997). *Border theory: The limits of cultural politics.* Minneapolis, MN: University of Minnesota Press.

Miller, M. A. (1995). Technoliteracy and the new professor. *New Literary History, 26,* 601–611.

Mirabito, M. (1996). Establishing an outline educational program. *THE (Technical Horizons in Education) Journal, 24*(1), 57–60.

Mohanty, C. T. (2003). "Under Western Eyes" revisited: Feminist solidarity through anticapitalist struggles. *Signs, 28,* 499–535.

Molnar, A. S. (1997). Computers in education: A brief history. *THE (Technological Horizons in Education) Journal, 24*(11), 63–68.

Myers, W. (1992). New applications for information technology. *IEEE Software, 9*(3), 102–103.

NEA (National Education Association). (2001). Focus on distance education. *Update, 7*(2).

Neale, R., & Mindel, R. (1992). Rigging up multicultural teamworking. *Personnel Management, 24*(1), 36–39.

Nissenbaum, H., & Walker, D. (1998). A grounded approach to social and ethical concerns about technology and education. *Journal of Educational Computing Research, 19,* 411–432.

Osland, J., Bird, A., Maznevski, M., McNett, J., Mendenhall, M., Scholz, C., Stein, V., & Brunner, D. (this volume). Global reality with virtual teams: Lessons from the Geographically Distant Multicultural Teams Project. In C. Wankel & R. DeFillippi (Eds.), *The cutting edge of international management: Research in management education and development* (Vol. 3, Ch. 6.) Greenwich, CT: Information Age Publishing.

Pauleen, D. J. (2003). Lessons learned crossing boundaries in an ICT-supported distributed team. *Journal of Global Information Management, 11*(4), 1–19.

Payne, S. L. (1998). Recognizing and reducing transcultural ethical tension. *The Academy of Management Executive, 12*(3), 84–85.

Phatak, A. V. (1997). *International management, concepts & cases.* Cincinnati, OH: South-Western.

Pieterse, J. N. (1995). Globalization as hybridization. In M. Featherstone, S. Lash & R. Robertson (Eds.), *Global modernities* (pp. 45–68). London: Sage.

Redding, S. G. (1994). Comparative management theory: Jungle, zoo or fossil bed? *Organization Studies, 15, 323–359.*

Rice, C. D. (1996). Bring intercultural encounters into classrooms: IECC electronic mailing lists. *THE (Technological Horizons In Education) Journal, 23*(6), 60–63.

Saldívar, J. D. (1997). *Border matters: Remapping American cultural studies.* Berkeley: University of California Press.

Schallert, D. L., & Reed, J. H. (2003). Intellectual, motivational, textual, and cultural considerations in teaching and learning with computer-mediated discussion. *Journal of Research on Technology in Education, 36*(2), 103–118.

Schank, R. C. (2001). Revolutionizing the traditional classroom course: Is the computer the device that can change the campus as we know it? *Communications of the ACM, 44*(12), 21–24.

Schneider, S. C., & Barsoux, J.-L. (1997). Citizens of the world: Business ethics and social responsibility (Ch. 10). *Managing across cultures.* New York: Prentice Hall/Financial Times.

Schneider, S. C., & Barsoux, J.-L. (2003). *Managing across cultures* (2nd ed.). New York: Prentice Hall/Financial Times.

Schutte, J. G. (1996). *Virtual teaching in higher education: The new intellectual superhighway or just another traffic jam?* Northridge, CA: California State University, Department of Sociology. Retrieved February 9, 2004 from http://www.csun.edu/sociology/virexp.htm

Secretary's Commission on Achieving Necessary Skills (SCANS). (1991). *What work requires of students.* Washington, DC: U.S. Department of Labor.

Shirts, R. G. (1977). *Bafá-Bafá: A cross-culture simulation.* Del Mar, CA: Simile II.

Simons, R. L., & Bartlett, C. A. (1992). *Asea Brown Boveri: HBS Case 9–192–139.* Cambridge, MA: Harvard Business School.

Sinclair, J., Jacka, E., & Cunningham, S. (Eds.). (1996). *New patterns in global television: Peripheral vision.* New York: Oxford University Press.

Singelis, M. (2000). Some thoughts on the future of cross-cultural social psychology. *Journal of Cross-Cultural Psychology, 31*, 76–91.

Sitze, A. (2002). Language of business: Can e-learning help international companies speak a common language? Some say it can, but expect rough waters when it comes to getting learners to sign on. *Online Learning, 6*(3), 19–22.

Solomon, C. M. (1998). Building teams across borders. *Workforce, 3*(6), 12–17.

Søndergaard, M., & Naumes, W. (under review). ABB Transformers–Denmark (A+B). *North American Case Research Journal,* 1–13.

Stajkovic, A. D., & Luthans, F. (1997). Business ethics across cultures: A social cognitive model. *Journal of World Business, 32*(1), 17–34.

Taylor, C. (1985). Understanding and ethnocentricity. In *Philosophy and the human sciences* (pp. 116–133). New York: Cambridge University Press.

Trinkle, D. A. (1999, August 6). Distance education: A means to an end, no more, no less. *The Chronicle of Higher Education,* p. A60.

Victor, D. (1999). Electronic classrooms and virtual publishing: A look beyond the writing requirement. *Business Communication Quarterly, 62*(1), 74–81.

Vogel, D. (1992). The globalization of business ethics: Why America remains distinctive. *California Management Review, 35*(1), 30–49.

Walker, R., & Jeurissen, R. (2003). E-based solutions to support intercultural business ethics instruction: An exploratory approach in course design and delivery. *Journal of Business Ethics, 48*(1), 113–126.

Webster, J., & Hackley, P. (1997). Teaching effectiveness in technology mediated distance learning. *Academy of Management Journal, 40*, 1282–1309.

Wesley-Smith, T. (2003). Net gains? Pacific studies in cyberspace. *The Contemporary Pacific, 15*(1), 117–138.

Wheeler, D. L. (1998). Global culture or culture clash: New information technologies in the Islamic world—a view from Kuwait. *Communication Research, 25,* 359–376.

Yergin, D., & Stanislaw, J. (1998). *The commanding heights: The battle between government and the marketplace that is remaking the modern world.* New York: Simon and Schuster.

Young, J. F. (2001, June 29). Logging in with ... Farhad Saba: Professor says distance education will flop unless universities revamp themselves. *The Chronicle of Higher Education, p. A33.*

section III

TEACHING PERSPECTIVES

CHAPTER 8

GAINING A GLOBAL MINDSET

The Use of Stories in International Management Education

Mila Gascó-Hernández and Teresa Torres-Coronas

Most ideas about teaching are not new, but not everyone knows the old ideas
—Euclid, 300 BC

INTRODUCTION: THE INTERNATIONAL MANAGER
AND THE NEED FOR A GLOBAL MINDSET

A new revolution is taking place in our societies—a digital revolution. Different from the precedent industrial one, this transition toward a digital era is characterized by the spread of new information and knowledge technologies, globalization, and networking activities. This new environment is giving rise to numerous transformations in different fields, one of which is corporate human resources strategy. Specifically, global businesses are taking very purposeful steps to develop what have been called *global executives*.

Not much consensus exists on what global managers are, although everybody agrees that they are not just expatriates. Ferraro (2002) argues that global managers are "those who have the agility to operate in a rapidly

The Cutting Edge of International Management Education, pages 203–222

changing marketplace and those with the experience at working with different legal systems, political structures, languages, tax systems, customs, and ethical systems" (p. 158). In addition to this, Dalton, Ernst, Deal, and Leslie (2002) explain that global executives today must have a set of capabilities that allows them to successfully manage the complex challenges that attend today's global business environment. These authors identify four categories of skills which they call *pivotal capabilities*: (a) the ability to understand how business is conducted in each country and culture in which global managers have responsibilities (international business knowledge); (b) the knowledge of cultural differences (cultural adaptability); (c) the ability to know, understand, and act in accordance with the deeply held values and beliefs of people from other cultures (cultural empathy); and (d) the ability to be creative (innovation).

Indeed, global managers must have global mindsets. They must possess the "tendency to scan the world from a broad perspective" (Srinivas, 1995, p. 30). That is why, in addition to the pivotal capabilities listed above, global managers are characterized by the following attributes: (a) curiosity and concern with context; (b) acceptance of complexity and its contradictions; (c) consciousness of and sensitivity to diversity;[1] (d) ability to seek opportunity in surprises and uncertainties; (e) faith in organizational processes; (f) a focus on continuous improvement; (g) possession of an extended time perspective; and (h) an emphasis on systems thinking (Srinivas, 1995).

Although several books have been written on the needs and attributes of global managers in today's business world, most international management university courses have not been adapted accordingly. For one thing, course content remains largely unchanged. What is needed is new coursework and direct experience in management of cultural diversity, implementation of global strategies and structures, and expertise in dealing with ethical issues in global management and international manufacturing. Also, no matter where business schools are located, the same North American and European textbooks and case studies are used. Consequently, the authors' assumptions and cultural perspectives (which are usually ethnocentric) influence students' perception processes while, on the other hand, students' motivation to learn declines. Leavitt (1989) summarizes these ideas:

> Among the right things that we already teach quite well . . . are analytical methods.... We also do a pretty good job of teaching, descriptively, about business.... But there are many right things we don't teach adequately. We don't, for example, teach our rather chauvinistic American students to think globally. (p. 39)

Cavusgil and Ghauri (1990) add: "We often accept our own culture and its ways as the norm and tend to judge others by our own standards"[2] (quoted in Maclachlan, 1993, p. 168).

Despite this situation, the fact is that intercultural education for managers matters. In this sense, Ojile (1986) states that this type of education should be a structured learning experience that increases the sensitivity of individuals in cross-cultural situations. This structured learning experience should combine knowledge and skills from the fields of communications, psychology, management, and cultural anthropology in order to improve adaptation to new cultural environments, including interethnic and inter-class situations. According to the author, this structured learning experience is not merely a guide to or list of appropriate cultural conducts, because it aims to provide the training required to evaluate a wide range of cultural interactions and the flexibility to respond to specific events and situations. With these skills, specialists and professionals reduce their chances of (a) offending foreign colleagues, (b) making interpersonal errors, (c) making financial errors, and (d) misunderstanding the signals that may lead to future business opportunities. The teaching associated with intercultural education is based on adult education methods. The cognitive-experiential models combine factual information with exercises—including case studies, critical incident analysis, and simulations—through which the participants learn about their feelings and experiences

It is therefore the intention of this chapter to show a new methodology, based on anthropological method, for teaching international management. Particularly, the focus will be on the ways that stories and storytelling can help business professors worldwide train their students in innovative and creative ways to develop a global mindset while avoiding ethnocentrism.

STORIES AS A PEDAGOGICAL TOOL IN MANAGEMENT EDUCATION AND DEVELOPMENT

Both innovative and creative pedagogical tools for enhancing the effectiveness of management education and development have been developed during the last few decades. Music and the mystique of magic as proposed by Wheatley (1998) are two first-class examples. Other methodologies are related to the use and analysis of movies (Champoux, 1999); the use of novels as proposed by Knights and Willmott (1999) in their book, *Management Lives: Power and Identity in Contemporary Organizations;* the use of folklore (Torres & Arias, 2003); and the use of modern history to analyze what contributes to leader effectiveness and cultural diversity, as proposed by Mello (1999). Examples of how arts-based learning is being practiced in management education can be found in Nissley (2002). All of these new pedagogical tools can be seen as "other ways of communicating, creating knowledge, and making sense of the complexities of managing in the New Economy" (Nissley, 2002, p. 46).

Particularly expert in the field of developing a global mindset is Srinivas (1995), who proposes such training approaches as video cases, simulations, specific language training, anthropology courses, sensitivity training, and intercultural workshops. The main problem when applying these techniques is that they have been generated in the West. This is precisely where the techniques are being used, so a major question is whether such methods are appropriate in all cultural contexts (Srinivas, 1995).

To answer this question requires analyzing those elements that all nations and cultures have in common, such as stories, legends, myths, and folktales.[3] As the American writer Ursula K. LeGuin once said:

> The story—from Rumpelstiltskin to *War and Peace*—is one of the basic tools invented by the mind of man, for the purpose of gaining understanding. There have been great societies that did not use the wheel, but there have been no societies that did not tell stories. (LeGuin, 1970, p. 31)

Every civilization has constructed stories and myths. For most of human history, oral tradition has been the best medium for communicating a particular viewpoint or idea about life and culture. Romance songs used in the medieval era in Europe and Native American folktales are two examples of oral tradition. Because myths and stories are vehicles of communicating values and role models (Olsson, 2002, 2000), storytelling is one of the best tools for developing the explicit dimension of a global mindset (i.e., being sensitive to the needs of other people through an understanding of their cultures).

In management development, an organizational story is defined as "a tale about a person caught in one situation unfolding from start to climax to resolution" (Boje, 1991, quoted in Morgan & Dennehey, 1997, pp. 497–498), or a "narrated or written information that serves to enrich the understanding of an organization and its people" (Kaye, 1996, quoted in Forster, Cebis, Majteles, Mathur, Morgan, and Preuss et al., 1999, p. 11). In recent years, management researchers, consultants, and practitioners have become increasingly interested in the importance of stories to represent what goes on inside organizations (a) to motivate and educate employees; (b) to consolidate corporate culture by illustrating how things are done; (c) to adapt to change (Kaufman, 2003; Collison & MacKenzie, 1999; Kaye & Jacobson, 1999; Hansen & Kahnweiler, 1996; Wilkins, 1984); (d) to communicate values[4] (McCollum, 1992); and (e) to act as a sense-making device within organizations (Gabriel, 2000).

Generally speaking, "stories tell us about the nature of organizations as distinct forms of human collectivity" (Gabriel, 2000, p. 2), or as it can be appreciated in Denning's book *The Springboard: How Storytelling Ignites Action in Knowledge-Era Organizations* (2000), stories help us understand relationships from the point of view of a participant who is acting in the world. Stories are a source of data whereby researchers can capture organizational life and a management learning tool (Gold, 1996). Thus, stories can provide unique insights into managerial action and thinking. Studies by Hannabuss (2000), Morgan and Dennehy[5] (1997), and Greco[6] (1999) have all confirmed this. These studies help us to understand why "narrative has played a central part in the well-established tradition of case-study teaching in management education" (Watson, 2001, p. 388). The art of storytelling is an essential managerial skill for organizational leaders (Forster et al., 1999). Stories can encourage behavioral and attitudinal mind-shifts (Brown, 1995), so they have been used to teach business ethics (see Watson, 2003).

Although many authors agree about how powerful stories are when teaching management-related concepts, not much research has been carried out that emphasizes the use of storytelling as a pedagogical tool. According to Greco (1996), stories have not been studied as learning tools in management education settings, although in organizational settings, the use of stories and metaphors in teaching is now well-documented (Greco, 1996; Phillips, 1995; Barley, 1983; Morgan, 1980).

The few studies which have been found have produced the following results (Zemke, 1990): (a) Stories told with words of high visual imagery stimulated better long-term retention than did repetition; (b) students who were instructed to visualize the action and content of a story were better able to remember its key ideas that students who were instructed to memorize sentences from the story; (c) students who were taught principles through storytelling rather than through straight exposition were more creative in applying the principles; and (d) both students and instructors reported that using stories makes learning more meaningful and fun (Morgan & Dennehy, 1997).

From a pedagogical point of view, storytelling is the transformation of analytical thinking; it takes students onto a more imaginative level, from left brain thinking to right brain thinking. By telling the right kind of story, instructors can cause profound changes. Because stories stir emotions, they are likely to be remembered. In Bell's (1992) words: "A good story can touch something familiar in each of us and, yet, show us something new about our lives, our world, and ourselves" (p. 53). And that is why stories are so powerful, because they are capable of appealing to both hearts and minds (McConckie & Boss, 1994).

As stated in Vance (1991), the potential learning contribution of story-telling includes concept learning, vicarious learning,[7] learner expectations for success, and learner attention. The first two areas involve learning within the cognitive domain (Bloom, 1956), while the next two areas fall within the affective domain (Krathwohl, Bloom, & Masia, 1964). Vance's message (1991) is that "storytelling, which is widely recognised as having a powerful influence upon informal learning in organisations, should be formalised" (p. 56) as a way to facilitate understanding and to help to build knowledge. In organizational learning, the value and meaning of a story-telling workshop is illustrated by Abma (2003). In this kind of workshop, people come together to exchange stories, "to relate stories to each other and collaboratively create meaning" (Abma, 2003, p. 223).

When teaching international management, all the above applies. Stories in general, and folktales[8] in particular, have a significance due to their direct relationship to culture and cultural values that may help managers to develop a global mindset, enabling them to understand the roots of local workers' behavior (Grimaldi, 1986). As Geertz (1973) points out, a thorough understanding of the details of any specific culture can help to gain understanding of the very nature of the human being:

> Whatever else modern anthropology asserts . . . it is firm in the conviction that men unmodified by the customs of a particular place do not in fact exist, have never existed, and most important, could not in the very nature of the case exist. (Geertz, 1973, p. 36)

The use of stories and narratives[9] is one of the best ways to facilitate under-standing and to develop a global mindset. According to Carter (1993),

> [Stories and narratives capture] in a special fashion the richness and nuances of meaning in human affairs . . . [which] can not be expressed in definitions, statements of fact, or abstract propositions. . . . From this perspective, story is a distinctive mode of explanation characterized by an intrinsic multiplicity of meaning. . . . (Carter, 1993, pp. 1–8 as quoted in Jabri & Pounder, 2001, p. 683)

In summary, members of any culture can understand stories and narra-tives, because all over the world, from early childhood,[10] storytelling is a common practice. Stories are not a *new pedagogical tool, but a tool that needs to be reinvented.*

STORIES IN INTERNATIONAL MANAGEMENT EDUCATION
AND DEVELOPMENT

The purpose of this section is to show how to use storytelling when training and developing international managers, no matter what their culture is. This section is not about theories on how to gain a global mindset, but about a methodology that the authors have been using with management students, particularly with MBA course participants. The authors of this chapter will discuss their own experiences related to (a) how stories are used in a class context, (b) how stories are presented, (c) how students work with them, and (d) what students really learn.

Storytelling is a pedagogical tool that can be used successfully in international management courses. In such courses, several seminars take place, each of them focusing on a particular culture. The objective of these seminars is to help students gain cultural understanding as well as to break cultural assumptions down. This section will explain how the module about Japanese culture, "Building awareness about Japanese culture," is developed by means of folktales. The authors used a module on Japanese culture because Japanese culture is one of the most analyzed cultures and is likely to be more familiar to students than other cultures. A brief example about "Building awareness about African culture" can be found in Appendix B.[11]

Learning Objectives

The overall goal of the "Building awareness about Japanese culture" seminar is to involve participants in an engaging learning activity that illustrates basic principles of the Japanese culture as well as their implications for international management. The different activities and the final discussion should enable students to achieve the following objectives:

- To make implicit assumptions about Japanese culture explicit.
- To understand the key attributes of Japanese culture.
- To evaluate and interpret the differences between the assumptions and the real characteristics of Japanese culture.
- To discuss how cultural misconceptions influence international management.

Conducting the Seminar

Ideally, there should be no time constraints for a seminar like this one. However, instructors should allow a minimum of one and one half hours as a minimum for an introductory explanation, the development of the exercise, and an adequate discussion afterwards. The only materials needed are the story or stories to be analyzed and a flip chart. The seminar has four distinct parts as described below.

Part 1. Unleashing Assumptions about Japanese Culture

After asking the students to gather in teams, the instructor explains how the seminar will be conducted. The first task for each team is to expose the assumptions the team members have about Japanese culture. The instructor should emphasize that, in a seminar about a less familiar culture (such as the Nigerian culture), it may be extremely difficult for the students to make any assumptions. In a case like that, the whole class will participate as a group in the exercise, and the instructor will facilitate the exercise by referring to the broader culture instead of to the specific culture. For example, the instructor will focus mainly on African culture rather than on Nigerian culture.

Part 2. Reading the Story and Discussing the Findings

Next, the students will read a story set within the culture of focus for the seminar. If possible, someone should tell the story. It would be particularly enriching to have someone from the country that is being considered tell the story.

In the Japanese culture seminar, one of the stories the authors use is "The Story of Prince Yamato Take." The participants receive a piece of paper that contains the following information:

> **Source**: Amy Blom's Web page http://students.ou.edu/B/Amy.C.Blom-1/folklore/story3.htm
>
> **Origin**: This story was originally from the Kojiki, a collection of Shinto myths and stories about the origin of Japan, dating from 712 AD. The exploits of Yamato Take, who was supposedly the son of one of the first Emperors in Japan, are explored in much greater detail in the Kojiki. This particular tale recounts Yamato Take's earliest days and demonstrates many of the qualities inherent in the Samurai tradition; thus, this story illustrates some of the more important values that prevail in Japanese culture.
>
> **The Story**: (See Appendix A).

Part 3. What We Thought versus What We Think

The whole group of students working together is asked to compare the results of Part 1 and Part 2 (each part has generated a different list). This is one of the most important parts of the seminar because one of its main goals is to identify and eliminate cultural barriers and assumptions.

Once Part 3 is finished, the instructor explains the implications of the Japanese values found throughout the story—in this case, implications for Japanese management.[12] Thus, the instructor emphasizes those elements that must be taken into account when Japanese firms are analyzed from the perspectives of other cultures or when executives from outside Japan want to deal with Japanese managers. Some of these elements are summarized in Table 8.1.

Table 8.1.   Comparative Analysis: The Samurai versus Japanese Management Culture

Endless Loyalty	
The Samurai world	"*Samurai still hold great fascination for the Japanese, influencing national thought today. One extreme example of modern ideas echoing the way of the Samurai is the methods of Japanese kamikaze pilots in World War II. Their choice to sacrifice life for the sake of honor and country came directly out of the old Samurai tradition*" (Blom, 2003). http://students.ou.edu/B/Amy.C.Blom-1/folklore/story3.htm
	"*Shintoism, another Japanese doctrine, gives Bushido its loyalty and patriotism. Shintoism includes ancestor-worship which makes the Imperial family the fountainhead of the whole nation. It awards the emperor a god-like reverence.*" (http://mcel.pacificu.edu/as/students/bushido/bindex.html).
Japanese management	In the Japanese business culture, there is a strong sense of loyalty to the company one belongs to. Once a worker joins a firm, s/he stays there for a long period of time. Some years ago (before the economic crisis that hit all societies), the Japanese had lifelong jobs and they could easily spend thirty or forty years in the same company.
	Japanese are loyal to the company they work in but they also develop a strong feeling of belonging to the company. Therefore, many times, when a Japanese is asked for her/his occupation, s/he usually replies that s/he is a Sony or Hitachi woman/man instead of an accountant, a sales person, or a business manager.
	This loyalty principle gives rise to the importance of seniority and age in Japanese management. Thus, the wages of employees in the Japanese recruitment system are linked to the number of years worked. This is based on the premise of securing long-term loyalty to the firm. Finally, tight and long bonds with providers and customers are also a consequence of the Samurai loyalty value.

Table 8.1.   Comparative Analysis: The Samurai versus Japanese Management Culture (Cont.)

Concentration and focus on a goal

The Samurai world	"*Zen Buddhism became widely adapted by the Samurai later on during the Warrior Period. Zen Buddhism focuses on the discipline of individuals, one of the many reasons why Samurai are seen as very refined warriors. They are often portrayed as being able to sense an enemy's attacks before they actually happen. This is an exaggeration of a Samurai's ability to concentrate and focus on a goal.*" (http://www.wowessays.com/dbase/af1/arm191.shtml).
Japanese management	The goal of Japanese businesses is to serve society. Therefore, they pay extra attention to the customer and the market.

Courage and honor

The Samurai world	"*The Samurai Spirit (bushi-dou)* involved not only skills with martial arts, but also absolute loyalty, a strong sense of personal honor (mei-yo), devotion to duty, and courage, if required, to sacrifice one's own life in battle" (http://www.chicagotribune.com/business/showcase/chi-020901measelle,0,2084666.story? coll=chi-newsspecials-hed).
Japanese management	Japanese management prompts ordinary workers to respond with readiness to share the burden of risk and responsibility for the company's affairs. This shows, in particular, in the fact that no union puts forward demands for higher wages when their company is going through hard times.

Social obligation

The Samurai world	"The Samurai does not always pursue profits, which are necessary in one's life, but are only secondary in the life of a Samurai" (http://www.chicagotribune.com/business/showcase/chi-020901measelle,0,2084666.story?coll=chi-newsspecials-hed).
Japanese management	Japanese firms do not only pursue an economic benefit but a social one. They measure their contribution more by the quality of service rendered than by whether they are making a good living out of it.

Benevolence

The Samurai world	"Samurai are leaders in a society. They have three codes: (1) giri—social obligation; (2) on—the concept of benevolence and thus obligation to the lesser status; (3) ninjo—a human feeling—a kind of tolerance for human nature" (http://www.digitalessays.com/ geography/009.shtml).
Japanese management	Disciplinary measures are very uncommon in Japanese firms since top level managers are always trying to keep the social harmony in the company. In fact, workers tend to be treated as family members so that the harmonic environment is kept.

Source: Gascó and Torres

Finally, the instructor provides the students with additional bibliography such as *Theory Z: How American Business Can Meet the Japanese Challenges* by William Ouchi, and *The Mind of the Strategist: The Art of Japanese Business* by Kenichi Ohmae. Other books on Japanese management are listed at http://www.clearbridge.com/Bibliography/aow_bibliography4b.htm).

The magazine *Japanese Management Today can be found at* http://www.apmforum.com/japan/jmt.htm

Part 4. Debriefing

To help connect the students' past experiences with future experiences, it is useful to have students think carefully about what has been discussed. Students thus gain a deeper understanding of the role that stories and storytelling have in building a global mindset. The seminar is successful when the students, on their own, are able to draw conclusions about the need

- To understand better what culture awareness is and what culture awareness is not
- To understand the impact of cultural awareness on international management
- To understand a new model of cultural learning
- To become aware of their own culture
- To start building a global mindset and become less ethnocentric

CONCLUSION

Neither formal nor in-depth research about the specific use of folktales in international management education and development has yet been conducted, and this chapter was not written to address this issue. The chapter was designed to highlight the ease with which stories from all around the world can be used to foster a global mindset. Stories and folktales can be used to fill up gaps in intercultural training programs.

Humankind possesses a unique pedagogic tool. From the beginning, the most complex training has used stories. The experience of the authors has demonstrated the viability of using storytelling in international management education and development. This approach, although it needs further development,[13] provides international management educators with a wonderful and powerful teaching method that is particularly appropriate for those educators wishing to encourage and motivate graduate students and international managers. One of the most important aspects of this approach is that students learn that there is no "superior" culture. By learning something about other cultures, students can understand that our own realities and truths are not the only ones.

Two interesting aspects about stories used as pedagogical tools need to be emphasized. First, stories "travel easily, mutating along the way, resurfacing in unexpected places in unexpected shapes" (Gabriel, 2000, p. 13). Second, as stories are passed on, they are heard differently by different people, depending on their own culture and experience. This is the case with "The Frog and the Scorpion"[14] story:

> A scorpion wanted to cross a stream and to go to the other bank. He approached a frog and requested a ride on his back. The frog said he would oblige if the scorpion promised not to sting. It was duly agreed upon, and they started the journey. Sure enough, half way across the stream, the scorpion could control himself no longer and stung the frog on his back. Despite the pain, the frog said nothing, continued the swim, and reached the other bank with his rider. The scorpion was very thankful and asked the frog whether he was not annoyed that he had been stung despite the promise. The frog politely said, "Stinging is in your nature. No, I did not expect to be able to change your basic nature so easily." The surprised scorpion shot back, "When you knew that you were going to be stung, why did you still agree to transport me?" The frog replied, "Obliging others is in my basic nature, and I could not change it!"

The story of the Frog and the Scorpion is a crystallized fable about humankind. It carries a basic message common throughout the globe, and it is a way of handing down wisdom from generation to generation—despite some important cultural differences.

NOTES

1. This provides the strength to question one's own assumptions, values and beliefs as well as sensitivity to the assumptions and needs of others.
2. A good example can be found in the movie *My Big Fat Greek Wedding* directed by Joel Zwick. When the Greek family of the main character, Toula, meets the US family of her boyfriend everybody judges the other's family by their own standards. They try to be polite but they find very difficult to forget they own cultural background.
3. In his book *Storytelling in organizations*, Yiannis Gabriel gives a thoughtful overview of stories starting with folktales and how they differ from other narratives. As he explains legends have a historical grounding. Myths carry grand sacral meaning that are alien to stories, they seek to explain, justify, and console. Within this folkloric universe storytelling is a process whose primary aim is entertain audiences.
4. Because "narrative consists of events and evaluations: what happened and what its moral meaning is" (Linde, 2001, p. 163) it becomes a powerful mean of transmitting social knowledge within organizations.

5. They pointed out that through storytelling managers can learn more about their organizations, interpret behaviors they observe, and understand the organization's culture.

6. His results show that participants view stories as a way to handle reality, to bring theory and application nearer to congruence and, to short circuit the defenses that keep behavior more constant in response to increasing pressure for change. "As familiar, user-friendly packets of complexity, experience of meaning, stories have practical value as a learning device in the workplace" (Greco, 1999, p. 48).

7. Fox (2003) proposed a new methodology to teach cultural issues. He calls it "vicarious culture learning". This proposed methodology builds on the strengths of simulations learning and go beyond it introducing detailed cross-cultural elements and life situations presented in literature, taking into account that "the use of cross-cultural literature must be chosen and reflected with intentionality" (p. 105).

8. A folktale is a story that, in its plot, is pure fiction and has no particular location in either time or space. However, despite its elements of fantasy, a folktale is actually a symbolic way of presenting the different means by which human beings cope with the world in which they live. Every folktale or story has a typical sequence (Haye and Jacobson, 1999): the story, the understanding, and the meaning. The meaning is directly related with the learning outcome.

9. As defined in Jabri and Founder (2001), "narrative is the expression of actual human experience, in the form of personal stories (p. 682)." Boje (2003) splits the concepts of story and narrative: "Story is an account of incidents or events, but narrative comes alter and adds 'plot' and 'coherence' to the story line". Gabriel (2000) also agrees that stories should no be equated with narratives. As summarized in Matzdorf and Ramage (2003) Gabriel's story definition is "story = narrative + plot + entertainment + personal experience + sense-making."

10. For example, the use of fairy tales helps build metaphorical knowledge through analogies. Fairytales are an important means of learning and communication, and because "they bypass defensive barriers we may have, they therefore are powerful educational tools" (Öztel & Hinz, 2001, p. 163). They represent both a form of entertainment and a way of learning about moral, other cultures and acceptable standards of behavior and conduct. They are part of the learning process and new life experiences can be given meaning and context (Kaye, 1996).

11. It is necessary to point out that that to speak of "Japanese culture" and "African culture" is, to a large extent, a generalization that may even be stereotyped, abstract, and even incorrect, although it may be licit and pedagogical, in the same way that Weber makes use of ideal types. Actually, anthropologists distinguish different levels of cultures: International culture, national culture and subcultures (Kottak, 1994). An international culture gathers cultural traditions that expand beyond the national frontiers. The term national culture is used to refer to experiences, beliefs, learned behaviour patterns and values shared by the citizens of a country. Because all cultures are diverse (a society is formed by numerous different groups of people), a culture can be divided into subcultures, that is, traditions and patterns based in different symbols which are associated to subgroups in a

complex society. For example, in a complex country such as the United States, Canada or even Spain (a much smaller country), there are multiple subcultures according to race, ethnicity, region or religion.

12.   Sometimes, an executive from a Japanese company is invited so s/he can conduct this part of the seminar. This experience is usually more enriching both for the students and the instructor. If a third person cannot join the class, expatriates' stories as a learning reference material available on the Internet are also recommended as suggested by Glanz (2003).

13.   Several issues have not been addressed in this introductory chapter to storytelling. The Internet as the most significant medium for storytelling, the good and erroneous information conveyed by the entertainment media, the possibility of using stories derived from reality, the manipulation of storytelling through interactive media (Stapleton and Huges, 2003), the different translations of a unique story or the language employed in storytelling only a few examples. We have not addressed either the use of storytelling in other disciplines such as legal practice (Mansfield, 1995); nursing (in order to identify careers' needs such as Wilcock et al., 2003, mention); or other educational settings such as English composition (Blaisdell, 2003), business ethics (Watson, 2003) or primary schools where storytelling has been used, for example, to improve childrens' self-concept (Mello, 2001). And last, but not least, another interesting issue is the potential of narratives as a research tool in accounting and management research (Llewellyn, 1999). There is no doubt that storytelling is a worthy world to explore.

14.   This story was submitted to us by Professor R. Ramamurthy from India, and it has been tested with both Indian and Spanish students. The general conclusions by Indian students were: (a) The frog had an orientation of selfless service, (b) noble persons remain noble irrespective of the action of knaves, (c) it is not easily possible to change the basic nature of individuals; it takes a long time, if at all and (d) when you deal with people, examine the compatibility of basic natures and be prepared for eventualities in case of disharmony. The basic conclusions by Spanish students were: (a) The frog wasn't very clever and (b) it is not worthy to behave in a way that is profitless for us.

APPENDIX A
BUILDING AWARENESS ABOUT JAPANESE CULTURE:
THE STORY OF PRINCE YAMATO

The Emperor was very proud of his son. He always had been. The boy was courageous and strong, almost to the point of being brutal, and never hesitated to prove his devotion to his father, the Heavenly Sovereign of Japan. In fact, it was exactly this tendency that sometimes alarmed the Emperor. He watched his brave young son as the boy bowed low, begging for permission to take care of the thieves Kumaso and Takeru.

"It is not your affair; others can solve this problem," he began weakly, but his son interrupted. "Why? I simply wish to serve you and bring honor to your venerable name!" complained the prince Yamato. His father knew this was true, but also suspected that the Prince wished to stir up trouble. "You're only sixteen, there will be time later . . ."

"By sixteen, I am a man by law. Your Highness, please . . ."

And so it went, until finally the Emperor agreed, wearily ordering many of his men to join the prince on his journey. Ecstatic about his upcoming adventure, Yamato ran to visit his aunt, the Princess Yamato. As he left, she caught his sleeve and gave him a gift to bring him luck on his trip. Although grateful, the prince didn't see how her finely spun silk *kimono* was going to help him much in fighting outlaws.

The next morning, the prince and his father's soldiers set out, riding quickly to where the criminals had last been seen. Before long, they were in a thick wilderness, and it was difficult for the soldiers to follow him through the forest. Instead of slowing down, Prince Yamato sped up, announcing that he would kill the evildoers himself while the others could rest. Perhaps they didn't like the idea, but there was really nothing else they could do.

Before long Prince Yamato heard music, and discovered the outlaws he sought in a clearing, celebrating their last raid. There were several frightened women there, who had been kidnapped by Kumaso and Takeru that very night. They huddled outside and shivered whenever the outlaws' laughter bellowed out from within their cave. Leaving his horse in the forest, Yamato walked purposefully toward them, now certain of how to make use of his aunt's gift. He changed into her clothing, and although the women were surprised and a little confused, they did help him to comb out his hair and dress properly. Once completely attired, even they were shocked by how beautiful and feminine Prince Yamato looked. The next time a girl came out of the cave to get another saké bottle, Prince Yamato took it from her and returned in her place.

He sat down next to the larger thief, chuckling inside at their jeering comments about his loveliness, for he knew that what lay close to his heart was a dagger. "Would you like for me to pour your saké, honorable sir?" he asked politely.

"Oi! This one is bolder than the others, and more charming besides. Where did you come from, little flower, and why did you take so long to arrive?" Prince Yamato laughed his most delicate giggle, and tried to seem bashful. "No need to be shy, come sit between us!" continued the large outlaw.

They let "her" pour cup after cup of saké for them, enjoying the view as this girl poured in a graceful, enchanting manner. When the bottle was empty, Kumaso called out for more, so the girl rose to exit . . . and said in a rather manly voice, "I think you've had quite enough." Turning, she drew a dagger from her robes and stabbed him through the heart before the drunken Kumaso could even move to defend himself. Seeing what happened, Takeru shrieked and ran for the entrance, but Prince Yamato caught him by his collar and tripped him. The blood-stained dagger flashed near, but Takeru caught the Prince's hand at the last instant. "Wait! Please!" he gasped. "I see no reason to," Yamato said calmly. "At least give me your name . . . Are you truly a man?" implored the thief. "I am the Son of the Heavenly Sovereign Obo-tarashi-hiko-oshiro-wake, the Prince Yamato!" he replied happily. "That name is too long," said the thief. "I thought that my brother and I were the strongest men in Japan, but now I see it was you all the time! Since you have defeated me, please take my title, and be 'Yamato-Take' from now on."

Once the Prince was done slicing up the bandit, he decided that was exactly what he would do, to honor Takeru's memory. Also, it would forever serve to remind him of his first adventure. He couldn't wait to tell this story to the Emperor!

APPENDIX B
BUILDING AWARENESS ABOUT AFRICAN CULTURE

Theme
The sense of what is fair.

Source
Five Ethiopian tales—The Donkey Who Sinned; The Goats Who Killed the Leopard (reproduced below as an example); The Judgment of the Wind; Fire and Water, Truth and Falsehood; Justice. In Harold Courlander (1996), *A Treasury of African Folklore* (pp. 542–547). New York, NY: Marlowe & Company. These tales are also available at Marcus Garvey's Web site http://www.marcusgarvey.com

The Goats Who Killed the Leopard

Once a leopard cub wandered away from his home into the grasslands where the elephant herds grazed. He was too young to know his danger. While the elephants grazed one of them stepped upon the leopard cub by accident, and killed him. Other leopards found the body of the cub soon after, and they rushed to his father to tell him of the tragedy.

"Your son is dead!" they told him. "We found him in the valley!" The father leopard was overcome with grief. "Ah, who has killed him? Tell me, so that I can avenge his death!" "The elephants have killed him," the other leopards said. "What? The elephants?" the father leopard exclaimed with surprise in his voice. "Yes, the elephants," they repeated. The father leopard thought for a minute. "No, it is not the elephants. It is the goats who have killed him. Yes, the goats, it is they who have done this awful thing to me!"

So the father leopard went out in a fit of terrible rage and found a herd of goats grazing in the hills, and he slaughtered many of them in revenge. And even now, when a man is wronged by someone stronger than himself, he often avenges himself upon someone who is weaker than himself.

A Short Debriefing

As Courlander states in the introduction to *A Treasury of African Folklore*, there is no better way to learn about Africa and its people than through the oral literature they have created and preserved. These five stories can rightly be seen as masterpieces of African folklore, whose analysis can yield substantial ideas about the nature of African culture. One of the important conclusions is that "the similarities of outwardly contrasting societies are more impressive that the differences" (Courlander, 1996, p. 2).

REFERENCES

Abma, T. A. (2003). Learning by telling: Storytelling workshops as an organizational learning intervention. *Management Learning, 34*(2), 221–240.

Barley, S. (1983). Semiotics and the study of occupational and organizational cultures. *Administrative Science Quarterly, 28*(3), 393–413.

Bell, C. R. (1992, September). The trainer as storyteller. *Training and Development,* 53–56.

Blaisdell, B. (2003). Around the world with the Odyssey. *Changing English, 10*(2), 195–198.

Bloom, B. S. (Ed.). (1956). *Taxonomy of educational objectives: Handbook 1. Cognitive Domain.* New York: McKay.

Boje, D. M. (1991). Learning storytelling: Storytelling to learn management skills. *Journal of Management Education, 15*(3), 279–294.

Boje, D. M. (2003, August 10). Narrative and antenarrative methods for organizational and communication research: Introduction to narrative and antenarrative methods (Revised version.). Retrieved March 26, 2004, from http://cbae.nmsu.edu/~dboje/

Brown, A. (1995). *Organizational culture.* London: Pitman.

Carter, K. (1993). The place of story in the study of teaching and teacher education. *Journal of Organizational Change Management, 4*(3), 106–126.

Cavusgil, S. T., & Ghauri, P. N. (1990). *Doing business in developing countries: Entry and negotiation strategies.* London: Routledge.

Champoux, J. E. (1999). Film as a teaching resource. *Journal of Management Inquiry, 8,* 206–217.

Collison, C., & MacKenzie, A. (1999). The power of story in organizations. *Journal of Workplace Learning, 11,* 38–40.

Courlander, H. (1996). *A treasury of African folklore.* New York: Marlowe & Company.

Dalton, M., Ernst, C., Deal, J., & Leslie, J. (2002). *Success for the new global manager: How to work across distances, countries and cultures.* Hoboken, NJ: Jossey-Bass.

Denning, S. (2000). *The springboard: How storytelling ignites action in knowledge-era organizations.* Boston: Butterworth-Heinemann.

Ferraro, G. P. (2002). *The cultural dimension of international business* (4th ed.). Upper Saddle River, NJ: Prentice Hall.

Forster, N., Cebis, M., Majteles, S., Mathur, A., Morgan, R., Preuss, J., et al. (1999). The role of story-telling in organizational leadership. *Leadership & Organization Development Journal, 20*(1), 11–17.

Gabriel, Y. (2000). *Storytelling in organizations. Facts, fictions, and fantasies.* Oxford, England: Oxford University Press.

Geertz, C. (1973). *The interpretation of culture.* New York: Basic Books.

Glanz, L. (2003). Expatriate stories: A vehicle of professional development abroad? *Journal of Managerial Psychology, 18*(3), 259–272.

Gold, J. (1996). Telling stories to find the future. *Career Development International, 1*(4), 33–37.

Greco, J. (1996). Stories for executive development: An isotonic solution. *Journal of Organizational Change, 9*(5), 43–74.

Grimaldi, A. (1986, Winter). Interpreting popular culture: The missing link between local labor and international management. *Columbia Journal of World Business,* 67–72.

Hannabuss, S. (2000). Telling tales at work: Narrative insight into managers' actions. *Library Review, 49*(5), 218–229.

Hansen, C., & Kahnweiler, W. (1996). Storytelling: An instrument for understanding the dynamics of corporate relationships. *Human Relations, 46*(12), 1391–1409.

Jabri, M., & Pounder, J. S. (2001). The management of change: A narrative perspective on management development. *Journal of Management Development, 20*(8), 682–690.

Kaufman, B. (2003). Stories that sell, stories that tell. *Journal of Business Strategy,* 11–15.

Kaye, B., & Jacobson, B. (1999). True tales and tall tales. The power of organizational storytelling. *Training and Development, 53*(3), 45–50.

Kaye, M. (1996). *Myth-makers and story-tellers.* Melbourne, Australia: Business & Professional Publishing.

Knights, D., & Willmott, H. (1999). Management lives: Power and identity in contemporary organizations. London: Sage.

Krathwohl, D. R., Bloom, B. S., & Masia, B. B. (1964). *Taxonomy of educational objectives: Handbook 2. Affective Domain.* New York: McKay.

Kottak, C. P. (1994). *Antropología. Una exploración de la diversidad humana* [Anthropology. The exploration of human diversity]. Madrid, Spain: McGraw-Hill.

Leavitt, H. J. (1989, Spring). Educating our MBAs: On teaching what we haven't taught. *California Management Review, 31*(3), 38–50.

LeGuin, U. K. (1970). Prophets and mirrors: Science fiction as a way of seeing. *Living Light, 7*, 3.

Linde, C. (2001). Narrative and social tacit knowledge. *Journal of Knowledge Management, 5*(2), 160–170.

Llewellyn, S. (1999). Narratives in accounting and management research. *Accounting, auditing, and accountability, 12*(2), 230–236.

Maclachlan, M. (1993). Sustaining human resource development in Africa: The influence of expatriates. *Management Education and Development, 24*(Pt. 2), 167–171.

Mansfield, C. L. (1995). Deconstructing reconstructive poverty law. Practice-based critique of the storytelling aspects of the theoretics of practice movement. *Brooklyn Law Review, 61*, 889–929.

Matzdorf, F., & Ramage, M. (2003). Storytelling in organizations. Facts, fictions, and fantasies. [Book review]. *Management Learning, 34*(2), 271–275.

McCollum, M. (1992). Organizational stories in a family owned-business. *Family Business Review, 5*(1), 3–24.

McConckie, M., & Boss, R. (1994). Using stories as an aid to consultation. *Public Administration Quarterly, 17*(4), 377–395.

Mello, J. A. (1999). Reframing leadership pedagogy though model and theory building. *Career Development International, 4*(3), 163–169.

Mello, R. (2001, February). The power of storytelling: How oral narrative influences children's relationships in classrooms. *International Journal of Education and the Arts, 2*(1). Retrieved March 26, 2004, from http://ijea.asu.edu/v2n1

Morgan, G. (1980). Paradigms, metaphors and puzzle solving in organisation theory. *Administrative Science Quarterly, 25*(4), 605–622.

Morgan, S., & Dennehy, R. F. (1997). The power of organizational storytelling: A management development perspective. *Journal of Management Development, 16*(7), 494–501.

Nadkarni, R. P. (1992, December). Experience of 600 training programs for industrial workers: Lesson to learn. *Industrial Engineering Journal*, 22–24.

Nissley, N. (2002). Arts-based learning in management education. In C. Wankel and R. DeFillippi (Eds.), *Rethinking management education for the 21st century* (pp. 27–61). A volume in: Research in Management Education and Development. Greenwich, CT: Information Age Publishing.

Ojile, C. (1986). Intercultural training: An overview of the benefits for business and the anthropologist's emerging role. In H. Serrie (Ed.), *Anthropology and international business. Studies in Third World societies* (pp. 35–51). (Publication No. 28). Williamsburg, VA: College of William and Mary, Department of Anthropology.

Olsson, S. (2000). Acknowledging the female archetype: Women managers' narratives and gender. *Women in Management Review, 15*(5/6), 296–302.

Olsson, S. (2002). Gendered heroes: Male and female self-representations of executive identity. *Women in Management Review, 17*(3/4), 142–150.

Öztel, H., & Hinz, O. (2001). Changing organizations with metaphors. *The Learning Organization, 8*(4), 153–168.

Perry, C. (1993). Requirements and methods for management development programmes in the least developed countries in Africa. *Management Education and Development, 24*(3), 225–245.

Phillips, N. (1995). Telling organisational tales: On the role of narrative fiction in the study of organisations. *Organization Studies, 16*(4), 625–649.

Stapleton, C., & Hughes, C. (2003, September/October). Interactive imagination: Tapping the emotions through interactive story for compelling simulations. *IEEE Computer Graphics and Applications,* 11–14.

Srinivas, K. M. (1995). Globalization and the Third World. Challenge of expanding the mindsets. *Journal of Management Development, 14*(3), 26–49.

Torres-Coronas, T., & Arias-Oliva, M. (2003). Castles (or "human towers"): A metaphor to foster the human spirit within organizations. Paper presented at the 30th Organizational and Behavior Teaching Conference 2003, Springfield, MA.

Vance, C. M. (1991). Formalising storytelling in organisations: A key agenda for the design of training. *Journal of Organizations Change Management, 4*(3), 52–58.

Vance, C. M., & Paik, Y. (2002). One size fits all in expatriate pre-departure training? Comparing the host country voices of Mexican, Indonesian and US workers. *Journal of Management Development, 21*(7), 557–571.

Watson, C. E. (2003). Using stories to teach business ethics. *Teaching Business Ethics, 7,* 93–105.

Watson, T. J. (2001). Beyond managerialism: Negotiated narratives and critical management education in practice. *British Journal of Management, 12,* 385–396.

Wheatley, W. J. (1998). Enhancing the effectiveness of management education with a tone of music and the mystique of magic. *Journal of Workplace Learning, 10*(6/7), 342– 344.

Wilcock, P. M., Brown, G. C. S., Bateson, J., Carver, J., & Machin, S. (2003). Using patient stories to inspire quality improvement within the NHS Modernization Agency collaborative programmes. *Journal of Clinical Nursing, 12,* 422–430.

Wilkins, A. (1984, Spring). The creation of company cultures: The role of stories and human resource systems. *Human Resource Management, 23,* 45–57.

Zemke, R. (1990). Storytelling: Back to basics. *Training Magazine, 27*(3), 44–48, 50.

CHAPTER 9

COOPERATIVE LEARNING

Potentials and Challenges
for Chinese Management Education

Dean Tjosvold, Zi-you Yu, and Sofia Su

*The central task of the final years of this century is the creation of a new model
of co-existence among the various cultures within a single interconnected civilization.
Yes, it is clearly necessary to invent organizational structures appropriate
for the multicultural age.}*

—Vaclav Havel

INTRODUCTION

In one of the world's most audacious experiments, China is transforming
itself from a centrally controlled economy and socialist society to a market-
driven economy and open society. The thrust is economic, but the reform
affects the daily lives of over a billion people. Chinese educators realize
that they must update their methods to prepare their students to negotiate
this changing, demanding world.

Management education in particular is widely believed to be critical for
successful reform. Chinese universities are joining forces with Western

The Cutting Edge of International Management Education, pages 223–242
Copyright © 2004 by Information Age Publishing
All rights of reproduction in any form reserved.

business schools to offer MBA degrees as well as their own management courses. In 1986, there were only 38 MBA graduates from one program offered by the State University of New York. In 1991, nine Chinese universities, including Tsinghua, Peiking, and the China Peoples' University, began MBA programs. By 1999, there were more than 23,000 MBA students and 5,000 graduates. In 2003, more than 44,000 students took the entrance examination and applied for MBA programs in 62 universities.

Based on research and our professional experiences in teaching managers in Hong Kong and mainland China, we argue that cooperative learning techniques can contribute very much to educational reform in China and, in particular, to management education. Cooperative learning is a research-based approach to developing and utilizing the relationships among students to promote educational objectives. Typically, it involves small groups of students with the goal of helping each student learn and master the course content. It is more than group learning as students develop relationships where they feel they are on the same side and have a vested interested in promoting each other's learning. Students are expected to support each other and engage in intellectual controversies to explore and question ideas. Professional experience has developed many practices—such as cooperative note-taking and peer discussion—that can be applied even in large lecture-oriented classrooms (Johnson & Johnson, 1991). Educators can help students learn with and through each other by using cooperative learning techniques.

Some researchers have objected to applying Western ideas and practices in China and, specifically, have questioned the cultural appropriateness and utility of high student-involvement approaches like cooperative learning in Chinese classrooms (Earley, 1997; Earley & Gibson, 1998; Hofstede, 1993). Many practical challenges exist in implementing cooperative learning. Although assigning students to groups is straightforward, helping them develop their relationships and interactions so that they all learn is a complex challenge for instructors and students alike. Many students who have adopted traditional Chinese classroom values—such as trying to outdo each other—have little experience and few skills in supporting each other's learning, discussing and debating ideas together, and resolving conflicts.

In this chapter, we review research support for the benefits of cooperative learning in management education in China and present ways to overcome barriers and implement cooperative learning successfully. In the first section, we discuss how cooperative learning can contribute to the reform of management education in China. In the second section, we review objections to cooperative learning as culturally inappropriate—versus our view that cooperative learning is compatible with Chinese values. In the third section, we argue that Chinese values can support cooperative learning. In the fourth section, we review research and the rationale for cooperative learning in China. In the fifth section, we use recent studies to show how Chinese values can support spirited, productive, cooperative teamwork. In the final section, we note procedures that we have found particularly useful in Hong Kong and mainland China classrooms.

THE NEED FOR COOPERATIVE LEARNING
IN MANAGEMENT EDUCATION

Surges in foreign investment figures, entry into the World Trade Organization, and dramatic increases in trading volume capture Western headlines about reform in China; These changes, while offering great opportunities, also impose great demands on managers. Beijing has passed sweeping reforms, but the success of those reforms depends upon the abilities and persistence of managers and their employees throughout China. Companies, managers, and students recognize the need to strengthen their management capabilities to take advantage of emerging opportunities. These constituents are pressing universities not only to enlarge their offerings but also to strengthen and modernize their educational methods.

Pearce (2001) has recently shown that government policy and regulations powerfully affect dynamics within organizations. Pearce described the Chinese government as non-facilitative in that it required managers first and foremost to maintain relationships with government officials and bankers who hold the purse strings. State Owned Enterprises (SOEs) were expected to provide for the welfare of their employees, while the state was responsible for losses. Managing was not easy since there were seldom enough funds to support the schools, hospitals, homes, and wages of employees while living up to the socialist ideals of fairness and equality. Employees in turn lobbied their managers for better treatment. These relationship-building activities distracted managers and employees from developing customer-oriented, productive organizations.

SOEs are now responsible for their own budgets and face bankruptcy unless they sell their products. Many managers, professionals, farmers, and laid-off employees are forming their own private ventures. Multi-national corporations are establishing subsidiaries and joint ventures in order to participate in China's manufacturing capabilities and market opportunities. Provinces, cities, and towns also have more authority and responsibility and are under pressure to earn income. Especially after entrance to the World Trade Organization, Chinese organizations are increasingly oriented toward performance and customer value as they recognize that they cannot rely on government protection. They are eager to employ modern management methods to enhance their productivity and profitability.

Managers of SOEs, as well as private enterprises and joint ventures, want to learn from international companies and to integrate themselves into the global marketplace. Chinese managers feel considerable pressure to develop the skills to work in a new system and, simultaneously, to develop this new system. The Chinese education system had earlier concentrated on the natural sciences and engineering, leaving few educators equipped to teach social sciences and management. As Chinese managers are emulating Western business practices, they naturally have been turning to Western management knowledge.

Recognizing that they cannot simply imitate the West, Chinese managers want to modify Western ideas and methods to fit Chinese culture and circumstances. The Cultural Revolution was an extremely painful, costly experiment in trying to purge Chinese values to create a modern society. Therefore, the necessity of integrating Western ideas and methods into Chinese organizations is another demand on Chinese managers.

Chinese students recognize the emerging demands on managers and employees and realize that they must develop their own capabilities in order to do well in the competitive job marketplace in China. They are pressuring their educators to experiment with new learning methods that will help them develop their people skills, among others. Teaching only from the textbook is no longer acceptable. Educators from primary schools to universities are devoted to searching for new, effective ways to help students learn.

Cooperative learning can play a central role in the reform of management education in China to help Chinese managers and management students strengthen their leadership capabilities. Tjosvold et al. have found that strong cooperative learning techniques, in strategic management courses, support Chinese students learning important business ideas and methods (Tjosvold, Wong, Nibler, & Pounder, 2002). Contemporary organizations have discovered that they must create new products through cross-functional teams if they are to use their resources effectively and serve their customers with value. Cooperative learning techniques help managers and students strengthen their teamwork and leadership skills as they learn business disciplines which are so valuable to their organizations. The method of cooperative learning reinforces the message of the value of teamwork.

Chinese students are welcoming cooperative learning as opportunities for them to work with each other. For example, in a class at Shanghai University of Finance and Economics, 62 percent of the students wanted their instructor to use cooperative learning so that they could discuss case studies and other issues with each other. Less than 10 percent of the students wanted the instructor to lecture. At the end of cooperative learning classes, the students applauded the instructor to express their appreciation.

IS COOPERATIVE LEARNING CULTURALLY APPROPRIATE?

Researchers have raised objections about applying Western ideas and practices in general in China and specifically to cooperative learning. Researchers have argued that China has its own cultural traditions that should be respected and nurtured, and that the utility of Western ideas should be severely limit limited. (see Hofstede, 1993). Chinese students are expected to be highly respectful of their instructors and oriented toward passive approaches to learning. To be in accord with Chinese values, classrooms should be instructor-dominated and student participation should be minimized. Applying the Western-developed approach of cooperative learning is considered imperialistic and ineffective in that it is inconsistent with Chinese values. (Earley, 1997; Earley & Gibson, 1998).

Researchers have argued that China is a collectivist society where closely linked individuals see themselves as belonging to one or more groups (e.g., family, tribe, coworkers, groups, and organizations) and are motivated by norms, duties, and obligations imposed on them (Hofstede, 1980,1991; Triandis, 1990, 2000). Individualistic countries like the United States have loosely linked individuals who view themselves as independent of collectives, and who are motivated by their own preferences, needs, rights, and contracts. Collectivist values have been found to induce Chinese people to be conforming and submissive in that they want to avoid face-to-face confrontation, while individuals are characterized as favoring direct give-and-take collaboration (Tang & Kirkbride, 1986). Similarly, high power distant values are thought to make Chinese people oriented toward and accepting of dominating leadership styles (Leung, 1997). These values appear to indicate that Chinese students prefer and benefit more from didactic educational methods rather than participative educational methods (Earley, 1997; Earley & Gibson, 1998).

Our position is that Chinese values themselves are not so highly restrictive and inimical that students cannot participation in their own education. For example, although traditional values reinforce submissive acceptance of authority, other values support inquiry and debate. For example, Mencius, an influential Confucian scholar, argued that wise rulers should adopt ideas that may oppose their own. He himself was famous for his eagerness to debate and challenge rulers and people as he tried to teach them the right ways:

> Indeed, I am not fond of disputing, but I am compelled to do it.... I am alarmed by these things, and address myself to the defense of the doctrines of the former sages.... I also wish to rectify men's hearts, and to put an end to those perverse doctrines, to oppose their one-sided actions and banish away their licentious expressions.

Befitting an ancient, ongoing culture, Chinese people have many values. In the twentieth century alone, the nationalist movement, the revolution of 1949, the Great Leap Forward, the Cultural Revolution, the Gang of Four movement, and the reforms since 1979 have engendered a whole host of new values and traditions. In China, socialist and nationalistic values now co-exist with free market and international values.

COOPERATIVE LEARNING

In their focus on curriculum and their own interaction with students, educators have traditionally neglected the relationships among students. However, student-student interaction may be particularly important in management education with its emphasis on case studies and group projects. Cooperative learning techniques show educators ways to help students make their learning groups effective and enhance their knowledge.

Beginning in the 1940s, Morton Deutsch (1949, 1973) argued that how people believe their goals are related is a useful way to understand the dynamics and outcomes of interaction. Because interaction can take on very different characteristics, people's beliefs about how they depend upon each other drastically affect their expectations, communication, exchange, problem solving, and learning. What is critical is how people believe their goals are predominantly linked, because these perceptions affect their expectations and actions. Deutsch identified three models of interaction: cooperation, competition, and independence.

Models of Interaction

In cooperation, people believe their goals are positively linked so that as one moves toward goal attainment, the others also move toward reaching their goals. They understand that one's goal attainment helps others reach their goals; as one succeeds, others succeed. People in cooperation appreciate that they want each other to pursue their goals effectively, because the effectiveness of others helps all of them reach their goals. Individual achievement depends upon the achievement of others. Cooperation is not based on altruism, but on the recognition that, with positively related goals, self-interests require collaboration. Cooperative learning team members want each other to develop useful ideas and work hard so that they all perform well and learn. Cooperative work integrates self-interests to achieve mutual goals.

Alternatively, students may believe their goals are competitive in that one's goal attainment precludes or at least makes less likely the goal attainment of others. If one succeeds, others must fail. If one wins, others lose. People in competition conclude that they are better off when others act ineffectively; when others are productive, they are less likely to be successful themselves. Competitive team members want to prove they are the most capable and their ideas superior; they are frustrated when others develop useful ideas and work hard. Competitive work pits each member's self-interest against other members' self-interests in a fight to win.

Independence occurs when people believe their goals are unrelated. The goal attainment of one neither helps nor hinders the goal attainment of others. Success by one means neither failure nor success for others. People in independence conclude that it means little to them if others act effectively or ineffectively. Independent team members care little whether others develop useful ideas or work hard. Independent work creates disinterest and indifference.

Advantages of Cooperation

According to Deutsch, people's beliefs that their goals are predominately cooperative, competitive, or independent profoundly affects their orientation toward each other. In cooperation, people want others to act effectively and expect that others want them to be effective because it is in each person's self-interest to do so. They trust that their risks and efforts will be supported and reciprocated.

Cooperative goals lead to constructive controversy, which is defined as the open-minded discussion of diverse views. Experimental research has documented that people with cooperative goals engage in direct discussions of conflict and full exchanges of views that lead to understanding of perspectives and issues (Tjosvold, 1998). Confronted with an opposing view and doubting that their own position is fully adequate, people with cooperative goals have been found to be curious and to seek to understand opposing views. They ask questions and demonstrate understanding of the other position. Through defending and understanding opposing views and rationales, protagonists begin to integrate ideas to create new, useful solutions. These dynamics lead to quality solutions that protagonists accept and implement when they emphasize their cooperative goals. Protagonists also develop confidence in working together in the future.

Competition and independence, compared to cooperation, typically restrict information and resource exchange, distort communication, and escalate or avoid conflict (Johnson & Johnson, 1898). In particular, competitive and independent goals have been found to lead to closed-minded discussions.

Research Support

In a recent meta-analysis of more than 120 studies with adults, cooperative teams were found to result in higher level of procedural knowledge than individual learning structured competitively or individually (mean differences equal to 0.54 and 0.51 standard deviations respectively). These results held for verbal, mathematical, and procedural tasks (Johnson, 2003, Johnson & Johnson, 1994). Meta-analyses also indicate that people in cooperation discuss opposing ideas openly, use higher-quality reasoning, and manage conflicts constructively (Johnson & Johnson, 1989; Johnson, Johnson, Maruyama, Nelson, & Skon, 1981; Stanne, Johnson, & Johnson, 1999). These interaction patterns in turn result in task completion, problem solving, reduced stress, attraction, strengthened work relationships, and confidence in future collaboration. In contrast, competition and independence frustrate learning and productivity (except on some simple tasks), intensify stress, and lower morale. Research has not so clearly distinguished competition and independence, although generally independence has similar though not as negative an impact on interaction dynamics and outcomes as competition (Tjosvold, 1998).

Laboratory and field experiments conducted with elementary to adult students in various kinds of educational settings support the value of cooperative learning (Johnson & Johnson, 1998). Recent field studies also indicate that this value extends to management education in China (Chen & Tjosvold, 2002; Tjosvold et al., 2002).

COOPERATION AND COMPETITION RESEARCH IN CHINA

Cooperative learning is based on the theory of cooperation and competition. Despite considerable empirical support in the West, the theory cannot be assumed to apply in the collectivist society of China. To what extent do Chinese students recognize cooperative goals and how do they respond to them? Can managers also apply the theory and methods they use in their classrooms to their organizations? Should Chinese leaders be cooperative toward employees and have them work in cooperative groups?

This section reviews experimental and field studies on leadership and teamwork research conducted in Asia that can provide insights into these issues. A cooperative, bi-cultural network has tested the theory in Chinese and other Asian organizations. Trained both in the East and West and based in Hong Kong, mainland China, and other East Asian countries, researchers have debated the theory and developed research methods.

Leadership in Asian Organizations

A major goal of MBA education is to help professionals and specialists to become leaders. Research in the West has shown that developing high-quality productive relationships very much contributes to effective leadership (Graen & Uhl-Bien, 1995). Chinese employees with high-quality relationships with leaders performed their own jobs well and were willing to contribute as good citizens to the organization (Hui, Law, & Chen, 1999). Strong cooperative relationships helped Hong Kong managers and employees believe they were powerful, productive, and democratic (Tjosvold, Hui, & Law, 1998).

Managers and their employees in a watchcase-manufacturing factory in southern China participated in a study of the leader relationship and employee citizenship (Tjosvold, Law, & Hui, 1996). Structural equation analysis confirmed the hypothesis that strong cooperative goals—not competitive or independent ones—as measured by the employees, promoted a high-quality relationship between leader and employee, which in turn led to high levels of job performance and citizenship behavior as described by their manager.

In today's global economy, leaders must at times supervise employees working in another country. Hong Kong senior accounting managers were found to be able to lead employees working in mainland China effectively when they had cooperative goals, but not when their goals were competitive or independent (Tjosvold & Moy, 1998). Then they were able to discuss their views open-mindedly, leading to stronger relationships and productivity, consequences that in turn induced future internal motivation. Managers in the Hong Kong parent company who had cooperative links with new product specialists in Canada discussed issues open-mindedly and developed productive, trusting relationships despite their cultural differences and geographic separation (Tjosvold, 1999).

Chinese employees with cooperative goals with their American or Japanese manager open-mindedly discussed their views that led to productive collaborative work and strengthened relationships (Tjosvold, Sun, & Chen, 2002). Experimental studies in China show that managers with cooperative (compared to competitive) goals with their employees used their valued resources to assist and support employees, especially employees who demonstrated high needs by being unable to complete the task themselves (Tjosvold & Sun, 2000, 2001; Tjosvold, Coleman, & Sun, 2003).

Teamwork in Asian Organizations

Field and experimental studies have also demonstrated that cooperative goals and constructive controversy help colleagues work productively and innovatively (Tjosvold, 2002; Tjosvold, Tang, & West, in press; Tjosvold, Yu, & Hui, in press; Chen, Liu, & Tjosvold, in press). Experiments have shown, for example, that cooperative goals compared to competitive goals promote the open-minded consideration of opposing ideas (Tjosvold & Sun, 2001). Chinese participants in an experiment were interested in learning more about the opposing views, considered these views useful, came to agree with them, and tended to integrate them into their own decisions in cooperative situations compared to competitive situations. They were more attracted to the other protagonists and had greater confidence in working together in the future than participants in the competitive situation.

Experimental studies have documented the processes by which cooperative goals contribute to leadership and teamwork, and field studies suggest that these dynamics occur in many Chinese organizations. However, it may be that traditional Chinese values make establishing spirited cooperative groups difficult. The following section reviews research indicating that Chinese values can be applied to reinforce cooperative teamwork.

CHINESE VALUES: ORGANIZATION AS FAMILY

Researchers have emphasized that collective societies believe that organizations should be families (Farh & Cheng, 2000; Westwood, 1997). Organization as family is a metaphor that orients managers' and employees' expectations of each other. The organization, as a family, should be tightly knit and managed by the father. The in-group of actual family members and long-term employees accepted as family is considered entitled to power and special treatment. This section discusses how Chinese values of collectivism, social face, and communication—when appropriately applied—promote cooperative teamwork.

Relationships and Collectivism

As argued above, researchers have long proposed that Chinese people are collectivists who value a socially defined *self*. They give priority to in-group goals and accept that social norms should determine behavior (Sampson, 2001; Triandis, 1995). Collectivism has generally been assumed to lead to conflict avoidance, not the constructive controversy of cooperative teamwork. However, in a study in State Owned Enterprises in three regions of China, 689 employees in 194 teams indicated that their group's values were goal interdependence, constructive controversy, and productivity (Tjosvold, Law, & Sun, 2003). Their managers also reported on the extent that these teams were productive. Structural equation analysis indicated that collectivist values reinforced cooperative goals and an open-minded discussion of views. This, in turn, resulted in strong relationships and team productivity, as experienced from both the team and the manager's perspectives. Individualistic values had contrasting effects through fostering competitive goals and closed-minded discussion. These results suggest that collectivist values can reinforce cooperative goals and constructive controversy for productive teamwork in China.

Studies have shown that collectivist values strengthen the leader relationship. Employees who indicated that their relationship was collectivist with their managers also indicated that they were very open to their manager and, as a result, were committed and effective organizational citizens as rated by their manager (Tjosvold, Yu, & Liu, 2001). Similarly, Chinese employees with collectivist relationships with their Japanese managers were able to discuss their differences open-mindedly and productively (Tjosvold, Wong, & Liu, 2002).

Social Face

Social face assumes that people attempt to project a desirable image and want assurance that their image is accepted (Tjosvold, 1983). Chinese people have been found to be particularly alert to protecting social face to promote relationships (Ho, 1976). Given their sensitivity to the collective and relationships, they seek harmony and communicate that they respect their partners as capable and worthy (Ting-Toomey, 1988). Their collectivism and their understanding of social face lead them to be hesitant about engaging in aggressive interaction that may challenge the face of others. They want to avoid conflict and, once engaged, use compromise and accommodation to deal with conflict (Kirkbride, Tang, & Westwood, 1991; Tse, Francis, & Walls, 1994).

However, Chinese values related to social face may not inevitably make managing conflict more indirect and difficult. Indeed, sensitivity to protecting face can make discussions of differences more constructive (Tjosvold, Hui, & Sun, 2000). For example, Chinese leaders are expected to protect social face by discussing problems with employees privately. When employees feel their social face is protected or confirmed, they may then openly discuss differences without experiencing social or psychological threat (Tjosvold, Hui, & Sun, 2000). Consequently, the problem and conflict are solved, and the relationship between employees and managers deepens.

Social face has been found, under certain conditions, to promote open-ness. Chinese negotiators who confirmed social face were able to discuss their opposing views open-mindedly (Tjosvold et al., 2000; Tjosvold & Sun, 2000). Chinese participants taking the role of managers emphasized their cooperative goals with the employee learned, considered the opposing views useful, and came to agree with some of them.

A field study also indicated that confirmation of face helped Chinese people to discuss their opposing views cooperatively and productively. Contrary to traditional reasoning, open discussion in China (compared to avoiding conflict) can strengthen relationships and induce curiosity so that Chinese people asked questions, explored opposing views, demonstrated knowledge, and worked to integrate views (Tjosvold, Hui, & Sun, 2000; Tjosvold & Sun, in press). People who disagreed directly and openly were characterized as strong persons and competent negotiators whereas protagonists who avoided conflict were considered weak and ineffectual. Thus, open discussion and social face, when effectively communicated, appear to reinforce each other in China.

Persuasion and Implicit Communication

Chinese leaders, as well as others, are expected to be reserved, consider carefully the best way to express their ideas, and avoid expressing potentially hurtful ideas directly. This tendency to use skilled discussion and persuasion rather than coercion can be very useful. A recent experiment conducted in Guangzhou, China, found that persuasive influence resulted in feelings of respect, cooperative relationships, and openness to the other persons and their positions (Tjosvold & Sun, 2001). Leaders who were targets of persuasion—compared to coercion—sought mutual benefit in the discussion, were open to listening to the other, and were interested in learning more about the opposing view. Leaders in persuasion, compared to coercion, were also more attracted to and more confident in their relationship with the opposing negotiators.

Traditional Chinese values have proved to be flexible. Research has underlined that collectivism, social face, and persuasion can be applied in ways that promote cooperative goals and constructive controversy. Chinese educators are open to new Western methods like cooperative learning, but they realize that they must adapt them for their students in order to uphold Chinese values.

Confucius (trans. 1979) emphasized intellectual honesty coupled with respectful, humane treatment of others. He believed that every person is engaged in a lifelong striving to improve (known as *ren*) and, therefore should be open and ready to learn from anyone, even from those with opposing ideas. Confucius advised listening attentively and responding only after one understands others. He was fond of saying that if a person is in a group of three, one of the other members knows something the first person does not. Cooperative learning with its emphasis on open-minded discussion may not only be useful but also culturally appropriate for Chinese students.

APPLYING THE THEORY OF COOPERATION AND COMPETITION

Research has shown that cooperative goals are an important basis both for effective learning and for organizational productivity. Educators and managers should develop the conditions that help students and employees make their cooperative teams work. Students by themselves cannot be expected to make their groups effective but need assistance and guidance to develop cooperative relationships and give-and-take interaction.

Making Cooperative Learning Work

Johnson and Johnson (1999) have outlined basic conditions for making cooperative learning effective. With cooperative goals, team members perceive that they need each other in order to complete the group's task (sink or swim together). Instructors may structure positive interdependence by (a) establishing mutual goals (maximizing one's own productivity as well as that of the other members of the group); (b) giving joint rewards (if all group members achieve above the criteria, each will receive bonus points.); (c) sharing resources (members have different expertise); and (d) assigning roles (summarizer, encourager of participation, elaborator, etc.).

Educators should also structure individual accountability. Groups should assess the quality and quantity of each member's contributions. After studying in groups, students may be asked to perform individually on a test; each group member receives increased marks when all their group members achieve an established standard.

Students should interact face-to-face. Team members promote each other's productivity by helping, sharing, and encouraging efforts to produce. Members explain, discuss, and teach what they know to teammates. Instructors structure teams so that members sit knee-to-knee and talk through each aspect of the tasks they are working to complete.

Educators can help students develop interpersonal and small group skills. Groups cannot function effectively if members do not have and use social skills. Instructors emphasize these skills as purposefully and precisely as job-performance skills. Collaborative skills include instructorship, decision-making, trust-building, communication, and conflict-management skills.

Group processing also contributes to making cooperative learning effective. Groups need specific time to discuss how well they are achieving their goals and maintaining effective working relationships among members. Instructors structure group processing by assigning tasks such as listing at least three member actions that helped the group be successful and listing one action that could be added to make the group even more successful in the future. Instructors also monitor the groups and give feedback on how well the groups are working together.

At times, educators should structure competition and independence when the task and situation are appropriate. All students should become knowledgeable and skillful in competing and working independently. However, considerable research indicates that for most purposes and situations, cooperative interaction promotes important educational objectives.

Team Organization

Tjosvold (1991) used the theory of cooperation and competition and its research to develop an overall model of team effectiveness. The Team Organization model integrates the conditions and processes that contribute to effective cooperative teamwork. *Envision, unite, empower, explore,* and *reflect* are mutually reinforcing steps to an effective group. Managers and employees are committed to their vision. People understand how their own efforts fit into the objectives of their department and the goals of their company. Specifically, a team vision provides a common direction for team members and helps them believe that their goals are cooperative rather than competitive or independent.

Cooperative group members feel more capable and able to utilize each other's abilities and resources to accomplish their goals. They feel powerful and confident they have the technical skills and interpersonal abilities to combine their resources to accomplish tasks and move toward goal attainment. They explore problems by exchanging information and discussing opposing views openly to dig into issues and create solutions. They are also prepared and able to express and integrate their divergent views to identify and solve problems. They use their experiences and conflicts to reflect, learn, and adjust so that they can continue to work together and move toward their vision. They reflect on their experiences to celebrate progress and learn from conflicts and mistakes. This model applies to small groups and to the organization as a whole.

A key advantage of this integrated model of team effectiveness is that all members can use it to develop a set of ideals for how they can develop their team and to develop the common skills they need to work productively together. Group members are often frustrated because they have incompatible notions of the kind of team they should be. They want to develop a productive team but have opposing views of the methods to do so. Some group members may assume that they must work harmoniously to be cooperative; others assume that they must confront conflict. Discussing and using the framework can help team members become co-oriented with a consensus about how they should strive to work together. They reach agreement about when and how they are going to use conflict to be cooperative and productive. They learn key skills together and use the cooperative model to develop the norms and contexts that support the use of these skills.

Management educators have recognized the value of group learning and team training. The research that has been reviewed indicates that cooperative teams are useful for learning *in* teams and learning *for* teams. Learning in teams emphasizes taskwork—the specific ideas, procedures, and skills needed to get the job done. Learning for teams emphasizes teamwork skills. Yet, taskwork and teamwork are highly related because few organizational tasks can be accomplished with complete independence. An operator may be able to keep one machine working, but teamwork skills are relevant as operators discuss ways to improve quality. Employees who lack confidence in their teamwork skills may be unable to engage in appropriate taskwork. Learning in and for teams will become more critical so that employees will have the well-learned teamwork skills needed to concentrate on complex, demanding tasks and to work in team-based organizations. The theory of cooperation provides a common foundation for learning in and for teams.

EXPERIENCE WITH COOPERATIVE LEARNING

The authors have used cooperative learning both in Hong Kong and mainland Chinese management courses and have worked with other instructors. Overall, our experience is consistent with the evidence. There is considerable value in cooperative learning, but developing effective cooperative learning is challenging for students and instructors alike. We are impressed that Chinese students, though accustomed to didactic teaching, are open to cooperative learning. We note several aspects of making cooperative learning particularly useful in Chinese classrooms.

Individual accountability needs to be emphasized in mainland China and perhaps especially in Hong Kong. Hong Kong students are famous for their pragmatism, and they often assume that group projects are opportunities to divide up the work to complete the tasks efficiently rather than opportunities for everyone to learn all aspects of the task. They assign the persons they consider to be best for each task, they work individually, and then they put everything together. But this procedure means that students are not working on developing their abilities and confidence on all the tasks or helping each person learn. Instructors can call on individuals at random and have each group member complete the full task, which can help Chinese students recognize that the goal of cooperative learning is to make each student stronger, not simply to get the group task done efficiently.

Although collectivists recognize the importance of their relationships, Chinese students are often reserved and introverted. Group members often do not know each other's names. However, since cooperative learning is based on students knowing each other as individuals, what we have found effective is to give students activities and time for personal disclosure so that they will know each other as individuals. For example, the students might begin each meeting by discussing their favorite activities, career goals, and so on. These activities are useful for Western students, and structuring them in for Chinese students appears to be particularly appropriate.

Chinese people want to be respectful and avoid appearing to be particularly critical. Guidance as to how to provide feedback without showing disrespect needs to accompany the opportunities to give feedback. Explicitly defending the usefulness of feedback and structuring times to give feedback and to process their group functioning can develop openness. Emphasis should be put on providing positive feedback to help students build upon their strengths.

Chinese people have been characterized as avoiders of conflict. However, Chinese students, especially in mainland China but also in Hong Kong, are eager to discuss opposing views through structured controversy. For example, we have successfully used advocacy teams by dividing groups of four into two sub-groups, giving them time to prepare the pro and con positions, and then having them discuss their opposing views.

The Hong Kong Cooperative Learning Center has developed workshops in Hong Kong and mainland China since 1997. Hundreds of university instructors and school educators are experimenting with cooperative learning. The Center also sponsored the translation and publication by the Machine Press of Beijing in 2001 of Johnson and Johnson's *Active Learning: Cooperation in the College Classroom*, 1991 (Interaction Book Company: Edina, MN).

THE POSSIBILITY OF INTEGRATION

Traditionally, either-or thinking has dominated educational and organizational theory. Educators and managers value either learning or performance, individual well-being or organizational productivity. Organizations prosper through discipline and conformity, whereas individuals thrive on self-expression and relationships.

Research on cooperation and competition reveals the limits of this either-or thinking. Although there may be some trade-offs, the individual learns and flourishes, and the organization delivers value through open, spirited cooperative work. Cooperative relationships contribute to getting things done in business and to learning in and out of the classroom. Cooperative learning reinforces the teamwork abilities that managers and employees must have to make modern team-based organizations effective.

China is thought to have a collectivist and supportive culture, whereas the West is individualistic and innovative. Not only do these contrasting cultures make joint work difficult, but it is believed by some that ideas and methods developed in one culture should not be applied in the other. Indeed, researchers have argued that collectivist and individualist cultures have distinct psychologies, although a recent meta-analysis provides little support for this view (Oyserman, Coon, & Kemmelmeier, 2002).

However, research indicates that the theory of cooperation and competition, although developed in the West, is applicable to China and to cross-cultural relationships. Both Chinese students and Western students, Chinese employees and Western employees can use the theory of cooperation to understand and strengthen their joint learning and common work.

The global economy has brought fresh opportunities and agonizing challenges. Our economic and technological developments seem to be far outdistancing our knowledge and abilities to work together to exploit opportunities and deal with threats. Cooperation theory presents the conditions and dynamics by which diverse people can together learn and solve common problems.

ACKNOWLEDGMENT

The authors thank the Hong Kong University Grants Council for its support of this chapter, grant project TDG2001-04LC-2.

REFERENCES

Chen, G., Liu, C. H., & Tjosvold, D. (in press). Conflict management for effective top management teams and innovation in China. *Journal of Management Studies.*

Chen, G., & Tjosvold, D. (2002). Conflict management and team effectiveness in China: The mediating role of justice. *Asia Pacific Journal of Management, 19,* 557–572.

Confucius. (1979). *The analects* (D. C. Lau, Trans.). New York: Penguin Books (Original work published c. 479 BCE)

Deutsch, M. (1949). A theory of cooperation and competition. *Human Relations, 2,* 129–152.

Deutsch, M. (1973). *The resolution of conflict.* New Haven, CT: Yale University Press.

Earley, P. C. (1997). *Face, harmony, and social structure: An analysis of organizational behavior across cultures.* NY: Oxford University Press.

Earley, P. C., & Gibson, C. B. (1998). Taking stock in our progress on individualism-collectivism: 100 years of solidarity and community. *Journal of Management, 24,* 265–304.

Farh, J. L., & Cheng, B. S. (2000). A culture analysis of paternalistic leadership in Chinese organization. In A. S. Tsui & J. T. Li (Eds.), *Management and Organizations in China.* London: Macmillan.

Graen, G. B., & Uhl-Bien, M. (1995). Relationship-based approach to leadership: Development of leader-member exchange (LMX) theory of leadership over 25 years: Applying a multi-level multi-domain perspective. *Leadership Quarterly, 6,* 219–247.

Ho, D. Y. (1976). On the concept of face. *American Journal of Sociology, 81,* 867–884.

Hofstede, G. (1980). *Culture's consequences: International differences in work-related values.* Thousand Oaks, CA: Sage.

Hofstede, G. (1991) *Cultures and organizations: Intercultural co-operation and its importance for survival.* New York: HarperCollins.

Hofstede, G. (1993). Cultural constraints in management theories. *The Academy of Management Executive, 7,* 81–94.

Hui, C., Law, K. S., & Chen, Z. X. (1999). A structural equation model of the effects of negative affectivity, leader-member exchange, and perceived job mobility on in-role and extra-role performance: A Chinese case. *Organizational Behavior and Human Decision Processes, 77,* 3–21.

Johnson, D. W. (2003). Social interdependence: Interrelationships among theory, research, and practice. *American Psychologist, 58,* 934–945.

Johnson, D. W., & Johnson, R. T. (1989). *Cooperation and competition: Theory and research.* Edina, MN: Interaction Book Company.

Johnson, D. W., & Johnson, R. T. (1991). *Learning together and alone.* Englewood Cliffs, NJ: Prentice Hall.

Johnson, D. W., & Johnson, R. T. (1994). Learning together in the social studies classroom. In R. J. Stahl, (Ed.), *Cooperative learning in social studies: A handbook for teachers.* Menlo Park, CA: Addison-Wesley.

Johnson, D. W., & Johnson, R. T. (1998). The three Cs of effective schools: Cooperative community, constructive conflict, civic values. *Australasian Association for Cooperative Education, 5*(1), 4–10.

Johnson, D. W., & Johnson, R. T. (1999). *Learning together and alone: Cooperative, competitive, and individualistic learning* (5th ed.). Englewood Cliffs, NJ: Prentice Hall.

Johnson, D. W., Johnson, R. T., Maruyama, G., Nelson, D., & Skon, L. (1981). Effects of cooperative, competitive and individualistic goal structures on achievement: A meta-analysis. *Psychological Bulletin, 89,* 47–62.

Johnson, D. W., Johnson, R. T., & Smith, K. A. (1991). *Active learning: Cooperation in the college classroom.* Edina, MN: Interaction Book Co.

Kirkbride, P. S., Tang, S. F. Y., & Westwood, R. I. (1991). Chinese conflict preferences and negotiating behaviour: Cultural and psychological influences. *Organization Studies, 12,* 365–386.

Leung, K. (1997). Negotiation and reward allocations across cultures. In P. C. Earley & M. Erez (Eds.), *New perspectives on international industrial/organizational psychology* (pp. 640-675). San Francisco: Jossey-Bass.

Oyserman, D., Coon, H. M., & Kemmelmeier, M. (2002). Rethinking individualism and collectivism: Evaluation of theoretical assumptions and meta-analyses. *Psychological Bulletin, 128,* 3–72.

Pearce, J. L. (2001). *Organization and management in the embrace of government.* Mahwah, NJ: Lawrence Erlbaum Associates.

Sampson, E. E. (2001). Reinterpreting individualism and collectivism: Their religious roots and monologic versus dialogic person-other relationship. *American Psychologist, 55,* 1425–1432.

Stanne, M. B., Johnson, D. W., & Johnson, R. T. (1999). Does competition enhance or inhibit motor performance? A meta-analysis. *Psychological Bulletin, 125,* 133–154.

Tang, S., & Kirkbride, P. (1986). Development of conflict management skills in Hong Kong: An analysis of some cross-cultural implications. *Management Education and Development, 17*(3), 287–301.

Ting-Toomey, S. (1988). A face negotiation theory. In Y. Y. Kim & W. B. Gudykunst (Eds.), *Theory and intercultural communication* (pp. 47–92). Thousand Oaks, CA: Sage.

Tjosvold, D. (1983). Social face in conflict: A critique. *International Journal of Group Tensions, 13,* 49–64.

Tjosvold, D. (1991). *Team organization: An enduring competitive advantage.* Chichester, England: Wiley.

Tjosvold, D. (1998). The cooperative and competitive goal approach to conflict: Accomplishments and challenges. *Applied Psychology, 47,* 285–313.

Tjosvold, D. (1999). Bridging East and West to develop new products and trust: Interdependence and interaction between a Hong Kong parent and North American subsidiary. *International Journal of Innovation Management, 3,* 233–252.

Tjosvold, D. (2002). Managing anger for teamwork in Hong Kong: Goal interdependence and open-mindedness. *Asian Journal Social Psychology, 5,* 107–123.

Tjosvold, D., & Moy, J. (1998). Managing employees in China from Hong Kong: Interaction, relationships, and productivity as antecedents to motivation. *Leadership & Organization Development Journal, 19,* 147–156.

Tjosvold, D., & Sun, H. (2000). Social face in conflict among Chinese: Effects of affronts to person and position. *Group Dynamics: Theory, Research, and Practice, 4,* 259–271.

Tjosvold, D., & Sun, H. (2001). Effects of influence tactics and social contexts: An experiment on relationships in China. *International Journal of Conflict Management, 12,* 239–258.

Tjosvold, D., & Sun, H. (2003). Openness among Chinese in conflict: Effects of direct discussion and warmth on integrated decision making. *Journal of Applied Social Psychology, 33,* 1878–1897.

Tjosvold, D., Coleman, P. T., & Sun, H. (2003). Effects of organizational values on leaders' use of information power to affect performance in China. *Group Dynamics: Theory, Research, and Practice, 7*, 152–167.

Tjosvold, D., Hui, C., & Law, K. S. (1998). Empowerment in the leader relationship in Hong Kong: Interdependence and controversy. *Journal of Social Psychology, 138*, 624–637.

Tjosvold, D., Hui, C., & Sun, H. (2000). Building social face and open-mindedness: Constructive conflict in Asia. In C. M. Lau, K. S. Law, D. K. Tse, & C. S. Wong (Eds.), *In Asian management matters: Regional relevance and global impact* (pp. 4–16). London: Imperial College Press.

Tjosvold, D., Law, K. S., & Hui, C. (1996). *Goal interdependence, leadership relationship, and citizenship behavior in China.* Paper presented at the International Association for Conflict Management, Ithaca, NY.

Tjosvold, D., Law, K. S., & Sun, H. (2003). Collectivistic and individualistic values: Their effects on group dynamics and productivity in China. *Group Decision and Negotiation, 12*, 243–263.

Tjosvold, D., Sun, H., & Chen, Y. F. (2003). *Effects of employee achievement and social context on the use of power to affect performance in China.* Paper presented at the International Association for Conflict Management, Melbourne, Australia.

Tjosvold, D., Tang, M. L., & West, M. A. (in press). Reflexivity for team innovation in China: The contribution of goal interdependence. *Group & Organization Management.*

Tjosvold, D., Wong, M. L., & Liu, C. H. (2002, June). *Collectivist values and open-mindedness for Chinese employees' trust of their Japanese leaders.* Paper presented at the Academy of International Business, San Juan, Puerto Rico.

Tjosvold, D., Wong, A. S. H., Nibler, R., & Pounder, J. S. (2002). Teamwork and controversy in undergraduate management courses in Hong Kong: Can the method reinforce the message? *Swiss Journal of Psychology, 61*, 131–138.

Tjosvold, D., Yu, Z. Y., & Hui, C. (in press). Team learning from mistakes: The contribution of cooperative goals and problem-solving. *Journal of Management Studies.*

Tjosvold, D., Yu, Z. Y., & Liu, C. H. (2001). *Collectivist and individualistic values in the leader relationship: Openness and employee commitment and performance.* Paper submitted for publication. Lingnan University, Hong Kong.

Triandis, H. C. (1990). Cross-cultural studies of individualism and collectivism. In J. Berman (Ed.), *Nebraska Symposium on Motivation, 1989* (pp. 41–133). Lincoln, Nebraska: University of Nebraska Press.

Triandis, H. C. (1995). *Individualism and collectivism.* Boulder, CO: Westview Press.

Triandis, H. C. (2000). Culture and conflict. *International Journal of Psychology, 35*, 145–152.

Tse, D. K., Francis, J., & Walls, J. (1994). Cultural differences in conducting intra- and inter-cultural negotiations: A Sino-Canadian comparison. *Journal of International Business Studies, 24*, 537–555.

Westwood, R. (1997). Harmony and patriarchy: The cultural basis for "paternalistic headship" among the overseas Chinese. *Organization Studies, 18*, 445–480.

CHAPTER 10

CREATING A MULTI-SITE SUMMER STUDY ABROAD PROGRAM

Thomas M. Porcano, William B. Snavely, David M. Shull, and Wayne Staton

ABSTRACT

The purpose of this chapter is (a) to show the benefits of a multi-site program relative to a single-site program and (b) to provide a comprehensive guide to the development, organization, administration, and maintenance of a multi-site program. Based on the success of our own programs, in particular the multi-site model, we believe that faculty from other universities could develop multi-site programs. We discuss all program aspects, including choosing the academic focus, selecting locations, marketing the program to students and parents, pre-departure preparation for students, running the program, follow-up and evaluation, and year-to-year continuity.

The Cutting Edge of International Management Education, pages 243–283
Copyright © 2004 by Information Age Publishing

CREATING A MULTI-SITE
SUMMER STUDY ABROAD PROGRAM

Advocates for international education express the opinion that the United States educational system has a great need to address the increasingly interdependent global economy and resulting global interconnections. Collins, Czarra, and Smith (1998) argue that no institution in the United States needs to respond more to the global challenge than does the United States education system. The benefits accruing to student and faculty education on aspects of life in other countries have created an educational imperative that is almost no longer a topic of debate (Kwok & Arpan, 2002). The focus is on how best to increase international literacy for United States students and faculty. In this chapter, we present the details of one approach: a multisite summer study abroad program. We will provide readers with detailed guidance toward creation of similar programs.

Numerous United States colleges and universities include study abroad programs to foster the internationalization of students. Hopkins (1999) believes a study abroad program is invaluable in providing both experiential learning and a new cultural context for students. Barker (2000) suggests that the importance of providing study abroad programs to students cannot be overvalued. Unfortunately, the number of United States students studying abroad is still relatively small—less than 10 percent of undergraduates at four-year colleges and universities. However, according to the Institute of International Education (2003a), the number of United States students studying abroad doubled from 1992 to 2002. Social sciences accounted for the largest proportion at 22 percent, followed by business/management at 18 percent (Institute of International Education, 2003b).

United States business educators advocate recognition of the importance of international literacy for students and faculty. The accreditation process of the Association to Advance Collegiate Schools of Business International (AACSB International)—formerly the American Association of Collegiate Schools of Business—has increased the emphasis on internationalizing the business curriculum. Learning experiences in multicultural environments and in understanding diversity are general knowledge and skill areas for undergraduate business programs. Learning experiences in domestic and global economic environments of organizations are general knowledge and skill areas for both undergraduate and master's level business programs (Association to Advance Collegiate Schools of Business International, 2003). The AACSB International accreditation process serves as a de facto mandate to internationalize United States business school programs.

Business schools use various approaches to internationalize United States business students and faculty. Most business schools have infused their curricula with international content. The content may be a single international business class, a sequence of classes, and/or "internationalization across the curriculum" (i.e., an attempt to inject international topics into the spectrum of appropriate courses). Some business schools also use study abroad programs perhaps as a substitute for international business courses (Trevino & Melton, 2002). Study abroad programs have a variety of approaches. United States business schools can partner with foreign schools—allowing students to matriculate while at foreign campuses. Some United States business schools offer courses where United States students and United States faculty are domiciled in foreign countries.

At this time, little research exists about business study abroad programs. Several articles relate faculty members' experiences with a specific type of study abroad program (e.g., Praetzel, Curcio, & Dilorenzo, 1996; Wymar, 1996; and Keillor & Emore, 2003). Several articles describe planning and/or assessing study abroad programs (e.g., Tashakori & Dotson, 1989; Porth, 1997; Thomas & McMahon, 1998; Duke, 2000; and Bailey & Harbeck, 2002). A study by Holland and Kedia (2003) suggests how to make study abroad programs more attractive and effective for United States students.

Our goal in this chapter is to document our experiences in establishing a multi-site program in Europe and to compare its benefits relative to the more typical single-site program. The goal of such a program is to provide students with meaningful exposure to European culture and business. With appropriate planning and effort, the various interactions with individuals and institutions across Europe provide students with a range of insights not easily obtained from a single-site program. For example, the cultures, lifestyles, and attitudes of British, French, German, Italian, Spanish, and Swiss nationals (and United States expatriates domiciled abroad) can be more directly compared and contrasted via a multi-site approach. Differing viewpoints about the United States, the European Union (EU), other European countries, foreign workers, and a plethora of cultural differences become dramatically more apparent in the multi-site approach.

The obvious trade-off is that a single-site program offers more immersion in the culture of the country where the student is domiciled. A student seeking to become an expert on a particular country would be better suited to a single-site program. A potential problem with a multi-site program is that the exposure to each culture may be too superficial to be meaningful. Careful advance planning and the following program design attempt to mitigate this potential problem. While we strongly support the benefits of single-site programs for study abroad, we favor the multi-site approach for the reasons given above and in greater detail in following sections.

Historical Perspective

The authors have extensive experience in teaching multi-site European programs and single-site summer business courses in London, Luxembourg and Russia. The multi-site European program was developed during 1995–1996. The inaugural program occurred in summer 1996 with two faculty members and 65 students attending classes throughout Western Europe. The program grew to four faculty members and 144 students by 2001.

Prior to the establishment of our multi-site summer business in Europe program in 1995, each faculty member had taught in a single-site study abroad program for either a summer term or an academic year. Almost all students in the program each year came from the same school in the United States (Miami University in Ohio). Single-site programs at this university occur in a wide variety of formats. They vary with respect to duration, classes offered, location, dates offered, and so forth. A typical summer study abroad program occurs during a summer term of five to eight weeks at a single site. Miami University offered two single-site summer study abroad programs in 1995. One was located in London, and one was located in Luxembourg.

At that time, we believed that a multi-site program would be more beneficial, enjoyable, and efficient for students and faculty than a program stationed in one locale only. The program itinerary was initially developed during the summer of 1995. Base cities were selected, hotel accommodations were reserved, field trips were planned, potential guest speakers were contacted, and so on. Advertising for the program was conducted during the early part of fall semester 1995; an ad was placed in the student paper, and posters were placed throughout the school of business. The ads and posters provided general information and indicated the times and places of four informational sessions. Students were required to attend one of the sessions and then to attend a general presentation (with their parents) during the university's Parents' Weekend (held in early October). During the informational sessions, students were given handouts regarding the proposed itinerary, estimated costs, course information, and so forth. In October, approximately 65 students had signed up for the inaugural program in summer 1996.

The inaugural program included two courses—Comparative Accounting and Comparative International Business Law. Students were required to enroll in both courses. The program was expanded to 72 students in 1997, with full enrollment and a large waiting list by October 1996 for the summer 1997 session. The program size was thereafter maintained at 72, and the waiting list continued to expand significantly. The waiting list for the summer 2000 program was more than 200 students. Consequently, we expanded the program for summer 2001 and added two additional courses, International Organizational Behavior and International Business. Thus, the summer 2001 program contained two tracks: (1) the original track (Accounting and Business Law) and (2) the new track (International Organizational Behavior and International Business). Students had to enroll in one track and take the two courses in that track. Regardless of the track, all faculty members and students were in the same cities at the same time. Each track had 72 students enrolled in it (a total of 144 students), and there still was a waiting list.

Logistics

Briefly, the logistics of the multi-site program are as follows. There are five base cities: London, Paris, Zurich, Munich, and Rome. We reside in hotels in each base city, with two students per room with breakfast and dinner included. Classes and professional visits/presentations usually take place in the morning; thus, the students are free to explore each base city during the afternoon and after dinner. Sometimes there are afternoon or evening trips (e.g., theater), but for the most part, students are free during these times. In general, we are in a base city for three or four nights; then the students travel during the weekend to arrive at the next base city (usually on Sunday night in time for dinner). Where students go during weekends is their choice, but the advantage is that they do not have to return to the same city. They can visit other places while traveling toward the next base city. Thus, in five weeks, they can experience many different villages, towns, and cities. At the end of the five-week program, the students are free to go home or travel independently. Some of them will meet family or friends and will continue to travel through Europe. Many of our students went to Greece for a week to experience the Greek Isles on sailboats before they went home.

Selecting the Academic Focus

Great care should be given to the choice of academic focus. We have chosen courses that either have international content by nature or have an international component embedded into a typically non-international course. Comparative Accounting, ACC 383, illustrates the former while International Organizational Behavior and Theory, MGT 291.I, exemplifies the latter. MGT 291.I is a business core course (typically numbered MGT 291 and titled Organizational Behavior and Theory) required by all majors in the business school with an additional credit hour of international topics integrated into the course. It is important that the courses in which the students enroll count for credit in their academic program; therefore, the courses we have chosen satisfy core business requirements or major/minor requirements. This is important to students and to whomever is paying for the program because they want to know that the money spent provides a unique experience and adds to the student's degree progress. A study abroad program that does not contribute to the student's timely degree progress has an extremely high hidden cost. The hidden cost consists of the possibility that the student will need an additional term of coursework to graduate, which could result in lost income and/or job experience while the student is still attending school.

One key issue in structuring these programs is that the two courses in a track should logically fit together. For example, we designed two tracks. One track especially appeals to accounting and finance majors between their junior and senior years, and the other fits all business majors between their sophomore and junior years. What makes the most sense at other universities depends on student make-up and academic requirements. A program consisting of pure elective courses should be avoided because many students do not need additional electives by junior year. For these students, pure electives in the program hours do not provide any matriculation benefits. Thus, they typically constitute unnecessary hours for students who have already fulfilled their electives.

Another key issue is course rigor. It is important to have appropriate academic content and rigor, especially with required courses. In addition to the material that needs to be covered to satisfy requirements of the school—major or minor—the subject matter must be internationalized. As mentioned above, the three-hour core requirement in organizational behavior can be expanded by one hour to allow for substantial international topics in the form of business interactions, field trip experiences, speakers, and team projects. At least one course in each track should have flexibility for emphasis on international topics of opportunity. The BUS 371 course covers a wide range of international topics and provides a vehicle for integration of a wide range of international experiences. BUS 371 and MGT 291 complement each other in providing international experiences and matriculation progress from the track. Further, the choice of courses allows varying levels of integration between courses within a track. Greater integration enhances student learning.

ACC 383 and FIN 483 are integrated in several ways. In ACC 383, tax treaties are discussed, and in FIN 483, treaties in general are discussed. In FIN 483, general legal aspects of doing business abroad (including entity structure) are discussed, and in ACC 383, the specific accounting and tax issues (and planning opportunities) of these concepts are discussed. In FIN 483, general aspects of the World Trade Organization (WTO) are discussed, whereas in ACC 383, the WTO is discussed as it relates to recent income tax and tariff issues. Similarly, the European Union (EU) and the European Monetary Union (EMU) are discussed in general terms in FIN 483, and in specific terms (e.g., accounting harmonization) in ACC 383. MGT 291 and BUS 371 are integrated across several topics, such as Hofstede's Model, international issues in management and marketing, course presentation assignments, and research papers. Primary coverage for a topic can be given in either course with appropriate supplemental coverage occurring in both courses.

While academic rigor is essential, instructors must make a strong effort to encourage travel and incorporate it into the international experience. Study abroad students should be expected to travel abundantly since different perspectives provide a better-rounded set of experiences for the students. Students are not expected to spend their entire weekend with their noses in a book or writing assignments. Students are expected to read and study for exams during time in each base city and during travel time on the weekends (i.e., during long train rides). Weekend assignments other than the preparation for Monday course coverage as established by the syllabus should be avoided, since time is the most precious resource for students studying abroad. Courses that are too time-consuming while the students are abroad are ill-planned and should be avoided. If courses are too time-consuming, the students will miss out on seeing and enjoying the great locations you select, and the reputation for the program will diminish quickly.

Some textbook and course material (as much as reasonably possible) should be taught in the term prior to departure. Any research projects should be due (and graded) prior to departure since resources to produce these papers will likely be unavailable once the students have left the United States. This involves teaching in the spring term and working with students on research papers during this period. Students must be encouraged to keep appropriate time slots open during the spring term. This information should go out to students in the fall prior to their registration for spring schedules. Front-loading the course in this way requires coordination and effort by instructors and students prior to departure. In return, it unlocks precious time abroad.

A final consideration is the faculty who teach in the program; they must enjoy teaching and interacting with students. Faculty in the multi-site program usually spend more time with students than do those in a single-site program. In addition to class meetings, they have breakfast and dinner together, and attend many field trips (business, cultural and social). There is also an opportunity to travel with some of the students during the weekends. Thus, it is imperative that student-friendly faculty participate in the multi-site program.

Choosing the Locations

Our primary focus has been a "Summer Business in Europe" program that utilizes five Western European cities as base cities. However, a similar approach also can work for other parts of the world. Using our multi-site program as an inspiration, one of our colleagues developed a Pacific Rim program that is based in several countries (South Korea, Japan and China) during a five-week term. However, Western Europe works especially well because of the ease of independent weekend travel and because many students like it as a travel destination.

One of the primary considerations, of course, is finding a location where you can effectively hold classes. Depending on the time of year and the schedules of local universities, you might be able to choose locations at universities. Our choice is normally a hotel located in a safe, convenient part of the city. The hotel must have adequate conference facilities, excellent sleeping accommodations, and a good menu for breakfast and dinner. These accommodations will increase the program costs, but most students and parents have appreciated knowing that the rooms and meals will be of high quality during base city stays.

The next consideration is whether the chosen city has plenty for the students to see and do during their free time after classes. An especially good choice is a city where you have business contacts (alumni or others) who can either visit your classes, host a class field trip, or be dinner guests (so that the students and guests can have informal conversations). Examples in our experience have been corporate offices of banks, accounting firms, other businesses, stock exchanges, the International Court of Justice, the WTO, etc. We also try to include other excursions (a show in London, a boat cruise in Paris, museums, a German concentration camp, a tour of the Vatican, and so forth).

The geographic order for your cities also is very important. The cities should logically follow each other (in a geographical sense) to allow for more effective and efficient use of travel time. For example, our program usually goes from west (e.g., starting in London) to east (e.g., ending in Rome). This allows students to travel northeast and/or southeast on weekends without backtracking or spending too much free time in transit. If you are going to allow weekend travel, you need to think about where the students might reasonably go so that the students get the most from their weekend travel.

Marketing the Program to Students and Parents

Program costs are an important concern. Courses that assist students' timely degree progress overcome the hidden costs mentioned previously and make the study abroad program more feasible and attractive. Although some schools advertise study abroad programs for the same costs as a typical term, a study abroad program will cost more than a regular term at home. Our experience suggests that a study abroad program, even a single-site program, should include the costs of travel and weekend activities. To leave them out of advertised costs is less than complete disclosure. Students in single-site programs usually travel on weekends, paying for their food, shelter, and travel costs (typically a Eurail Pass). The comparison of advertised costs should be made very carefully across programs. The cost of our multi-site program is reasonably similar to the cost of the single-site programs at our school.

After courses, faculty, and locations for the program have been selected, the next step is to find the students. Marketing the program is an often over-looked aspect of a successful study abroad program. Program marketing should begin as early as possible. Ideally, initial marketing should occur during the spring term a full year or more before the summer program. For example, a one-page handout briefly describing the program and listing contact persons could be handed out in freshmen and sophomore classes during spring semester 2004 for a summer 2005 or 2006 program. This enables students to think about it during summer 2004 so that when they return for the fall 2004 term, they have already discussed it with their parents or guardians. It also enables students to more effectively register for fall 2004 and winter/spring 2005 classes (i.e., they know what they are taking in the summer). If it is not possible to advertise that early, then advertising should occur as early as possible in the academic year.

Advertising can be done in several ways. For new programs, an ad in the student paper is a good choice. This reaches a large number of students and usually is not too costly. Placing posters around campus (in dormitories, the student union and especially where business courses are offered) is a low-cost but effective means of advertising. Also, asking colleagues to distribute a handout in their classes works well (all sophomore and junior classes should be contacted). The one-page ad, poster, or handout should briefly describe the program, base city locations, field trips, and so forth, in addition to indicating dates, times, and places of informational meetings.

The informational meetings should take place on different days over several weeks. During these meetings, the program should be described completely. Students should receive handouts that provide an indication of program courses (and how the courses fulfill various degree requirements), program itinerary, cost estimates, contact persons, and so forth.

Also, a general letter providing background information about the program should be prepared for students and their parents or guardians. Students should take two or three copies of each handout, one for the student and one for each parent or guardian, because in most instances, parents or guardians must be sold on the benefits of the program.

The final informational session should be held on a weekend when a substantial number of parents/guardians will be on campus, such as football homecoming weekend or during Parents' Day weekend. This enables the parents to evaluate the cost-benefit of the program early in the academic year and to ask (in person) any questions that they may have. Advanced advertising of this special informational session is very helpful. In many instances, freshmen students and their parents or guardians also attend the sessions and start planning to enroll in the program when the students are eligible after their sophomore year.

Significant benefits accrue when the summer program roster is filled prior to the end of the fall term. Deposits can be collected so that contractual deposits can be made. Initial class rosters can be developed. Travel arrangements can be booked (e.g., air travel). Logistical meetings can be held before the end of the term. This allows the program coordinators to organize classes for the winter or spring term. Students can receive course syllabi to facilitate the inclusion of spring schedules in conjunction with meetings for the upcoming summer program. It also enables students to explore various funding sources. It is very common that some students' plans will change, and they will drop out during late fall or early spring. In that case, maintaining a good waiting list ensures that replacement students are available, and when it is time to depart, you will likely have a full program.

Pre-Departure Preparation

In most cases, it does not make sense just to drop a large group of ethno-centric American students into an international setting and expect everything to work. Preparation includes logistical meetings, social meetings, and pre-departure class sessions related to your courses.

Logistical meetings address all aspects of the program's itinerary:

- Orientation and informational meetings during the fall term
- Class meetings during the spring term preceding the summer departure
- Payments (when amounts are due, how much is due, what the payment covers, and to whom the checks are to be made)
- The day-to-day schedule while abroad

- Expectations regarding student behavior and performance
- What to pack
- Student pre-departure travel plans (e.g., it is best if the students at least know where they are going for the first "free time" weekend)

Social meetings enable students to get to know each other and the faculty. Two social meetings are recommended, which will help students and faculty break down barriers and become more willing to interact with each other. These meetings also can be used to help the students get ready for some of the cultural differences they will experience while abroad.

Pre-departure class sessions address academic content of the courses and provide other information and orientations:

- Academic subject matter that needs to be covered prior to departure
- Team assignments
- Discussion of team projects and progress reports
- Handouts to students
- Collection of all checks and other documents (e.g., emergency and medical forms)
- Cultural orientations (i.e., an indication of cultural differences and what to expect)
- Procedures to follow in case of an emergency

The pre-departure sessions should also be used to address any concerns or questions that the students may have. Doing this early (before the students go abroad) can reduce on-site problems and increase the program's effectiveness.

Running the Program On-Site

Pre-departure meetings and planning make on-site operations run more smoothly. However, much remains to be done during the program. Upon arrival at each base city hotel, faculty must meet with hotel staff to make sure that the correct arrangements are in place. Guest speakers and dinner guests should be contacted to reconfirm their visits. All field trips should be reconfirmed with personnel such as business contacts and guides.

Students must be reminded of what is expected of them regarding class sessions, field trips, behavior in the hotel, and during all scheduled activities. The faculty must interact with students to be sure that things are going well for them and be very observant in case a student is having a problem or becoming a loner. The faculty must be aware of what is happening in the base cities and address areas of concern, such as potentially threatening or dangerous events.

It is important to stress to the students that they must be flexible. The students must adapt to their environment and must be able to handle unexpected events. Contingency plans should be reiterated. The faculty should obtain weekend travel plans from students on the last day of class prior to the weekend and should provide a contact telephone number to all students prior to weekend departures. We recommend that all faculty have one or more international cell phones for emergency contact purposes. Upon arrival at the next city during dinner, faculty should be certain that all students have arrived and be prepared to investigate if some of the students have not arrived at the appointed time.

Evaluation and Follow-Up

Course/instructor evaluations and program evaluations are invaluable. They provide information that is needed to find out if all aspects of the multi-site program are running well. Additionally, insights can be gained from students with respect to their weekend travel plans.

Required university, school (college), and department course/instructor evaluations should be used. These evaluations are required for all courses taught by the faculty, and teaching in a multi-site program should not be an exception. The evaluations should be reviewed carefully to see if certain aspects of the course or something about the instructor need to be changed. The success of a multi-site program is highly dependent on the course and the instructor; so this feedback, and subsequent action based on it, is very important.

Program evaluations do not address course and instructor aspects; rather, they are concerned more with logistical aspects of the program. They should contain questions regarding the day-to-day schedule, the hotels (quality, convenience, etc.), the meals, sleeping arrangements, classroom arrangements, field trips, travel arrangements, pre-departure meetings and information, costs, and so forth.

Information about student activities during free time can be very useful in advising next year's students and possibly in revising the program. (For example, the initial program in 1996 did not include Munich as a base city. However, after obtaining feedback from students in the 1996 and 1997 programs regarding their experiences in Munich during weekend travels, Munich was added as a base city.)

BENEFITS OF THE MULTI-SITE
SUMMER STUDY ABROAD PROGRAM

Students in study abroad programs naturally have a strong desire to travel extensively on weekends, and they benefit immensely from their travel experiences. An appropriately designed multi-site program builds upon students' travel experiences to enhance the program's academic content, cultural exposure, efficiency, effectiveness, and appeal. In short, a multi-site approach dramatically enriches a student's international experience.

Most obvious is the more efficient and effective use of travel time with the multi-site approach. To illustrate, consider the potential travel of a student on the first weekend of a single-site program based in London. After the first week of classes, the student leaves for Paris on Thursday afternoon, usually with other students, and arrives after a three- to four-hour train ride. Finding a hostel or hotel and navigating the Metro may take until evening. Touring Paris and its environs can easily cover a weekend with the student returning late Sunday to the base city. An ambitious student might even travel to other locales on the same weekend, returning to the base city very late on Sunday or early Monday prior to class. The return travel duplicates the initial travel to get to Paris, and is dead time. This would occur for each weekend of travel, leading to a large amount of duplicated travel and dead time.

In a multi-site program, Paris could be the base city for the second week. This program's more efficient use of travel time is obvious. A student can travel to areas of greatest interest and arrive in Paris for Sunday dinner, probably with less train travel time than required by the single-site program and certainly with no duplicate travel and related dead time. A less obvious but equally important benefit is that with Paris as base city for the second week, the program coordinators can arrange for local speakers, field trips, and business interactions/experiences. Speakers in each base city should be prompted to provide both local and global opinions so that students can observe and reflect upon the different viewpoints espoused in different locales. For example, views and perspectives in London can differ dramatically from those in Paris. Students receive the benefits of comparing the insights and opinions of locals or United States expatriates in numerous base cities.

The students in a multi-site program are exposed to a broader range of views, both geographically and culturally, than are the students enrolled in a single-site program. A broader exposure seems especially desirable for business students. Also, a multi-site program uses the students' desire to travel to help expand on the students' experiences. Travel works in a symbiotic relationship with the program, which enhances the students' experiences and perceptions of the program.

Student Benefits

Based on our experiences with the program and the extensive feedback we have received, we believe that the students' educational experience and understanding of cross-cultural differences during their undergraduate studies is significantly enhanced by participation in a multi-site program. Instead of being exposed to only one country's viewpoint, students obtain perspectives from several countries. These perspectives enable the students to more fully understand the similarities and differences of the countries, even if these countries are united (e.g., EU countries). In their efforts to unite and harmonize the various aspects of daily life in other countries, students obviously benefit from the perspectives gained from enrollment in multi-site programs. In addition to the content knowledge the student receives, each student also grows in numerous ways. The cultural and social aspects of the program help the students learn to appreciate cultural differences and the fact that one culture, while different, is not necessarily "better" than another one. The overall multi-site experience helps our students understand how these differences affect perceptions of Americans (as well as intra-EU perceptions) and to understand why, for example, the French perceive Americans differently than do the Germans or Italians.

As the students learn to "navigate" various cities and learn how to travel from one country to another, their self-confidence also increases. They become more independent, more responsible for their actions, and better able to handle unstructured situations.

Finally, many of the students who have participated in our multi-site program have indicated that participation in the program positively affected their job placement prospects (e.g., interviewing with prospective employers, obtaining positions, and subsequently transferring to an office abroad). The perception of former students in our programs is that participation in a study abroad program provides several benefits to potential employers. Study abroad students have learning experiences with other cultures, and the ones who desire to return abroad are likely to have overcome culture shock and language barriers, to some degree. Assigning those who have previously participated in study abroad programs to overseas jobs may mitigate the cost of expatriate problems.

Benefits to the University

Numerous benefits accrue to the university. A high-quality international business program enhances a school's reputation. Also, international business education is a major concern of AACSB International. The multi-site study abroad program that we describe in this chapter provides a tested product that meets AACSB International standards for learning experiences in domestic and global economic business in addition to providing learning experiences in diverse multicultural environments. This is a popular program, and once the word "gets out," having a sufficient student base should not be a problem. The multi-site program allows faculty to use their entrepreneurial (and naturally competitive) skills to develop a first-class, highly-demanded program that should produce additional well-developed and highly-demanded courses. This competition can be very healthy, but it also can be perceived by some school of business faculty and administrators as unfair because it is so successful (sometimes educators do not practice what they teach).

The program has had a positive effect on the students who have participated in it, and prospective employers have looked favorably upon those students. Thus, job recruitment and placement have been positively impacted. Providing an exciting and positive international experience, not to mention a positive impact on prospective employment, will help the university attract more students.

The study abroad program has also had a positive impact on alumni and university relations. We contacted alumni in the base cities and asked them to be our dinner guests, because students benefit through the informal discussions that take place during dinner. The university benefits through the renewed contact with (and interest shown by) its alumni. In one instance, an alumnus (who had not heard from the university or school of business in a long time) we contacted volunteered to become more involved in courses and events on the main campus.

The program has had a positive impact on department faculty and business relations. We contact local firms who have a presence in the base cities to see if they are willing to provide speakers or site visits. This contact is perceived in a positive way, since company owners believe that the students' exposure to their personnel and facilities abroad will help in recruiting the students as potential employees.

The program also can be used to develop faculty members who might have an interest in "internationalizing" but do not have sufficient time and/or the means to do so by themselves. Such faculty could shadow the program faculty during part of the multi-site program and learn how things work. They also can be assisted in developing their own programs.

Why is This Program so Popular?

We believe the multi-site students abroad program is very popular for several reasons. First, the travel aspect of the program is very appealing. The arrangements in each base city provide students with excellent sleeping accommodations and excellent nourishment (breakfast and dinners); this is especially popular with parents. The arrangements also provide students with time to see each city. Also, because the students do not have to return to the same city (make a loop), they are able to see more of Europe at a less frantic pace; the inefficiencies of constantly leaving from and returning to the same city are eliminated. Second, the field trips provide the students with business, cultural, and social experiences that they might not otherwise experience. This is especially true when compared to programs that are based in only one city. Third, the courses in each track are "integrated" in that each course covers different aspects of similar subject items; this naturally enhances the learning process. Fourth, the team projects provide students with a general foundation for a specific country, and this foundation can be built on during class discussions. Finally, the teacher/student interaction is greater than in regular classes. Students and faculty are together more frequently, and students respond favorably to the increased interaction, guidance, and assistance.

GENERAL PROGRAM ITEMS

Example of Program Itinerary

What does the program look like? The following is a day-by-day example for a five-week program in Western Europe.

Friday	May 10	All fly to London
Saturday	May 11	Arrive in London—bus pickup at airport, tour Windsor Castle, then transfer to hotel
Sunday	May 12	London—morning classes*
Monday	May 13	London—morning classes; evening London theatre
Tuesday	May 14	London—morning classes
Wednesday	May 15	London—morning classes, then Eurostar to Brussels and free
Thursday	May 16	free
Friday	May 17	free
Saturday	May 18	free
Sunday	May 19	free—arrive at Paris hotel for dinner
Monday	May 20	Paris—morning classes
Tuesday	May 21	Paris—morning classes; evening Bateaux Mouches
Wednesday	May 22	Paris—morning classes
Thursday	May 23	Paris—morning classes then free
Friday	May 24	free

Saturday	May 25	free
Sunday	May 26	free—arrive at Zurich for dinner
Monday	May 27	Zurich—morning classes
Tuesday	May 28	Zurich—morning classes (exam in one course)
Wednesday	May 29	Zurich—morning classes (exam in other course); afternoon classes then free
Thursday	May 30	free
Friday	May 31	free
Saturday	June 1	free
Sunday	June 2	free—arrive in Munich for dinner
Monday	June 3	Munich—morning classes; afternoon Mike's Bike Tour
Tuesday	June 4	Munich—morning classes; afternoon Dachau trip
Wednesday	June 5	Munich—morning classes then free
Thursday	June 6	free
Friday	June 7	free
Saturday	June 8	free
Sunday	June 9	free—arrive at Rome hotel for dinner
Monday	June 10	Rome—morning classes; afternoon classes
Tuesday	June 11	Rome—Vatican trip
Wednesday	June 12	Rome—morning classes (exam in one course)
Thursday	June 13	Rome—classes (exam in other course)—then program ends

* *Note:* Classes may consist of regular material, a guest speaker, or a site visit.

Sample General Letter to Parents and Students

Dear Parents and Students:

The purpose of this letter is to describe briefly our summer international program that we (Professors Thomas Porcano, Accountancy; Wayne Staton, Finance; David Shull, Finance; and William Snavely, Management) are offering next summer and to provide a brief background on ourselves. The program is called "Summer Business in Europe Program."

Students in our program take one of two tracks—either the Porcano/Staton track or the Shull/Snavely track. The Porcano/Staton track includes ACC 383, Comparative Accounting, and FIN 483, Comparative International Business Law. Each course is four credit hours, and ACC 221 is the only prerequisite. The Shull/Snavely track includes MGT 291, Organizational Behavior, and BUS 371, International Business. Each course is four credit hours and ECO 201 and ECO 202 are prerequisites for this track. Each track covers various aspects of doing business abroad. Also, the courses meet a variety of requirements depending on the student's major, minor, or thematic sequence.

In addition to the uniqueness, timeliness, and importance of these course offerings, the travel arrangements also are unique. We believe that students benefit more from a foreign program if classes are taught in several countries, as opposed to being in one location for the entire period. Not surprisingly, we find that the students also share this belief, so our program is designed to maximize student exposure to several European countries. Classes take place in cities—London, Paris, Zurich, Munich, and Rome—in five different countries, and we generally spend four days at each location (Sunday evening until noon on Thursday). Students are then free to travel, and we all meet at the next location on Sunday evening. To supplement and enhance class materials, we have guest speakers and several field trips. We have also planned several cultural field trips (e.g., Windsor Castle, Dachau, the Vatican).

During our time in each city, we ask professionals to make presentations on various aspects of their accounting, legal, behavioral, and business systems. This enables us to take full advantage of being in Europe and provides an excellent base for a comparative analysis of each country's systems and international business in general. Also, since we are in each locale for four nights, students are able to explore each city and its environment in a relaxed manner. Finally, students are housed in three- or four-star hotels in each locale and are provided a full breakfast and a three-course dinner. Thus, you can be assured that the students' accommodation and nutritional needs will be met.

We have designed our program so that it begins on May 10, when everyone flies to London, and formally ends on June 13 in Rome. Since we are in Europe for only five weeks, this shorter time period provides more flexibility for students and reduces the costs of the program. We are able to accomplish this because we teach related materials during the fall and spring semesters prior to our summer program.

The professors of the Summer Business in Europe Program have been nominated for and have won a variety of teaching awards. In addition, each professor has extensive experience abroad.

The experience we gained while abroad and our extensive interaction with students and professionals lead us to the conclusion that a summer program located in one place for the entire summer period is not as beneficial as a multi-site program which is shorter in duration. The summer 2002 program will be the seventh time we have conducted this program. Programs during the previous six summers were very successful (based on feedback from students, parents, and business people. Please see the attached comments page).

Again, we believe that we have developed a summer business program in Europe that is unique, maximizes students' exposure to professionals in several countries, incorporates travel, and is student-friendly. In short, it is a good and enjoyable program. The program's tentative schedule is attached More information can be obtained from our website, www.sba.muohio.edu/finance/europe.htm

We hope that your son or daughter and you will find the program interesting and that you will attend our presentation. If you are unable to attend the presentation and/or have questions about the program, then please contact one of the professors.

Sincerely,

Thomas M. Porcano, Arthur Andersen Alumni Professor of Accountancy
David M. Shull, Associate Professor of Finance
William B. Snavely, Professor of Management
Wayne Staton, Associate Professor of Finance

A Selection of Comments from Business People, Parents, and Students

From a presenter in France and "Big 5" partner (a Miami alumnus):

As an alumnus, I am very pleased and proud to see that Miami continues to support faculty like you who seek to innovate, experiment, and keep the Miami program on the leading edge of undergraduate education. I hope that the students found the experience worthwhile, as it is undoubtedly one of their "life" experiences that will never be forgotten, either academically or personally.... Finally, speaking as an expatriate, the program is definitely right for the times given the continued globalization of the world business community.... It is important that Americans develop a broader knowledge of others, and your program is definitely a leading step in the right direction for a Miami business student.

From a presenter in Germany and "Big 5" partner (not a Miami University alumnus):

I think that you and Wayne have put together an excellent program for your students. Through the travel and interaction with professionals in the various European cities, they are not only intellectually exposed to accounting and legal systems, but they actually experience the different cultures. By directly experiencing these cultural differences, your students gain an appreciation for the reasons behind the different accounting and legal structures.

From the parents of several students in our programs:

Well, the pictures are developed, the stories told, and the dirty clothes all washed, and it's safe to say that our daughter has had the experience of her young life! Thanks for everything you did with/for these kids.

Our daughter's most memorable experience was her European trip. She was so full of excitement and delight about every aspect of the program. We thank you for giving her the highlight of her life.

From various students in our program:

Everything ran so smoothly, from all the great hotels to the tours. The trip was truly incredible, the best six weeks of my life. It gave me the chance to see so many great places and also to meet so many new friends that I will have for life. I will never forget the memories from all the countries from France to Italy. My friends from other schools couldn't believe how great this program is; it is truly the best European program in the country. Thanks again from both my parents and me; we truly do appreciate all the effort you put in for the many students each summer. I had the time of my life.

I would just like to thank you for the wonderful opportunity and experience of traveling through Europe. I am convinced that there is no other trip that will top the past six weeks of my life.... You are unique individuals, with very special qualities.

Thank you for all the time and effort you put into making our trip incredible. I am amazed by how much I learned and experienced. It would not have been half the fun without you to guide us. You've given me something I'll never forget. Thanks for the opportunity of a lifetime.

Thank you so much for the trip of a lifetime. I feel like I have been to the moon and back, and nothing else compares.

Thank you so much for coordinating such a great international program! I learned an awful lot on this trip, which extended far beyond the classroom. Before I went on the trip, I had heard other students talk about what an amazing time they had on this program. I knew I would have a good time, but I never thought I would have so many great experiences studying abroad. Thank you again for helping make the program so great! It is an experience I will never forget.

I would like to express my appreciation for the effort you made to make the program one of the most rewarding experiences of my life.... When asked about the program I cannot find enough good things to say. The one thing that stands out in your program, as opposed to other programs or traveling alone, is the extent to which we traveled Europe in just five weeks. No other program offered at Miami University offers such a thorough investigation of European nations within this period. Further, the program was beneficial for allowing the students to get to know their professors outside of a classroom. Once again, thanks for all your hard work.

Who needs or wants a home base! The multi-site way is the only way to go!

CONCLUSION

We have presented the details of one approach to increasing the international literacy of students and faculty: a multi-site summer study abroad program. The purpose of this chapter is to provide detailed guidance toward the creation of similar programs that can provide both experiential learning and a new cultural context for students. The multi-site study abroad program includes local speakers, field trips, and business interactions/experiences that are more difficult to provide in a single-site program. The experience allows students to observe and reflect upon different viewpoints in different locales. Overall, we believe that a multi-site program exposes students to a broader range of views, both geographically and culturally, than a single-site program does. The students' desire to travel works in a symbiotic relationship with the program to enhance their educational experience.

APPENDIX

Examples of Course Syllabi

ACC 383
Summer Business in Europe Program

ACCOUNTANCY 383—Comparative Accounting
Tentative Syllabus

Professor: Dr. Thomas M. Porcano

Course Prerequisites:
ACC 221 (Principles of Financial Accounting); permission of instructor

Course Fulfillment:
For all students, the course provides four hours of elective credit. For SBA majors, the course meets the SBA international requirement and also counts as a professional elective. For general business majors, the course counts as an upper-level accounting elective (in lieu of ACC 321, ACC 333, etc.). For finance majors, the course counts as an upper-level accounting elective (in lieu of ACC 321, ACC 333, etc.).

Course Objectives:
The primary objectives of ACC 383 are to introduce students to: (1) the financial accounting standard-setting process and general taxation aspects

of the United States and Western European countries; (2) general tax policy issues; (3) general issues in international taxation; (4) accounting and taxation issues as they affect and are affected by the European Union; (5) general aspects dealing with a firm's foreign direct investment (FDI) decision making; and (6) various professional, cultural, and social aspects of Western Europe. This introduction will enable us to perform comparative analyses of the various aspects of the United States and Western European countries.

Readings:

You must come to class prepared to discuss the assigned materials. Two reading packets will be handed out. The first packet (Packet A) contains articles that you must read during the spring semester prior to the summer program. The second packet (Packet B) contains articles and cases that you must read in Europe. In addition, there are readings from the books listed below (other reference materials are available).

Miller European Accounting Guide, 4th edition, edited by D. Alexander and S. Archer (Aspen Law 7 Business, 2001).

2002 Miller International Accounting Standards Guide, edited by D. Alexander and S. Archer (Aspen Law 7 Business, 2001).

Doing Business in _____ *Series* (for respective countries), Ernst & Young.

International Tax and Business Guide for _____ (for respective countries), Deloitte Touche Tohmatsu

The European Union: A Guide for Americans which can be downloaded at http://www.eurunion.org/infores/euguide/euguide.pdf

Grading:

Group project	100 points
Exam 1	100
Exam 2	<u>100</u>
Total	<u>300</u> points

The group project is due in April (see separate handout for requirements). Each exam contains 50 multiple-choice questions. The first exam is in Zurich (Tuesday or Wednesday—to be announced) and the second exam is in Rome (Wednesday or Thursday—to be announced). Each group will present the result of its project during classes in Europe (see the day-to-day schedule to determine which groups present on which days). Finally, you must read assigned materials by their due date and be prepared to discuss them in class. All borderline considerations will be based on your participation during class meetings.

Attendance:

You must attend all classes. However, I realize that there will be some conflicts for class meetings held during the fall and spring semesters on this campus. If you will miss a class during these times, then you MUST notify me PRIOR to the class meeting and you MUST turn in all items that were due that day. Additionally, you are responsible for all materials covered in any classes that you miss.

Attendance to all classes and field trips held in Europe is mandatory. There can be NO conflicts. If you miss a class or field trip held in Europe, then your grade will be lowered.

Behavior:

All Miami University rules apply while we are in a base city or on a field trip; thus, you must behave appropriately. You must be respectful of all hotel personnel, hotel guests, field trip guides, etc. Any behavior that is detrimental to the program will not be permitted, and if this occurs then the student(s) responsible will be dismissed from the program immediately and sent home at his/her (their) expense.

Anytime you attend a program function (i.e., breakfast, class, dinner, and company visits) you may NOT wear caps or hats. When you leave the table after breakfast or dinner, please push in your chair and place your napkin on the table. Also, remember to pay for any drinks you order PRIOR to leaving the dinner table and do NOT bring your own drinks to the restaurant.

Class Meetings:

Fall 2001 and Spring 2002—on Campus
See separate handout for fall/spring meetings
Summer 2002—in Europe

Day	Time	Place	Topic
Sa 5/11	8:30 a.m.	arrive in London	bus pickup at airport and tour of Windsor Castle and Windsor then transfer to hotel
Su 5/12	a.m.	London	IASC; harmonization; Ireland*
M 5/13	a.m.	London	Harmonization; Belgium; p.m. London Theatre
T 5/14	a.m.	London	Presentations—site visit
W 5/15	a.m.	London	Harmonization; UK; After class bus pick up at hotel to Waterloo Station for Eurostar to Brussels
M 5/20	a.m.	Paris	European Union; Luxembourg; Sweden
T 5/21	a.m.	Paris	Presentations—site visit; p.m. Bateaux Mouches
W 5/22	a.m.	Paris	European Union; France; Norway
R 5/23	a.m.	Paris	European Union; Denmark

Day	Time	Place	Topic
M 5/27	a.m.	Zurich	European Union; Finland
T 5/28	a.m.	Zurich	Comparative taxes; Switzerland; Italy**
W 5/29	a.m.	Zurich	Exam 1**
M 6/3	a.m.	Munich	Comparative taxes; Netherlands, then Mike's Bike Tour
T 6/4	a.m.	Munich	Presentations—at hotel, then Dachau
W 6/5	a.m.	Munich	Comparative Taxes; Germany; Austria
M 6/10	a.m.	Rome	Tax Treaties; U.S. citizens abroad; Spain; Portugal
T 6/11	a.m.	Rome	The Vatican
W 6/12	a.m.	Rome	Exam 2***
R 6/13	a.m.	Rome	Course/Instructor and Program Evaluations***

*Bold-faced country indicates group presentation made that day
**The topics might be in reverse order; e.g., Exam 1 will be on Tuesday or Wednesday
***The topics might be in reverse order; e.g., Exam 2 will be on Wednesday or Thursday

Group Project Requirements

1. See next three pages for specifics of the project
2. Written requirement due in April
   (a) Provide information on your country as indicated on the next three pages
   (b) Provide eight multiple choice questions (*with solutions*) on the information for your country—two questions for each section as indicated on the next three pages
3. Presentation requirement due in Europe
   (a) See the schedule for the date your assigned country is listed
   (b) You must present on all the aspects (background, financial accounting, tax, and incentives) of your country
   (c) You must use TYPED transparencies for the presentation
   (d) You must present unique aspects of the financial statements as part of your presentation
   (e) EACH member of the group must ask questions of the professionals when (if) they present on your country (e.g., United Kingdom, France, Germany)

Group Project Requirements
   I. General Background Information
      A. Location
      B. Official language(s)

C. Currency and exchange rate
D. Size (compare to similar-sized state in the United States)
E. Population (compare to similar-sized state in the United States)
F. Capital of the country
G. Major industries (the three largest ones)
H. Brief description of the country's history
I. Member of EU? If so, since when
J. Member of European Monetary Union? If so, since when
K. The economy (e.g., inflation rate, unemployment rate, cost of living index) [compared to whom?]
L. Political climate (e.g., stability, areas of political unrest)
M. Attitude toward foreign investment
N. Amount of foreign direct investment into and out of country
O. Any other information you would like to include

II. Financial Accounting System
A. Standard setting process (how "GAAP" are developed in your country)
   1. Agencies
   2. Influence of private and public sectors
   3. Indicate whether it is a macro-uniform or micro-uniform system
B. Annual reports
   1. Copy of annual reports from a firm in the country (you will be assigned a specific firm)
      – indicate the type of annual report (e.g., no accommodation, convenience translation, etc.)
   2. Compare to the annual report of a United States firm (you will be assigned a specific firm)
      – what is each firm's primary industry
      – who audited each firm's financial statements
      – is the terminology similar
      – is the general format similar
      – are the same financial statements used
      – do the financial statements use the same measurement (valuation) techniques (e.g., historical cost, current value)
      – is the level of disclosure similar
      – are footnotes used similarly (in content and frequency)
      – do the financial statements provide segment data, and if so, at what level (e.g., geographic area, product line, etc.)
      – do the financial statements use or mention IAS
      – which report uses more color photos/pictures
      – which report uses more graphs, and are they distorted
      – which annual report is more useful, and why

III. Tax System
   A. Corporations
      1. Types of taxes
      2. Tax rates of each type of tax
   B. Individuals
      1. Types of taxes
      2. Tax rates of each type of tax

IV. Tax and Nontax Incentives
   A. Types and rationale for tax incentives
   B. Types and rationale for nontax government incentives
   C. Does the country discriminate against foreign investment
      (i.e., provide more or better incentives to domestic firms)
   D. Does the country encourage foreign investment

V. Multiple Choice Questions
   Two good questions for each of the four areas (I–IV) above
   (Make sure you cover this information in your presentation.)

VI. General Requirements of the Written Paper
   A. Use headings and subheadings
   B. Use citations in the body of the paper
   C. Do not plagiarize
   D. Do not use contractions
   E. Do not use an informal tone
   F. Do not use different formats (font, margin, justification, etc.)
   G. Properly merge all sections
   H. As part of the annual report analyses, indicate the page
      number of each financial statement and the Auditor's Report
      for each firm

MGT 291
Summer 2003—Business in Europe Program
**MANAGEMENT 291.I—International Organizational Behavior
and Theory Tentative Syllabus**

Dr. Bill Snavely, Professor and Chair of Management

Course Prerequisite:
Admission to SBA Business in Europe Program

Course Fulfillment:

For SBA majors, this course is a SBA Core Course and counts the same as the normal MGT 291. It is also the first course in the Thematic Sequence (MGT–1) and counts toward each track of the Management Minor (for non-business students). Students desiring to complete the thematic sequence or minor in Management should have a form signed during sophomore year in order to enroll and ensure your ability to get senior level classes on the Oxford campus to complete the sequence and/or minor.

Description:

This is an introduction to the study of behavior in organizations. The emphasis is on the identification and application of behavioral science theory and research to the role of manager or leader in a contemporary organization. Students should gain an understanding of basic terminology, the findings of organizational behavior research, current thinking in the field, how that knowledge might be applied in work settings to improve the effectiveness and efficiency of the organization, and what the international implications of these topics are. While most of the course will be identical to what is offered in Oxford, we will take time to examine the international dimensions of organizational behavior.

Students in teams will conduct an intensive study of one of the countries within or bordering the European Union. Students will receive preparation for their field experience, including lectures and readings, during the spring term. Teams will begin independent work on their projects during spring term. While in Europe, students will be exposed to guest speakers in each of the host cities. Topics will include culture and international business practice. Site visits and cultural tours will also be a regular part of each class day in Europe. Students will make final team presentations in Europe.

Readings:

1. *Fundamentals of Organizational Behavior* (2nd Edition, 2002) by Andrew J. DuBrin
2. A readings packet will be handed out containing notes and cases

Grading:

The performance opportunities consist of the following items. This course will use plus–minus grades. The conversion of points earned to grades is provided below.

Performance Opportunities:

Pre-departure paper	50 Points
Exam #1	100 Points
Exam #2	100 Points
Exam #3	100 Points
Team presentation	50 Points
Engagement	100 Points
Total Possible	**500 Points**

Exams:

Each of the exams will consist of multiple-choice questions. My students in the past have described my exams as difficult but fair. You are responsible for all lectures, readings, and in-class discussions. Exam emphasis will be on lecture/discussion material. While some questions may address terminology of the field and what was said during class and in the readings, others will ask you to apply concepts.

One of the goals of this course is to provide you with the terminology and tools of the profession of management. Please be aware that you will need to understand concepts and theories and memorize models and definitions. I will not ask you to memorize meaningless lists, but you should know theories and models and their various components. While many do not like memorization, it is a useful skill and often a necessary requisite to learning.

Pre-Departure Paper

Due in April prior to the end of spring semester, this *team paper* (typed and double spaced, no covers) will enable students to process the lectures and discussions during spring class periods and to begin work on the team project. We will discuss the paper in more detail in class, but some of the specifics follow. You will be evaluated on both content and style (grammar, etc.). Teams will choose one of the countries in Europe (see schedule) and provide the following information:

General Background Information

Identify your assigned country. Where is it? What is the official language(s) used in business? What is the currency and what is the current exchange rate (check this carefully). Provide demographic information (e.g. size, population, capital, major industries, exports, and imports). Is this country a member of the EU? If so, when did it join? Evaluate the economy. Would you recommend American companies place a facility in this country? Why or why not? What are the current political issues in this country that could affect international business? What other relevant information have you found about this country?

Cultural and Behavioral Analysis

Apply one or more appropriate models to help understand the cultural and behavioral environment of this country (e.g. Hofstede, Kluckhohn & Strodtbeck, Trompenaar, Hall, and/or other sources). Choose the model(s) that will best help you analyze this country. Based on this detailed analysis, what will the most important issues be for Americans in adapting to and working with people in this culture?

Expectations/Reservations

Overall, what are your expectations for working and living in this country? What reservations would you have about companies in this country or working in this country? What questions do you hope to answer that cannot be easily answered by the research you have done if you visit this country?

Team Presentations:

Team presentations will be scheduled in Europe. See the schedule for the date your team will present. Your BUS 371 and MGT 291 assignments will be one combined presentation. You will present all the above information and whatever additional information you collect while in Europe pertinent to your assigned country. You will be evaluated on presentation style (i.e., communication skills, professionalism, interest level) as well as complete and accurate content. Be creative—you can use skits, visual aids, or anything else that will keep the interest of the students (and faculty) and communicate valuable information. If you want to use visual aids (they are not *required*) then you will need to bring them with you, as it is unlikely you will find facilities for visual aid production in Europe.

Attendance Policy:

You must attend all classes in Europe. However, if you have a conflict for a class meeting held during the fall or spring semesters on the Oxford campus, you must notify me PRIOR to the class meeting, and you MUST turn in all items that were due that day. If you miss a class, you are responsible for the material you missed. Seek out another student to catch up.

Attendance to all classes and field trips in Europe is mandatory. There can be NO conflicts short of a medical emergency. You must be on time to class.

If you are late to class in Europe, your participation grade will be automatically lowered up to 10 points. If you miss the majority (or all) of a class or field trip held in Europe, then your participation grade will be lowered 40 points. If you fall asleep in class, you will also lose points. If you are on time and attend every class in Europe, you will likely maintain all or most of your 100 points for engagement.

Dishonesty:

The Management Department encourages all students to become familiar with PART V—Academic Misconduct—of the Student Handbook. Please note that all Management Department faculty take issues of academic misconduct very seriously and will pursue severe penalties against those guilty of such acts. If you are not sure what the University and Department consider to be academic misconduct, please ask so you don't find out the hard way. All sources (including internet sources) used in the preparation of any written work for this course must be fully cited. This is true whether direct passages are used or whether you are just paraphrasing. Claiming credit for words or thoughts that are not your own is one type of academic misconduct. This includes having any name appear on a team project/paper when that individual did not fully participate in completion of the project/paper.

Behavior:

All Miami University rules apply while we are in a base city or on a field trip—and you are an "ambassador" of the university and your country; thus you must behave appropriately. You must be respectful of all hotel personnel, hotel guests, field trip guides, etc. Any behavior that is detrimental to the program will not be tolerated. If such behavior occurs, the student(s) responsible will be dismissed from the program immediately and sent home at personal expense. Due to safety concerns, your parent(s) or guardian(s) will be notified. No program fees will be refunded.

The moment you enter any of our hotels, you must be quiet and respectful of others. You may not have loud parties in your rooms that could disrupt other guests. You may not yell, etc. in the hallways. The continuation of this program depends on maintaining good relations with the hotels. If you seriously threaten that relationship, you will be dismissed from the program.

Any time you attend a program function (i.e. breakfast, class, dinner, business visits) you may NOT wear caps or hats. When you leave the table after breakfast or dinner, please push in your chair and place your napkin on the table. Also, remember to pay for any drinks you order PRIOR to leaving the dinner table and do NOT bring in your own drinks to the restaurant. Under no circumstances may you order an alcoholic beverage during dinner or during a scheduled program event.

By following these simple rules of behavior, we believe the Europe program will continue to be successful and you will be able to have an outstanding experience. Thank you in advance for your cooperation.

Fall and Spring Meetings

The specific date you need to attend depends on which section you are assigned to—one section meets on Tuesday and the other meets on Wednesday. Class times for spring courses will be announced before the end of fall semester.

Dates	Topic	Reading/Assignment
M—11/4	Introduction to Program	1 Upham–$2200 payment due to Travel 4 U
R—11/14	The European Experience—Guest Speakers	—$1000 payment due to Travel 4 U *Travel Plans* Form Distributed
M—12/2	The European Experience—Guest Speakers	—$1000 payment due to Travel 4 U *Travel Plans* Form Due Scholarship Forms Distributed—Due 12/5
January 8/9	Introduction to Organizational Behavior	DuBrin—Ch. 1
January 15/16	Teams	DuBrin—Ch. 9
January 29/30	Managing Diversity	DuBrin—pp. 323–328 Team Assignments
February 5/6	Team Presentations/Information	
February 12/13	International OB Issues	DuBrin—pp. 328–341 Forms Distributed: Emergency Contact, Insurance, Risk Release
March 5/6	Theory & Research	Completed forms due; Final Payment to Travel 4 U due; Roommate & registration forms distributed
March 26/27	Personality	DuBrin—Ch. 2
W—4/2	Final Wrap-up & Review of Oxford material	Roommate & Registration Forms Due: Registration Fees to Miami U due

Summer 2003—in Europe

Dates	Time	Location	Activity	Team
S—May 10	8:30 am	London	Bus pickup@airport & tour Windsor Castle—Transfer to Hotel	
S—May 11	am	London	Perception/Attribution; DuBrin pp. 45–48	Ireland & UK
M—May 12	am pm	London	Cognition/Ethics; DuBrin pp. 48–58 Theatre Field Trip—CSFB	Spain Belgium
T—May 13	am	London	Field Trip—CSFB	
W—May 14	am pm	London	Exam #1; DuBrin Ch. *1–3, 9, 15* Bus pickup@hotel to Waterloo Station for Eurostar to Paris	
May 15–18	—	Free	Make your own travel arrangements	
M—May 19	am	Barcelona	Learning Theory; DuBrin pp. 96–97; 100–193; 117–127	France Luxembourg
T—May 20	am pm	Barcelona	Motivation; DuBrin pp. 87–100 Field Trip—TBA	Denmark Sweden
W—May 21	am	Barcelona	Motivation continued	
May 22–25	—	Free	Make your own travel arrangements	
M—May 26	am pm	Cannes	Job Design; DuBrin pp. 108–116	Germany Norway
T—May 27	am	Cannes	Exam #2; DuBrin Ch. 5–7	
W—May 28	am pm	Cannes Lauterbrunnen	Communication; DuBrin Ch. 8 Tour	Finland Switzerland
5/30–6/1	—	Free	Make your own travel arrangements	
M—June 2	am pm	Munich	Power & Influence; DuBrin Ch. 11 Mike's Bike Tour	Russia
T—June 3	am pm	Munich	Leadership; DuBrin Ch. 10 Field Trips—Dachau & Spaten Brewery Organizational Theory; DuBrin Ch. 12	
June 5–9	—	Free	Make your own travel arrangements	
T—June 10	am	Athens	Organizational Culture & Change; DuBrin Ch. 13	Greece
W—June 11	am	Athens	Field Trip—TBA	
R—June 12	pm	Athens	Exam #3; DuBrin Ch. 8, 10–13	
F—June 13	am	Athens	*Program Evaluations—Program Ends*	

Note: You are required to be in the host city at dinner on the evening before classes start in that city.

BUS 371
Summer 2002—Business in Europe Program
SBA 371.I—International Business
Syllabus

Instructor: David Shull
Office: 124-C Upham Hall
Hours: To be announced.
Phone: 529–1565; 894–5750
Email: shulldm@muohio.edu

Course Prerequisite:
Admission to SBA Business in Europe Program

Course Objectives:
The primary objective of SBA 371 is to introduce students to the issues and decisions facing companies as they expand from domestic to international markets; and to increase students' sophistication and awareness with respect to foreign cultures and other issues of importance. We will examine and discuss business functions of multinational corporations and their interaction with country characteristics in order to gain a broader understanding of both international business and foreign cultures. This introduction will enhance our ability to perform comparative analyses of various aspects of the United States and western European countries.

Textbook:
*International Business: Competing in the Global Marketplace Postscript 2002, 3rd ed.,*by
     Charles W. L. Hill

Books can be ordered by phone with a credit card through McGraw-Hill customer support service. The phone number is (800) 262–4729. The book's ISBN Number is 0-07-248545-0. The book will cost approximately $100 + shipping and handling.

Other Readings:
International Tax and Business Guide for _____ (Appropriate guide for each
     presentation country), Deloitte Touche Tohmatsu.
Doing Business in _____ (Appropriate guide for each presentation country),
     Ernst & Young.
"The European Union: A Guide for Americans," www.eurunion.org/infores/
     home.htm. This website contains many links to other relevant websites.

You should read the international sections in newspapers such as *Wall Street Journal* and *New York Times* (available on the Web) and magazines such as *Business Week.*

Grading:

Pre-departure paper	50
Exam 1	70
Exam 2	70
Exam 3	70
Team Presentation	50
Participation	100
Other assignments	??
Total	410 + ??

Each exam contains 35 multiple-choice questions. The first exam is on Wednesday, May 15, in London; the second exam is on Wednesday, May 29, in Zurich; and the third exam is on Thursday, June 13, in Rome. A team paper is due on April 17. The typed (double-spaced, no covers) paper will enable students to process lectures and discussions during the Spring class period and to begin work on the team project. Details of the paper are given in the handout entitled "Group Project Requirements."

Each group will present the project results during classes in Europe (see the day-to-day schedule to determine which groups present on which days). In addition, some guest presentations about international business and related items about a country will occur. The group assigned to that country MUST ask questions of the presenters. Finally, you must read assigned materials by their due date and be prepared to discuss them in class—your presentation grade will be based on this and your general participation during class meetings.

Grades: Your grade will be based upon the percentage of total possible points that you earn on the group project, exams, presentation/participation, and other graded assignments. The final course grade shall be determined as follows:

A: 90—100% of total possible points.
B: 80—89.9% of total possible points.
C: 70—79.9% of total possible points
D: 60—69.9% of total possible points.
F: < 60% of total possible points.

Attendance:

You must attend all classes. However I realize that there will be some conflicts for class meetings held during the spring semester on the Oxford campus. If you will miss a class in Oxford, you MUST notify me prior to the class meeting, and you MUST turn in all items that were due that day. Additionally, you are responsible for all materials covered in the class you miss.

Attendance of all classes and field trips held in Europe is mandatory. There can be NO conflicts. If you miss a class or field trip held in Europe, then your grade will be lowered by loss of participation points. If you are late for class or fall asleep in class, your grade will be lowered by loss of participation points. If you are on time and attend every class and designated event in Europe, you will likely maintain all or most of your 100 participation points.

Behavior:

All Miami University rules apply while we are in a base city or on a field trip; thus, you must behave appropriately. You must be respectful of all hotel personnel, hotel guests, field trip guides, etc. Any behavior that is detrimental to the program will not be permitted, and if this occurs, then the student(s) responsible will be dismissed from the program immediately and sent home at his/her (their) expense.

Please be quiet and respectful from the moment you enter any of our hotels until the time you leave. You can not make loud noises in your rooms that could disrupt other guests. The continuation of this program depends on maintaining good relations with the hotels. If you threaten that relationship, you will be dismissed from the program.

Anytime you attend a program function (i.e., breakfast, class, dinner, and company visits) you may NOT wear caps or hats. When you leave the table after breakfast or dinner, please push in your chair and place your napkin on the table. Do NOT bring your own drinks to the restaurant.

Dishonesty:

I encourage all students to become familiar with PART V—ACADEMIC DISHONESTY of the Student Handbook. I have no tolerance for academic dishonesty. I will enforce university regulations and seek maximum penalties.

Finally, I reserve the right to amend this syllabus at any time. Any changes to the syllabus will be announced in class, so don't miss class. Again, contact me in advance if you cannot attend a class.

Class Meetings:

Fall Semester 2001—in Oxford

Day	Time	Place	Topic
M—11/08	4:00–5:30	100 Laws Hall	General Introduction Payment Due—Check made out to Travel 4 U
T—11/06	4:00–5:30	116 Pearson Hall	Handout—Travel Plans Handout—Syllabus Handout—Group Project Discussion of Group Project
W—11/28	4:00–5:30	1 Upham Hall	Payment Due—Check made out to Travel 4 U Collect Travel Plans Topic—Introduction to International Business

Spring Semester 2002—in Oxford

Day	Time	Place	Topic
W—2/13	4:00–5:15	TBA*	Introduction; and Ch.1 Globalization
W—2/27	4:00–5:15		Ch. 2 National Differences in Political Economy; Ch. 3 Differences in Culture
W—3/20	4:00–5:15		Ch. 4 International Trade Theory
W—4/03	4:00–5:15		Ch. 5 The Political Economy of International Trade
W—4/17	4:00–5:15		Ch. 6 Foreign Direct Investment: PAPER DUE

* Meeting places to be announced during Dr. Snavely's class on February 6

Summer 2002—in Europe

Day	Time	Place	Activity
S—5/11	8:30 am	Arrive in London	Windsor Castle and Windsor Tour
S—5/12	am	London	Ireland; United Kingdom: Ch. 7 The Political Economy of Foreign Direct Investment
M—5/13	am	London	Spain, Portugal; Ch. 8 Regional Economic Integration
T—5/14	am	London	Field Trip
W—5/15	am	London	Exam 1; Belgium
M—5/20	am	Paris	France; Luxembourg; Ch. 9 The Foreign Exchange Market; Ch. 10 The International Monetary System
T—5/21	am	Paris	Denmark; Sweden; Ch. 11 The Global Capital Market
W—5/22	am	Paris	Field Trip: TBA
R—5/23	am	Paris	Guest Speaker

Summer 2002—in Europe (Cont.)

Day	Time	Place	Activity
M—5/27	am	Zurich	Switzerland; Norway; Ch. 12 The Strategy of International Business
T—5/28	am	Zurich	Ch. 13 The Organization of International Business
W—5/29	am	Zurich	Exam 2
M—6/03	am	Munich	Germany, Russia; Ch. 15 Exporting, Importing, and Countertrade
	pm	Munich	Mike's Bike Tour
T—6/04	am	Munich	Austria, Finland; Dachau Field Trip
W—6/05	am	Munich	Ch. 16 Global Manufacturing and Materials Management
M—6/10	am	Rome	Italy, Greece; Ch. 17 Global Marketing and R&D, Ch. 20 International Financial Management
T—6/11	am	Rome	Vatican Field Trip
W—6/12	am	Rome	Exam 3
W—6/13	am	Rome	Exam 3 returned

Group Project Requirements

- See the next page for specifics of the project.
- Written requirement due April 17, 2002.
- Provide information on your country as indicated on the next three pages.
- Provide me with six multiple choice questions (with solutions) on the information for your country—two questions for each section as indicated on the next three pages.
- Presentation requirement due in Europe—See schedule for the date your country is listed. You must present on all the aspects (background, foreign investment, structure of business entities, labor force) of your country Also, you must ask questions of the professionals when (if) they present on your countries (i.e. United Kingdom, France, Switzerland, and Germany).

Group Project Requirements

1. General Background Information
    A. Location
    B. Official language(s)
    C. Currency, exchange rate, cost of living
    D. Size

E. Population
F. Capital
G. Major Industries
H. Brief description of country's history
I. Member of EU? if so, since when
J. The economy
K. Political climate
L. Attitude toward foreigners (and especially the United States)
M. Amount of FDI into and out of country
N. An evaluation of the best investment possibility in your country
O. Any other information you deem relevant.

2. Business Environment and Foreign Investment
    A. Economic trends and performance
    B. Economic structure
    C. Government and business relationship
    D. Financial sector
    E. Essential industries
    F. Exchange controls
    G. Restrictions on foreign investment
    H. Investment incentives
    I. Importing and exporting
    J. Registration of intellectual property

3. Structure of Business Entities and Labor Force
    A. Types of Business Entities
    B. Establishing a Corporation
    C. Labor Supply and Relations
    D. Social Security
    E. Other Payroll Taxes and Employee Benefits

4. Multiple Choice Questions
    A. Two good questions for each of the three areas (I–III) above; make certain that you cover this information in your presentation to class.

FIN 483
Summer 2002—Business in Europe Program
FINANCE 483—Comparative International Law
Four (4) credit hours

Wayne Staton

Objective:

To provide a framework for understanding International Business and the legal environment within which it operates. Extensive comparison of the United States legal system with numerous European legal systems. Study traditional commercial law topics, such as rights of buyer and seller under contract for international sale of goods. Attempt to provide a European prospective, rather than a United States prospective. Study of private law of international business transactions and public law of international trade. Analyze United States enterprises' transport of goods to another country. Analyze doing business overseas. Current events will be addressed as the course progresses.

Week One: (conducted in the United States):

1. The students are assigned a group research paper. Students must research a specific European country, analyze the legal system of that European country, and compare that legal system to the United States legal system. Students meet with instructor as their research progresses. The research paper is turned in to the instructor prior to departure to Europe and discussed in Europe. The students lead the discussion when we discuss their country.

Other topics covered during the first week are:

1. Introduction to International Business
2. International Law and Organizations
3. European Union and Development of Trade Areas

Week Two:

1. Extensive coverage of the English legal system. English Barristers/ solicitors supplement the discussions. Coverage of a few other European legal systems.
2. International Disputes Resolution
   (a) Jurisdiction
   (b) Enforcement of foreign judgments
3. Convention on International Sale of Goods

Week Three:

1. Extensive coverage of the French legal system: French Advocate supplements the discussion. Coverage of a few other European legal systems.
2. International Trade and Shipping Terms
3. International Risk of Loss
4. International Letters of Credit

Week Four:

1. Extensive Coverage of the Swiss legal system. Swiss Lawyer supplements the discussions.
2. General agreement on Tariffs and Trade
3. World Trade Organization—field trip for lecture held at WTO
4. North American Free Trade Agreement

Week Five:

1. Extensive Coverage of the German legal system. A German lawyer supplements the discussions.
2. Laws governing access to Foreign Markets
3. Fair Trade versus Unfair Trade Imports, Customs and Tariff Law
4. Imports, Customs and Tariff Law

Week Six:

1. Extensive Coverage of the Italian Legal System. An Italian lawyer supplements the discussions.
2. The Regulation of Experts
3. International Marketing Law
4. Political Risk of Doing Business Overseas
5. Privatization
6. International Environmental Law

Grading:

Research Paper	1/3
Midterm	1/3
Final	1/3

REFERENCES

Association to Advance Collegiate Schools of Business International (AACSB International). (2003). *Eligibility procedures and standards for business accreditation* (pp. 18–19). St. Louis, MO: AACSB International.

Bailey, B. A., & Harbeck, D. A. (2002, Fall). Liability issues associated with planning and executing a foreign study tour for undergraduates. *Journal of the Academy of Business Education,* 106–111.

Barker, C. M. (2000). Education for international understanding and global competence: Report of a meeting convened by Carnegie Corporation of New York (pp. 1–15). New York: Carnegie Corporation of New York.

Collins, H. T., Czarra, F. R., & Smith, A. F. (1998). Guidelines for global and international studies education: Challenges, culture, and connections. *Social Education, 62*(50), 311–317.

Duke, C. R. (2000). Study abroad learning activities: A synthesis and comparison. *Journal of Marketing Education, 22*(2), 155–165.

Holland, K. M., & Kedia, K. L. (2003). Internationalizing business students through the study abroad experience: Opportunities and challenges. *Advances in International Marketing, 13,* 115–139.

Hopkins. J. R. (1999, Summer). Studying abroad as a form of experiential education. *Liberal Education,* 36–41.

Institute of International Education (2003a). Open doors: Americans studying abroad. IIE Network. Retrieved from http://opendoors.iienetwork.org/?p=36524

Institute of International Education (2003b). Open doors: Fields of study. IIE Network. Retrieved from http://opendoors.iienetwork.org/?p=35944

Keillor, B. D., & Emore, J. R. (2003). The structure and process of curriculum integration in study abroad programs: The University of Akron international business model. *Advances in International Marketing, 13,* 227–245.

Kwok, C. C., & Arpan, J. S. (2002). Internationalizing the business school: A global survey in 2000. *Journal of International Business Studies, 33*(3), 571–581.

Porth, S. J. (1997). Management education goes international: A model for designing and teaching a study tour course. *Journal of Management Education, 21*(2), 190–199.

Praetzel, G. D., Curcio, J., & Dilorenzo, J. (1996). Making study abroad a reality for all students. *International Advances in Economic Research, 2*(2), 174–182.

Tashakori, A., & Dotson, M. (1989, November). Study abroad programs in business: Planning, organizing, and marketing. *Journal of Education for Business,* 74–78.

Thomas, S. L., & McMahon, M. E. (1998). Americans abroad: Student characteristics, pre-departure qualifications and performance abroad. *International Journal of Education Management, 12*(2), 57–64.

Trevino, L. J., & Melton, M. (2002, March/April). Institutional characteristics and preconditions for international business education—an empirical investigation. *Journal of Education for Business,* 230–235.

Wymar, B. (1996, March). Twenty-five years: European business and economic studies tour. *South Dakota Business Review,* 1–6.

CHAPTER 11

TEACHING INTERNATIONAL BUSINESS THROUGH INTERNATIONAL STUDENT CONSULTING PROJECTS

The GCP/JSCP at Ohio University

Gary Coombs and Ed Yost

INTRODUCTION

The goals of teaching international business may vary. They may be driven by environmental changes, constituent pressure, and/or accreditation mandates (Kaynak & Schermerhorn, 1999). Objectives might include bringing students to an understanding of strategic approaches to going international, appreciating socio-cultural differences in doing business, understanding risks and rewards of conducting business internationally, managing expatriates versus locals, and attaining "global competence" (Sherman, 1999). Similarly, approaches to teaching international business run the gamut from traditional classroom instruction and exercises, country studies (cf. Keys, 1995), international study projects (cf. von Eije, 1998),

The Cutting Edge of International Management Education, pages 285–305
Copyright © 2004 by Information Age Publishing
All rights of reproduction in any form reserved.

and extended overseas internships. Along this continuum from information-giving to immersion (Mendenhall, Dunbar, & Oddou, 1987), there are many options that vary significantly in cost, time, complexity, effort, and effectiveness—and trade-offs abound. Most would agree, however, that immersion in a different cultural setting adds something that classroom exercises, no matter how well designed, cannot adequately reproduce. As a result, opportunities for such immersive experiences have become increasingly commonplace at most universities through study abroad programs (SAPs), exchange programs, and international tours. Additionally, as Mendenhall and his colleagues have pointed out, immersive experiences better prepare potential expatriates to adapt and to be productive once placed in an overseas assignment (Mendenhall, Dunbar, & Oddou, 1987). For business students, it might be expected that immersive experiences while in school may create some lasting benefits toward any future international experiences. However, the goals of an educational program do not clearly align with the goals that a company might have in preparing employees for extended overseas assignments.

Henthorne, Miller, & Hudson (2001) discuss some of the benefits and challenges of conducting a short duration SAP as one means by which students can experience cultural immersion and some level of experiential learning. Their offering combines business tours with lectures by both home faculty and local experts. Students conduct research projects into an aspect of business in the host country that, ideally, includes some aspect of direct observation of business processes. Porth (1997) provides an example of a study tour course for international management education that combines pre-departure study about a country and international business issues; in-country business tours and interactions with business leaders; and post-travel reflection and assessment. Each of these examples addresses some aspects of both information-giving and immersion but still lacks in direct application of content and concepts through student experience.

Making the connections among cultural exposure, business theories and concepts, and practical application is more challenging. Ohio University's College of Business has more than 15 years experience using a collaborative international consulting project (ICP) with students at both the undergraduate and graduate levels as a means of making the desired connections. This project, called the Global Competitiveness Program/Joint Student Consulting Project, draws on the benefits of an immersive international experience with the strengths of a problem-based pedagogy to create rich learning opportunities that are likely to be better retained as a result of the experiential element. Our approach contextualizes learning about international business both in location and in practice. When our students engage in business consulting projects in another country, working collaboratively with peers from both home and the host country, they are provided with a learning opportunity that triggers the types of *situated cognition* (Brown, Collins, & Duguid; 1989) that are likely to result in both knowledge retention and ability to apply that knowledge.

Brown et al. (1989) have discussed the critical connection between what is learned and how it is learned and used, drawing on earlier work by Vygosky, Leontiev, and other activity theorists. As they state:

> The activity in which knowledge is developed and deployed . . . is not separable from or ancillary to learning and cognition. Nor is it neutral. Rather, it is an integral part of what is learned. Situations might be said to co-produce knowledge through activity. Learning and cognition . . . are fundamentally situated. (p. 32)

We believe that, by embedding students both in the national and business cultures of another country while they work intensively on a business problem with salience to the managers and employees with whom they are interacting, we have found a highly effective approach to teaching international business concepts and skills. Further, we believe that this approach is a means to internationalize the student instead of the curriculum (Beck, Whiteley, & McFetridge, 1996) by building student competencies in operating in the global arena and adapting their behaviors to cross-cultural situations.

At Ohio University we utilize a problem-based learning methodology, and we feel that this generates synergies when extended to the GCP/JSCP experience. Problem-based learning, or PBL, is pedagogy drawn from Constructivism, a philosophical view of the ways in which one comes to understand. Constructivists assert that individuals construct knowledge actively though sense-making of their current and past experiences. Drawn from the work of early educational theorists (including Jean Piaget, Jerome Bruner, John Dewey, and Lev Vygotsky), Constructivists emphasize the importance of the learners taking an active role in selecting and organizing information, constructing hypotheses, making decisions, and then reflecting on their experiences to determine the transferability of their learning to other settings.

PBL is a learner-centered (versus content- or instructor-centered) method that challenges the learners to take a progressively increasing responsibility for their own education and is therefore consistent with the Constructivist perspective. It was developed extensively in medical education, first during the 1960s at McMaster University, and later expanded to the University of Limburg, the University of Newcastle, the University of New Mexico, and Southern Illinois University. From medicine, it has been adopted by and adapted to other professional fields, including business. PBL is centered on the use of "real world" (authentic) problems that capture the complexity and ambiguity that learners will face in their careers, rather than being structured around separate academic disciplines. These problems form the context for learning within which both content knowledge and skills or competencies are developed.

Savery and Duffy (1995) state that (a) understanding derives from our interactions with the environment; (b) cognitive conflict both stimulates and structures the organization and nature of learning; and (c) knowledge evolves through a social process of testing individual understanding against the understanding of others in a learning group. Therefore, PBL calls for students to solve real or authentic problems in small groups, with a focus on helping the students learn how to direct their own learning. The faculty member is no longer the expert dispensing knowledge; instead the faculty member takes on the primary role of the coach or tutor. PBL aligns well with requirements for effective adult learning as described by Knowles (1980) and results in better retention in knowledge, transferability of learning to other situations, and development of self-directed learning skills (Norman & Schmidt, 1992).

The international consulting projects described below align well with the attributes of problem-based learning and are likely to generate the learning advantages described by Schmidt (1993) in the context of medical education. These consist of five cognitive effects:

1. Activation of prior knowledge through the initial problem analysis.
2. Elaboration on prior knowledge and active processing of new information through small-group discussion.
3. Construction of an appropriate semantic network by restructuring of knowledge to fit problem specifics.
4. Learning in the context of the problem presented, with extension of application to similar, future problems.
5. Emergence of epistemic curiosity as a result of perceived problem relevance and open-ended discussion.

What follows is a description of the lessons we have learned in conducting our Global Competitiveness Program and Joint Student Consulting Projects (GCP/JSCP). As we explore the program structure, we have attempted to indicate which of Schmidt's five cognitive effects are targeted at each stage of the process.

The International Consultancy Project

The GCP, offered to undergraduates, and the JSCP, for MBAs, share many commonalities in structure and delivery. Differences between the two will be noted along the way. Both involve preparatory work during the spring and travel in the summer. As indicated, the projects themselves are conducted using a PBL methodology, with the students working collaboratively in small, cross-cultural learning groups to address authentic business consulting projects.

Undergraduates are notified of the GCP opportunity during the fall along with a list of the sites being offered. Sign-ups occur on a first-come, first-served basis with a required deposit. Most sites sell out very quickly. Students who participate receive 12 hours of undergraduate credit and fulfill a College of Business requirement in the area of Global Perspectives. This is the equivalent of three undergraduate courses meeting four hours per week for a 10 week quarter. It is an entirely voluntary program and is only one of several ways that this requirement can be met. It is not restricted to College of Business students and many participants come from other programs of study, though often with Business minors or cognate areas. Students pay an established program fee that covers airfare, ground transportation, housing, some program events, and some faculty and program expenses. Students must also register for the 12 credit hours during the summer quarter and pay the associated tuition.

For the MBAs, the JSCP is a mandatory element of their program, and they are charged a JSCP fee in installments over the course of the year to cover the expenses mentioned above. MBA students are provided a list of sites and asked to rank order their preferences. Most are able to travel to their first or second choice location, though we do have some restrictions. First, international students are not allowed to choose their home location, as we believe that they will learn more in a location with which they are unfamiliar. Second, some sites have enrollment limits that we have to be aware of, and the MBAs therefore are distributed across sites within those parameters. The JSCP constitutes one project equivalent to 45 to 50 hours of contact, or approximately 25% of their summer workload, and is part of their normal 18-hour summer registration.

Site Selection and Establishing Partnerships with Host Institutions

It is exceedingly important to establish an effective partnership with host institutions in other countries in order to implement an international consulting project. We rely on our hosts to work with their local contacts to develop appropriate projects for the student teams to work on, to provide local students to partner with our students, to provide the facilities, and to handle a number of logistical elements of the program. Moreover, the site selected needs to match the learning objectives to be pursued. In our case, we want our students to experience business consulting in an emerging or changing economy and in a country where they are likely to face linguistic barriers and cultural differences. Some of the countries where we have conducted the GCP/JSCP include Brazil, China, France, Germany, Greece, Hungary, Italy, Macedonia, Malaysia, South Africa, Spain, and Thailand. Denmark and Estonia have been newly added. Each country offers unique learning opportunities and challenges, but we will concentrate on the common elements.

As in any joint venture, it is important to establish clear expectations and goals for the relationship, determining at the beginning what responsibilities each partner will accept in the planning and delivery of the program, who will pay for various elements, and so on. Our programs generally bear the costs of an opening reception and a closing banquet that includes students and client representatives, as well as participating faculty. We also pay for the rental of a bus and driver to transport student teams to client locations or other activities during the program, including local touring. Our partners often cover the costs of some local tourist activities or provide lunches or snacks for students and faculty at their institution. In rare instances, there may be a facilities charge to use the partner institution's computer labs or classrooms, though our partners usually include access to their facilities as part of their contribution.

Quality of the facilities at the partner institution is an important consideration. Access to computers with Internet connections, library resources, and meeting rooms is often necessary for project research, preparation of presentation materials, and production of consulting reports. The limitations on those resources can also be a source of learning for the students as they discover that there is a digital divide between countries with full and easy access to resources and those without. How they deal with the challenge of getting the work done with limited resources can be a powerful, and sometimes heated, discussion point. If the partner institution is lacking in critical resources, it may be incumbent on the faculty to locate alternatives, such as Internet cafés, or to supply basic reference materials.

We try to match the population of students to be sent on the GCP/JSCP to the type of students the partner will recruit (i.e., undergraduates with undergraduates and MBAs with graduate students). When groups differ widely in education and experience, it is more likely that one group will dominate in the team interactions, or that there will be a mismatch in goals or commitment level. By matching students with peer level partners, it is more likely that there will be balanced contributions.

Ideally, the host institution students will be receiving graded credit for their participation as this also tends to equalize the commitment level; however, we have run programs successfully where the partnering students were participating on a purely voluntary basis. One of the biggest challenges in such cases is matching the travel schedule against the host institution's academic calendar so that they have volunteer students available to participate.

It is very important to find a partnering institution where there is a champion for the project who will communicate regularly during the set-up phase. We have dealt successfully with champions who were senior administrators, faculty members, and even student-run organizations. In each case, however, our liaison was convinced of the value of the project and was committed to its success. Our partners have included such institutions as Cape Technikon in Capetown, South Africa; the Divisão de Relações Internacionais at União de Negócios e Administração (UNA) in Belo Horizonte, Brazil; Janus Panonius University in Pecs, Hungary; Università Politecnica delle Marche in Ancona, Italy; and Hubei University in Hubei, China.

Our contribution to the partner institution in many cases has included sharing of our expertise in Problem-Based Learning with their faculty, with the opportunity for them to observe it in action as we interact with the student teams during the project. In 2003, we were awarded a grant from the Department of State's Bureau of Educational and Cultural Affairs to extend our JSCP experience to the Former Yugoslav Republic of Macedonia with the explicit intent of training their faculty in the use of PBL. A group of 15 Executive MBAs were the trailblazing students in this effort, working in partnership with mixed teams of undergraduate and graduate students with seven of the largest companies in Macedonia. We expect that the relationship with our partner there, the University of Saints Cyril and Methodius, will continue and possibly expand to include students from our full-time MBA program.

We have been open to the possibility that a partnering institution might be interested in a reciprocal visit by their students to do similar consulting projects in the United States; but, to date, the financial costs of doing so have prevented our partners from taking advantage of the opportunity. However, we have had selected undergraduate students from several of our partners join our MBA program the following year, and we make every effort to facilitate their application process and assist them with finding necessary financial aid once they are accepted.

Project Selection, Structure, and Learning Outcomes

An important element of a successful agreement with a partner is clarity about the types of projects that are appropriate for the time frame the students will have to work on them. It is equally important to ensure that problems are neither too complex nor too simple for the types of students with whom one is working. If possible, it is very helpful if a faculty representative can travel to the site several months before the projects to pre-screen the clients and problem statements, though we have not always found this possible. Such visits allow time for the partner to find additional clients or to negotiate more appropriate projects if problems are identified.

The size and scope of projects needs to be tied to the learning objectives one has established for the project. In our case, our objectives (see Appendix A) are not content specific but instead focus on broad learning about international business and cross-cultural teamwork. Therefore, the projects do not have to fall into a specific functional area. Past projects have included operational problems, market research, consumer behavior questions, cost control measures, human resource issues, and strategic concerns. Projects have come from corporations of all sizes, including market leaders, and many different industries, including financial services, construction, confections, electronics, travel and tourism, brewing, and publishing. If the learning objectives are more tightly defined, greater selectivity in project definitions may be necessary. As these are real problems, some flexibility must be maintained in the expectations from the projects. At times, a project that appears on its face to be one thing transforms into something quite different once the students engage with the client.

Pre-Departure Preparation

Both the GCP and the JSCP officially begin on campus during the last weeks of spring quarter in preparation for travel in mid to late June through early July. In the pre-trip phase, student groups conduct research into the business and cultural environments of the country they will be visiting. The country analysis that they prepare and present focuses on economic, social, and political issues and trends; business practice and etiquette; and a cultural overview. Students will typically gather information from library resources, Internet research, country background notes from the State Department's Bureau of Public Affairs (http://www.state.gov/r/pa/ei/bgn/), and interviews with faculty and students who are either native to, or have expertise about, the target country. This phase starts the process of activating students' prior knowledge by utilizing their established research skills and general business background, and elaborates on that knowledge by adding new, specific information about the country to be visited (Schmidt, 1993). The deliverables in this phase include reports prepared by teams of three to five students and an oral presentation to the group as a whole. Students are subject to both formative and summative feedback as part of their overall grades for the projects.

Also during the pre-trip phase, students receive a variety of briefings on traveling abroad. For many of our students, this will be their first time outside the United States. Working closely with our Office of Education Abroad, students are informed about travel safety issues, emergency procedures, financial planning and monetary exchange, and inoculations and other medical issues. Another module centers on behavioral expectations and disciplinary consequences of violations of student conduct codes while abroad, conducted in association with our Office of Student Judiciaries.

Students are also given survival language instruction, phrase lists, and an overview of the site and the city they will be visiting, along with advice on post-project travel opportunities. Finally, they are given a thorough briefing on the parameters of the projects, expected deliverables, and grading criteria. We consider four main grading elements: the pre-departure country analysis, the on-site consulting project report and presentation, a post-project reflection paper, and professionalism. The first two are described in other sections of this article. The reflection paper assignment asks the students to articulate the learning they have done during the project about international business, business in general, and about themselves. The professionalism component is included to ensure that students do not allow the excitement of being abroad to overwhelm their better judgment about interacting with their teammates and with the client organizations.

As soon as problem statements become available from the partner institution, students are provided with an initial description of their clients, their host country partners, and the problem. This allows them to make contact with their teammates and begin background research into the industry and/or company. From a learning standpoint, the students begin to construct the necessary semantic network, fitting and adapting their current knowledge to the more specific details of the project (Schmidt, 1993). However, project definitions at this point are often vague and tentative, so students are warned not to focus too much on project specifics nor to jump to premature solutions. They can, however, collect industry level data and possibly gather benchmark information on similar companies.

Pre-Departure Logistics

Logistically, time during the spring is also used to ensure that students have acquired any necessary visas, a particular challenge if any travelers are international students, as about one third of ours are. Consideration must be given not just to the visas students need for the project site, but for any other countries they intend to visit during pre- and post-project tourism. For the international students, special attention must be paid to whether they will need a new visa to return to the United States post-project. This is becoming problematic for international students from some countries, who may arrive at a university with a single-entry visa or one that expires between the time they arrive at school and the planned return from the international project. Due to heightened security procedures, it is very difficult for such students to obtain a new visa in a third country. At minimum, it will require a visit to the embassy or consulate for an in-person interview, the needed paperwork and visa forms from the university, and passport-sized photographs. Several consulates advised us that the process could take a month or more and that the foreign student could end up stuck in the third country and eventually be sent to their home country. It may be necessary to require such students to obtain needed re-entry visas as a condition of participation in the international project. In 2003, we were forced to set up an alternative domestic consulting project for the six international MBA students who would have been at risk of not being able to return to the United States to complete their programs. The domestic project mirrored the JSCP in all aspects and turned out to be a highly successful experience for the six.

Another issue is ensuring that students have received any needed inoculations or boosters, have completed medical and emergency contact forms, acquired international student identification cards, and have arranged to bring needed prescription medications for the duration of their travels. Sites like the Centers for Disease Control Travelers' Health site (http://www.cdc.gov/travel/) and the World Health Organization's International Travel and Health site (http://www.who.int/ith/) are invaluable for identifying recommended or required vaccinations as well as general health advice when traveling in specific countries or regions. During the SARS outbreak in Asia and elsewhere, these sites became critical to decision-making about going through with a planned GCP/JSCP in China or canceling it. We chose to cancel and were able to reassign the students to alternate locations. Clearly, safety must be a primary concern when taking students abroad, and this extends beyond disease outbreaks to political instability and threats of terrorism. Working closely with the institution's Study Abroad office or the equivalent can be a crucial source of information and advice in these matters, as well as a connecting point with other faculty and administrators both at the home institution and at other universities who have experience to share.

Faculty participants need to make their own travel arrangements in consultation with the travel coordinator. While they are only required to follow the same itinerary as student groups on the outbound leg going directly to the site, many will also extend their stays to do touring after the project. Site coordinators must also communicate actively with the host institution to ensure that plans are in place for a variety of program elements. These include adequate numbers and quality of client projects, ground transportation to and from the airport and during the duration of the project, opening and closing events, and gifts for clients, hosts, student partners, and any dignitaries that might become involved in the program. Staff members from our Center for International Business Education and Development (CIBED) and our Office of Graduate Studies provide extraordinary support in this process, and also compile copies of student passports and visas, contact sheets, medical histories, and student travel itineraries for the faculty members who will be traveling to each site. Faculty participants are also provided with a Faculty Handbook that addresses frequently-asked questions about all phases of the project, faculty roles, on-line resources, report formats, grading rubrics, and foreign phrases. Faculty compensation is at our summer overload contract rate plus per diem and travel expenses.

During the pre-trip phase, groups of students also research, plan and book any pre- or post-project travel and finalize flight arrangements. Students are informed of a date and time that they must arrive in the host country if they will not be traveling as a group from the United States. Faculty members frequently travel with groups on the outbound leg of the journey if there are no pre-project tours planned. We have used flight consolidators to reduce flight costs with mixed success. At times, the cost savings came at the expense of flexibility and convenience. There is an ongoing debate here about whether students should book their own flight plans or work through a central travel planner. The advantage of using a single source is that departures and arrivals can be coordinated to minimize trips to the airport and fit within project dates. The downside is that students invariably shop the Internet and find single ticket deals at steep discounts and then complain when the airfares for the group are higher.

In-Project Processes and Post-Project Debriefing

Faculty and students typically fly into their countries at midmorning on a Friday in mid- to late June. They are met at the airport by representatives of the host institution along with transportation to the housing to be used during the student projects. Depending on the site, housing arrangements can vary widely. Our students have stayed in dormitories, hotels of far-ranging quality, and even a miners' orphanage. Adapting to the housing, in some cases, is the first eye-opener for students about socioeconomic and cultural differences. Faculty sometimes stay in the same facility as the students, but at times the host institution insists on placing faculty in better accommodations at a different location.

After move-in, there is an opening session scheduled for the afternoon of the first day (Appendix B provides an overview of the calendar of activities). At this session, students meet face-to-face for the first time with their host country teammates and faculty and staff from the host institution. A team-building activity designed to break the ice follows welcoming comments and introductions. The Ohio University faculty, using the PBL approach, officially launches the project. Students are asked to generate lists of things that they already know about the business problem they are facing and questions that they need to seek answers to in order to solve the problem. This continues the knowledge activation process begun with the Ohio University students during the pre-departure phase and introduces the host country students to PBL.

All students are informed of site-specific procedural issues and information resources that are available to them at the host institution. Teams then meet together to complete a project planning form describing initial plans for project task assignments, an assay of team members' strengths and skills, and a team contract that lays out behavioral expectations within the team (copies of forms used can be requested from the authors).

Later that day, a reception is scheduled, hosted by Ohio University, for teams to meet representatives of the client organizations. This reception serves as an opportunity for faculty to greet and thank the clients for their willingness to participate, as well as to introduce the students to their key contacts at the client organizations. Again, welcoming remarks and an overview of the project objectives are normally included.

The first weekend combines introduction to the host institution facilities, initial team meetings to socialize and plan for the project, and local touring. Monday is the teams' first opportunity to visit the client organization. Their task is to focus on the problem statement and arrive at a clear definition of what their project will entail. In some cases, teams discover that their understanding of the initial problem statement is at variance with that of the client's intentions or that the problem has been overtaken by events and changed. Just as professional consultants are called upon to do, they must adapt and negotiate an agreement about the problem and its parameters with the client, arriving at a revised problem statement that must be communicated to the faculty. This continues the process of restructuring of knowledge and the construction of the appropriate semantic network (Schmidt, 1993). The team will also offer the client a simple non-disclosure agreement form, restricting the teams from revealing any proprietary information to anyone outside the client organization other than the faculty who will be evaluating the reports. The outcome of the day is a report to the faculty that includes the finalized problem statement; an explanation of work accomplished that day, and a plan of attack for the next day.

The next five to seven days center on student teams engaging in whatever forms of research are necessary to solve the assigned problem and create the written report and presentation materials. Teams have used secondary sources from the Internet and books, but often find it necessary to conduct primary research, including employee and customer interviews and surveys, work process observation, and review of financial records. They also have to schedule time for follow-up meetings with the client. The students often have time in the evenings to socialize with their local partners or to attend cultural events, but their primary responsibility is to add value to the client.

Late in the afternoon or early in the evening of each project day, the faculty meets with the project teams either collectively or individually to discuss their progress, any obstacles they face, their plans to deal with those obstacles, and to determine if they need any faculty assistance or encouragement. The students are also asked to submit a short individually written report identifying what they learned about doing business in the host country that day, what surprised them, and what activities they would pursue the next day. Both the verbal debriefings and the written daily reports need careful faculty attention. There are times when faculty intervention is needed, particularly for teams of less experienced undergraduates. These situations might result from lack of client cooperation or refusal to share necessary information, team dynamics problems, or lack of access to resources. The faculty has to determine if the obstacle is one that the team can overcome after some coaching or whether it requires action by the faculty member in consultation with the host. Given the intensity of the process, timely intervention, if called for, is critical.

Throughout the project, the faculty role is to coach, ask questions, and to conduct the daily debriefings, but not to serve as co-consultants on the projects. Faculty members will typically only make visits to each client site to ensure that the client is satisfied with the student team's progress, to answer any questions the client may have, and to provide the client with a form for evaluating the team's performance.

Student learning is occurring in the context of the problem, with faculty assisting students to see both the potential impact of their emerging recommendations on their clients and how they might apply what they are learning to other problems in the future, triggering the epistemic curiosity that is, perhaps, the most critical cognitive effect of a PBL approach (Schmidt, 1993).

The middle weekend again combines project work with local touring, shopping, and social or cultural events. A significant portion of the cultural education occurs in these activities, as the students experience the culture first hand, often accompanied by their host country teammates who provide a different perspective on what they are seeing. Students are often exposed to aspects of the culture that traditional tourists never experience.

For example, many students will have meals with teammates' families in local neighborhoods.

The projects culminate with formal presentation of the consulting teams' reports and recommendations to the client and faculty. These are scheduled for Wednesday or Thursday of the second week and usually take place at the clients' facilities. We sometimes schedule presentations concurrently to get them completed in a timely manner, requiring the faculty to split up to cover the presentations. Transportation to get from location to location often requires careful planning and timing.

Written reports are expected to be in professional format, including an executive summary, although students are informed that the nature of the project and/or client may require modifications to standard report formats. While one copy of the report must be prepared in English for faculty grading, the team must determine whether the client wants the report in English or in the host country language. Similarly, the oral presentation to the client and faculty may be in either English, the host country language, or a combination of the two based on client preference. If the presentation is to be in English, the team must determine if translation will be required and make the necessary arrangements. If the presentation will be in the host's language, the students must arrange for the English-speaking members to receive translations of any questions that occur. Appendix C shows a grading rubric we have used for these deliverables.

The final major event is the closing banquet. Students, faculty, support staff, and clients join together to celebrate the shared experience they have just completed. It is our opportunity to thank the clients and our hosts for all that they have done to make the projects successful. It is at this event that our students normally give the gifts with which they were provided to their clients and to their teammates, and often receive gifts in return. The next morning we will have a last debriefing for the Ohio University students to capture any final observations and suggestions for program improvement; then they are free to embark on whatever post-project travel plans they have. Upon return to the United States, they are asked to submit a final reflection paper discussing their learning during the project and their suggestions for improving the program. This final reflection assists students in internalizing and concretizing the learning they have done.

Benefits for Student Learning and Faculty Development

Based on their reflection papers and feedback from alumni, our students, both undergraduates and graduates, often identify the GCP/JSCP experience as one of the peak experiences of their educations. They point to the intense cultural exposure, the opportunity to make a difference in solving a company's problems, and the application of the skills they have learned in their studies during the projects. They frequently comment on their enhanced self-confidence that results from discovering they are capable of not only surviving in, but also effectively working in, a different country and cultural setting. Many students develop lifelong friends and potential business contacts in their host country, and some receive offers of employment from their clients.

For the faculty there is similar enrichment. We, too, develop friendships with our peers that can often open up new research and publication opportunities. The experiences we have interacting with the client organizations enhance our ability to teach about international business with real examples that we have observed closely first-hand. The cultural exposure similarly increases our understanding of, and sensitivity to, our international students and colleagues. The internationalization of our faculty enhances our College and improves our overall offering of high quality business education.

It should be noted that the feedback we have received from our partners and the consulting clients also points to significant benefits that they derive from the experience. The host faculty and students derive similar enrichment to that experienced by our faculty and students. The host faculty is exposed to a pedagogical approach for which they often have no previous experience, and they often develop opportunities for collaborative research with American colleagues. Their own students, in some cases, are experiencing variously their first group projects, first consulting experiences, and/or their first time working in cross-cultural groups. Finally, the host clients almost uniformly report that the analyses and recommendations that they receive from the student consulting teams have real and immediate value to their business practices. In one recent case, the client estimated that the student recommendations could save them as much as US$400,000 per year.

Summary and Conclusions

As we have shown, an immersive international consulting experience can offer extraordinary learning opportunities for both student and faculty participants. The use of a problem-based learning approach enhances the richness of the experience by activating critical cognitive processes that contribute to more complete integration of the knowledge gained into the students' experience base and an enhancement of their ability to draw on that experience in future situations (Schmidt, 1993). As Rhem (1998) points out, excitement about PBL as pedagogy derives from research evidence that

Problem-based learning (PBL) ends up orienting students toward meaning-making over fact-collecting. They learn via contextualized problem sets and situations. Because of that, and all that goes with that, namely the dynamics of group work and independent investigation, they achieve higher levels of comprehension, develop more learning and knowledge-forming skills, and more social skills as well. This approach to teaching brings prior knowledge into play more rapidly and ends up fostering learning that adapts to new situations and related domains as quickly and with the same joyous magic as a stone skipped over a body of water. (p. 1)

Effective utilization of the PBL approach requires thoughtful faculty involvement in a less traditional role as coaches and tutors rather than information-givers. As Barrows (1988) indicates, the tutors' interactions should remain at a metacognitive level, assisting students to better structure their own learning rather than relying on the tutors for answers.

Our experience is approaching two decades with the Global Competitiveness Program and Joint Student Consulting Projects. It has been a challenging a rewarding journey. Approximately 400 undergraduates and almost as many MBA and Executive MBA students have now participated in one of these experiences, as well as dozens of faculty members and even a few executive advisors to the College. Each has come back with a greater understanding of international business based on first-hand experience with the challenges and rewards of doing business in another country. Each has developed a new appreciation for cultural differences, and, perhaps more importantly, similarities. Personal skills and professional competencies have been tested under fire and found to be successful, which builds self-confidence. We fully expect to continue and even to increase the opportunities for students to participate in these types of experiences in the future.

REFERENCES

Barrows, H. (1988). *The Tutorial Process.* Springfield, IL: Southern Illinois University School of Medicine.

Beck, J. E., Whiteley, A. M., & McFetridge, P. R. (1996). Internationalizing the business student. *Journal of Teaching in International Business, 7*(4), 91–105.

Brown, J. S., Collins, A., & Duguid, P. (1989, January/February). Situated cognition and the culture of learning. *Educational Researcher,* 32–42.

Henthorne, T. L., Miller, M. M., & Hudson, T. W. (2001). Building and positioning successful study-abroad programs: A "hands-on" approach. *Journal of Teaching in International Business, 12*(4), 49–62.

Kaynak, E., & Schermerhorn, J. R. (1999). Teaching and program variations in international business: Past, present, and future. In E. Kaynak and J. R.

Schermerhorn (Eds.), *Teaching and program variations in international business.* Binghamton, NY: International Business Press/Haworth Press.

Keys, J. B. (1995). A simulated action learning approach to teaching international management. *Journal of Teaching in International Business, 6*(4), 65–79.

Knowles, M. (1980). *Modern practice of adult education: From pedagogy to andragogy.* Cambridge Adult Education.

Mendenhall, M., Dunbar, E., & Oddou, G. (1987). Expatriate selection, training and career-pathing: A review and critique. *Human Resource Management, 26*(3), 331–345.

Norman, G. R., & Schmidt, H. G. (1992). The psychological basis of problem-based learning: A review of the evidence. *Academic Medicine, 67*(9), 557–565.

Porth, S. J. (1997). Management education goes international: A model for designing and teaching a study tour course. *Journal of Management Education, 21*(2), 190–199.

Rhem, J. (1998). Problem-based learning: An introduction. *The National Teaching & Learning Forum, 8*(1), 1–6.

Savery, J. R., & Duffy, T. M. (1995). Problem-based learning: An instructional model and its constructivist framework. *Educational Technology, 35*(5), 31–37.

Schmidt, H. (1993). Foundations of problem-based learning: Some explanatory notes. *Medical Education, 27*, 422–432.

Sherman, H. (1999). Pursuing global competence in undergraduate business education: Use of an international consulting experience. In E. Kaynak and J. R. Schermerhorn (Eds.), *Teaching and program variations in international business.* Binghamton, NY: International Business Press/Haworth Press.

von Eije, H. (1998). Learning from an international study and research project by undergraduate students. *Journal of teaching in international business, 9*(4), 21–38.

APPENDIX A
INTERNATIONAL BUSINESS LEARNING OBJECTIVES

1. Perform country analysis and determine the potential for products and services in non-United States countries.

2. Identify and consider the impact of disparate cultures, values, and behaviors on how one would design management systems (including motivation, organizational design, incentive systems, and leadership styles).

3. Identify and consider the impact of foreign trade issues, including the role of international organizations/trading blocks, foreign currency, and government regulations on a firm's operations.

4. Analyze the domestic and international issues involved with product development, distribution, promotion, and pricing

5. Identify and discuss the different types of strategic alliances and the management challenges they present.

APPENDIX B
REPRESENTATIVE CALENDAR OF ACTIVITIES

- Day 1 (Friday): Arrival at site, housing check-in, and opening reception.
- Days 2 & 3 (Saturday & Sunday): Local touring and cultural events.
- Day 4 (Monday): Initial client meetings, finalization of project charge, development of strategy for project completion, and first daily debriefing session with faculty.
- Days 5 through 8 (Tuesday through Friday): Team primary and secondary research, client meetings, drafting of report elements. Faculty visits clients, conducts daily team debriefings, and works with local faculty as trouble-shooters. Some cultural activities may be scheduled or arise spontaneously.
- Days 9 & 10 (Saturday & Sunday): Local touring and cultural events. Teams plan for final research and report development.
- Days 11 & 12 (Monday & Tuesday): Students do last minute research and analyses, finalize their recommendations and reports, and develop presentation materials. Faculty continues in coaching roles and conducting daily debriefings.
- Day 13 (Wednesday): Students present findings and recommendations to clients in both written and oral forms. Faculty assesses presentations and collects feedback from clients.
- Day 14 (Thursday): Faculty conducts a project debriefing session to focus on what was learned. Closing banquet will be held for students, client representatives, and host faculty.
- Day 15 (Friday): Student and faculty departure for post-project travel or return to United States.

APPENDIX C
GRADING RUBRICS
GCP/JSCP Presentation Rubric

Company_____

Introduction	Little or no description of company or project or introduction of group members.	Company and/or project discussed, group members introduced, but a sufficient outline of the presentation is not provided.	Excellent description of project and company. Members are introduced and an outline of presentation is given.
	2 4 6	8 10 12	14 16
Presentation Content	Content insufficient or with substantial problems	Information provided is relevant and on target for audience	Excellent presentation of issues relevant to this project
	2 4 6	8 10 12	14 16 18
Presentation Style	Presentation is sloppy, poor transition between speakers, and non presenters are detracting from presentation	Presentation is OK, some problems in transition, too much reading*, speakers are not talking to audience, some distractions in the presentation	Presentation is thorough with nice transitions between speakers, speakers talk to audience (little or no reading*) and have no distracting mannerisms. Non presenters are attentive to presentation
	2 4 6	8 10 12	14 16 18
Response to Questions	Group was not able to respond appropriately to questions	Group responded to questions adequately, but some uncertainty in response. Not sure who should answer questions. Directed questions had to be answered by another group member.	Group was well prepared to respond to questions. No uncertainty as to who should answer questions. All directed questions answered appropriately.
	2 4 6	8 10 12	14 16
Visual Aids	No use of visual aids	Visual aids were used but some problems occurred (timing of aids and presentation not in sync, hard to see or follow, etc.).	Visual aids appropriate and well done. Easy to follow and added much to the presentation.
	2 4 6	8 10 12	14 16
Organization and Completeness	Presentation is difficult to follow and/or is missing parts	Presentation is easy to follow and contains all assigned parts	Presentation contains all assigned parts, relationships among ideas and parts are clearly expressed, and presentation time is less than thirty minutes.
	2 4 6	8 10 12	14 16

* Italian students many use notes to present in English and OU students may use notes if presenting in Italian

GCP/JSCP Report Rubric

Company_____

Category	Level 1	Level 2	Level 3
Executive Summary	No executive summary or summary contains incorrect or incomplete information	Executive summary explains the purpose and some findings of the report	Executive summary gives a concise and thorough summary of the report including problem definition, objectives and findings or recommendations.
	2 4 6	8 10 12	14 16 18 20
Introduction/ Background/ Problem Definition/ Research Objectives	Little or no background, problem definition, research objectives or report outline.	Some background information provided, problem definition and research objectives are not clear, the report outline is not sufficient.	Excellent background provided, the problem definition and research objectives are clearly stated, and an excellent report outline is provided.
	2 4 6	8 10 12	14 16
Problem Analysis (Information here is problem specific. Could include market analysis, customer analysis, internal data analysis, competitor analysis, assumptions, etc.)	Insufficient analysis of the problem.	A reasonable problem analysis is provided but the team missed some key issues.	Excellent problem analysis. Teams considered all options and alternatives and demonstrated a thorough understanding of all relevant issues and limitations.
	2 4 6	8 10 12	14 16
Conclusions/ Recommendations	Conclusions and recommendations unclear with little or no justification.	Conclusions/recommendations are logical, well written, concise but lack sufficient justification.	Conclusions/recommendations are logical, well written, concise and with sufficient justification.
	2 4 6	8 10 12	14 16
Writing	Paper is sloppy, has no clear direction and contains multiple errors in spelling, grammar and punctuation.	Format is appropriate with not more than one spelling, grammar, or punctuation error and also transitions nicely.	Paper is well written, with no spelling or grammatical errors and ideas are expressed well through appropriate sentence structure and word choice.
	2 4 6	8 10 12	14 16
Organization and Completeness	Paper is difficult to follow and/or is missing parts.	Paper is easy to follow and contains all assigned parts.	Paper contains all assigned parts; relationship among ideas and parts is clearly expressed.
	2 4 6	8 10 12	14 16

Peer Evaluation Form

Required for All Group Projects: You must assess **each** team member and **yourself**.
A separate form is required for each evaluation. Deposit in Drop Box.
One letter grade penalty for failure to do peer evaluations!

S C O R E

Name of Assessor: _____ **Name of Assessee:** _____

1 Overall opinion of this person's contribution to the effort of the group.

Low   2   4   6   8   10   High

2 Came to group meetings prepared to solve the requirements of the project.

Low   2   4   6   8   10   High

3 Capacity to solve problems.

Low   2   4   6   8   10   High

4 Willingness to cooperate with others (if not at meetings the cooperation would be difficult).

Low   2   4   6   8   10   High

5 Willingness to listen to others.

Low   2   4   6   8   10   High

6 Attendance at group meetings.

Low   2   4   6   8   10   High

7 Attitude towards project.

Low   2   4   6   8   10   High

8 Leadership (i.e., provided some type of direction in project).

Low   2   4   6   8   10   High

9 Individual effort in getting things done as assigned.

Low   2   4   6   8   10   High

10 Contribution of time to overall group project.

Low   2   4   6   8   10   High

Total Points _____

Breinigsville, PA USA
22 August 2010
244011BV00002B/4/A